SWORDS AROUND THE CROSS

THE NINE YEARS WAR

Ireland's Defense of Faith and
Fatherland 1594–1603

TIMOTHY T. O'DONNELL

CHRISTENDOM PRESS ♦ **FRONT ROYAL, VIRGINIA**

Through storm and fire and gloom, I see it stand
    Firm, broad and tall,
The Celtic Cross that marks our Fatherland,
    Amid them all!
Druids and Danes and Saxons vainly rage
    Around its base;
It standeth shock on shock, and age on age,
    Star of our scatter'd race.

O Holy Cross! dear symbol of the dread
    Death of our Lord,
Around thee long have slept our martyr dead
    Sward over sward.
And hundred bishops I myself can count
    Among the slain:
Chiefs, captains, rank and file, a shining mount
    Of God's ripe grain.

The monarch's mace, the Puritan's claymore,
    Smote thee not down;
On headland steep, on mountain summit hoar,
    In mart and town,
In Glendalough, in Ara, in Tyrone,
    We find thee still,
Thy open arms still stretched to thine own,
    O'er town and lough and hill.

And would they tear thee out of Irish soil,
    The guilty fools!
How time must mock their antiquated toil
    And broken tools!
Cranmer and Cromwell from thy grasp retired,
    Baffled and thrown;
William and Anne to sap thy site conspir'd —
    The rest is known.

Holy Patrick, father of our faith,
    Beloved of God!
Shield thy dear Church from impending scaith,
    Or, if the rod
Must scourge it yet again, inspire and raise
    To emprise high
Men like the heroic race of other days,
    Who joyed to die.

Fear! wherefore should the Celtic people fear
    Their Church's fate?
The day is not — the day was never near —
    Could desolate
The Destined Island, all whose clay
    Is holy ground:
Its Cross shall stand till that predestin'd day
    When Erin's self is drowned.

The Celtic Cross
Thomas D'Arcy Magee

CONTENTS

CONTENTS

ILLUSTRATIONS

fOReWORO

The greatest current need in the study and writing of history is history written from some point of view other than turn-of-the-millennium materialism and moral relativism, from which almost all present history is being written. Some historians have kept some respect for objective truth, though by no means all; but even they generally shy away from points of view very different from their own, even when amply attested in the documents they use. They simply screen them out. And since all ages from the early fourth century of the Christian era to a little past the middle of the twentieth century were Christian ages, this practice of most historians screens out what the people of the West in all times more than forty years ago and less than 1700, whether Catholic or Protestant, regarded as the most important aspect of life.

It is absolutely false to say that history written by a self-proclaimed Catholic is biased while that written by a turn-of-the-millennium materialist and moral relativist is "objective." These commitments are every bit as much a "point of view" as that of the self-proclaimed Catholic historian. In fact, true history cannot be written without a world-view, for there must be a basis for the selection of facts, stories and analysis in a book of history, to determine which facts, stories and analysis are most important. Undigested history is not history at all.

For many years I have attempted, in many books, to present the Catholic view of history. Now my dear friend Dr. Timothy O'Donnell, third president of Christendom College, publishes this fine work applying the Catholic viewpoint to the central event in the history of Ireland from the English invasion under Henry II in the 12th century to the Irish wars of independence in the twentieth century; The Nine Years War (1594-1603) to save the Catholic Faith in Ireland. Under their two incomparable leaders, Hugh O'Neill and Red Hugh O'Donnell, Irish Catholics fought to the finish—and lost (as the world sees these events). But as Dr. O'Donnell points out in his stirring epilogue, in the end they won. For the Catholic Faith never died in Ireland. It endured through a century of vicious, systematic persecution (the 18th) and another century of desperate poverty and famine (the 19th), while its Catholic people spread all over the world, including my great-grandfather Robert Carroll, who died in the Battle of Cedar Creek near the Shenandoah River here in the United States, fighting for the liberty of black men even more oppressed than were his people—and including the forebears of Timothy O'Donnell. In what we have been able to build at Christendom College, with the ever-present help of God, we are both building on mighty foundations, laid more than any other men by Hugh O'Neill and Red Hugh O'Donnell.

Here is their story—an epic of valor, of love, and above all of faith, the Catholic truth of the Nine Years War. Most of this history is written from original sources, which are quoted at length, making clear how predominant the Catholic Faith was in all that these men did. Catholic historians do not relegate this to footnotes or less because it is "out of step with the times." They put it at the center where it belongs—and also because they know the Catholic Faith cannot die. Like its Founder, it can be buried, but it will always rise again.

Warren H. Carroll
FOUNDING PRESIDENT
CHRISTENDOM COLLEGE

preface

h ow can I ever forget the visit, which I made, with my mother and father, to Ireland back in 1969. Michael and Elizabeth nee McBreen had not returned home since their arrival in New York in 1926. Yes, many things had changed in the Republic of the Twenty-Six Counties but not so in the North!

As we drove from Donegal through the North in order to reach County Cavan for a special treat—a castle experience near my mother's hometown of Baileboro—we were stopped at the border by a squad of British B Specials. They ordered us out of the car, searched the interior and the trunk, and then proceeded to frisk my father and myself.

As my mother looked, with disbelief, at our arms extended against the wall of the Border Post, she suddenly began to cry and wail exclaiming: "Have I returned to an Ireland such as the one I lived through during the Trouble when I lost my beloved brother, Patrick, to a firing squad of the Black and Tans?" "And you, young lads," she continued, "you, with the map of Ireland on your faces, how can you serve a nation which enslaved your ancestors for centuries?"

We were quickly told to move on by these grim and shame-faced border guards, the B-Specials, who obviously were reminded of their ancestral roots by my mother's bold imprecations. And so we continued on our way. It was only after an hour that we broke silence, so shaken were the three of us, after this traumatic experience.

My mother spoke of how, when the casket of her slain brother was brought into the village church, the Pastor, Fr. McCormick, (who gave my mother, before she left for America, a copy of the prayer book entitled: *The Treasury of the Sacred Heart*), had to prevail upon Patrick's comrades-in-arms to open it. My mother recalled the Pastor's words— "Open this casket for this mother is not going to die without seeing the body of her son, a hero for Ireland!"

Arriving at Cabra Castle after the dinner hour, we were assured by the Manager that tea and sandwiches would be provided in our quarters. About five minutes after entering my room, I heard my mother exclaim across the hall from me: "Jesus, Mary and Joseph!" Realizing that my father had suffered a heart attack two years before, I naturally thought of the worst and straight away entered their room only to hear my mother say: "Michael, can you believe what you are seeing above our bed?" "Sure, it's a portrait of the dirty Cromwell!" "Don't fret," I replied. "Just let me take it off the wall and put it in the closet." I had no luck removing it and, at this point, my mother said to my father and me: "Well, that's it. I am not staying in a place, castle or no castle, which displays a portrait of this rascal, responsible for the destruction of every Chapel and Church in this vicinity of Cavan."

Driving through rainy windswept roads, we finally found shelter in Dundalk, an hour's drive from the Castle.

Fortunately, the rest of our trip throughout Ireland was a happy and pleasant one.

As I read   Dr. Timothy O'Donnell's *Swords Around the Cross: The Nine Years War, Ireland's Defense of Faith and Fatherland, 1594-1603*, I realized how deeply engraved in the "spiritual" genes of my parent's generation were the painful memories of the persecution and veritable slaughter inflicted upon Irish Catholics for centuries by *Perfide Albion*. Dr. O'Donnell's research into the exploits of O'Neill and O'Donnell opened for me, and this for the first time, an awareness that there is not one major sector in the whole of Ireland that has not been stained by the blood of those defending their right to practice their One, Holy, Roman, Catholic and Apostolic Faith.

Reading this work, I also came to realize that when next I travel there—now using a recently obtained Irish Passport—the rolling hills, and mountains, crossroads, glens and valleys, lakes, streams and ocean strands will remind me of the fallen heroes of 1594-1603; the generosity of Philip II, and his son Philip III and the ineptitude of Aquila which ultimately resulted in the Flight of the Earls.

Yes, a flight, but at last a safe haven for O'Neill and O'Donnell which resulted in a heroes welcome and ultimately a happy death and burial in the Holy City of Rome. How truly fitting that they should be buried there. Quite possibly their final resting-place in the Church on the Janiculum, close to the North American College, may have been the inspiration for the great Liberator Daniel O'Connell's deciding to have his heart entombed in Rome.

One of the most dramatic points made by Dr. O'Donnell, towards the conclusion of this riveting history speaks eloquently of how this war cemented the Catholic identity of the Irish people who, despite centuries of persecution, remained true to their Catholic Faith.

As the Republic of Ireland has enjoyed unheard of prosperity this past decade, and as rampant secularization along with decreasing church attendance seems to be taking root there, I pray that this scholarly work, filled with such faith in and love for Ireland and its history, will serve to remind the Irish of the next Millennium that not only was Ireland baptized by water and the Spirit but also by the "baptism" of blood flowing from the bodies of countless men and women who would not bow down to the Stranger's rule or his religion which sprang from the dissolute Henry VIII.

Henry VIII would leave, as his heir, *Elizabeth Regina*, whose raging hatred for Ireland's attachment to the Roman Catholic Faith would remain undaunted until that day, when attempting to stave off death by standing upright, supported by her attendants, she would finally swoon, thus joining the ranks of the infamous of human history!

Rev. Msgr. Michael J. Wrenn
PASTOR, ST. JOHN THE EVANGELIST
CHURCH, NEW YORK

acknowledgements

I would like to acknowledge those who introduced me to the Catholic vision of history, particularly the late Dr. John M. York and Richard H. Trame, S.J., of Loyola Marymount University. A special word of gratitude is also due to my dear friend Dr. Warren H. Carroll for his faith, inspiration and scholarship in the service of the Church. I would also like to acknowledge my debt to Fr. Denis Murphy, S.J., for his pioneering research at the archives in Simancas, Spain and his excellent introduction and treatment of O'Cleary's *Life of Hugh Roe O'Donnell*, which awakened and deepened my interest in the importance of this war. I would also like to thank the Franciscans in Rome at St. Isidore and San Pietro in Montorio, the library staff at Trinity College in Dublin, and particularly Mr. Stephen Pilon of the O'Reilly Memorial Library at Christendom College, who greatly assisted my research. A word of gratitude is also due to the staffs at the Lifford Heritage Center and at The Flight of the Earls Center in Rathmullen, who were also most gracious in their assistance along with Mr. Vincent O'Donnell of the Clan Odomhnaill Association for his conversation and erudition. I must also express my heartfelt gratitude to the late Fr. Seamus O'Reilly who reviewed the manuscript and made a number of helpful suggestions. A special word of thanks is also due to my assistant Miss Christina Lundberg who worked so graciously and faithfully on the numerous revisions of this manuscript.

I would also like to thank my wife Catherine for her tender support throughout the project and her proofing of the manuscript. Also, for my children, Colleen, Niall, Hugh, Bridget, Kathleen, Rory, Conor, Kieran, and Declan, who allowed their father to be a periodic hermit in his study.

Lastly, I would like to thank my parents Richard and Edna O'Donnnell, who raised and nurtured me in the faith brought from Ireland by William O'Donnell and Susan Devine O'Donnell in 1849.

SWORDS AROUND THE CROSS

IΠCROÒUCCIOΠ

C ommunication between Tudor England and Gaelic Ireland was frequent but often hampered by severe
prejudices which flourished on both sides of the Irish Sea.
Neither country truly understood or appreciated the culture of the other. This brooding cloud of ignorance and
suspicion lingered throughout the reign of Queen Elizabeth.[1] Tudor adventurers such as Sir Walter Raleigh, Edmund Spencer, Lord Borough, Sir Richard Bingham and the
Earls' of Essex paid dearly in purse, reputation and honor
as a result of their efforts in Ireland. Several paid with their
lives. Tudor propaganda, with all its disdain and contempt
for the Irish, is based primarily upon the experiences and
writings of these bitter men. It was difficult for these men
to comprehend that behind the impenetrable Irish forests,
dark sweeping glens, murky bogs, abundant rivers, streams
and shimmering lochs, there existed a civilization which
was as valid, noble, intricate and respectable as their own.
Most of the Elizabethan adventurers viewed the Irish as
nothing but "vermin," "savages," "beasts," "felons," and
"wild hares;" to be either "rooted out" or forcibly "civi-

---

[1]D.B. Quinn, *The Elizabethans and the Irish* (Ithaca: Cornell University Press, 1966), 38.

lized." At times both were sought simultaneously, as when Elizabeth, writing to her Lord Deputy in Ireland, pointed out that she wanted "the people to be trained from the inordinate tyranny of the Irish captains and to taste the sweets of civil order;"[2] this, as O'Faolain observes, after praising Walter Devereux, the elder Essex, for his slaughtering of helpless men, women and children on Rathlin Island, and as Lord President Malby reported to his satisfied Sovereign that in the past two years he had hanged over four hundred people in Munster alone for the sake of peace.[3] Despite overwhelming evidence to the contrary, the Irish, due to ethnic and cultural differences, were viewed as "unchristian" by these would be reformers and therefore uncivilized. This allowed for a more brutal treatment than was ethically permissible in English society.[4]

Fortunately, not all Tudor writers reacted as negatively towards Irish culture as did those adventurers. Men such as Fr. Goode and Sir John Harrington differed with their fellow countrymen in their assessment and degree of sympathy. Perhaps the most moderate description of the Irish during the reign of Elizabeth is that given by Edmund Campion:

---

[2]Sean O'Faolain, *The Great O'Neil* (New York: Duel, Sloan & Pearce, 1942), 14.

[3]*Ibid.*, 15.

[4]Nicholas Canny has chronicled the dramatic collapse in attitudes between the two peoples particularly during the crucial period from 1565-1576. Viewing the Irish as unchristian and uncivilized was essential to justify the seizure of land and conquest. See Canny, *Elizabethan Conquest of Ireland: a pattern established, 1565-76* (New York: Barnes & Noble Books, 1976), 117-136.

The people are thus inclined: religious, frank, amorous, ireful, sufferable, of pains infinite, very glorious; many sorcerers, excellent horsemen, delighted with wars, great almsgivers, passing in hospitality. The lewder sort, both clerks and laymen, are sensual and loose to lechery above measure. The same being virtuously bred up and reformed, are such mirrors of holiness and austerity that other nations retain but a show or shadow of devotion in comparison of them.

Abstinence and fasting is to them a familiar kind of chastisement. They are sharp-witted, lovers of learning, capable of any study whereunto they bend themselves, constant in travel, adventurous, intractable, kind-hearted, secret in displeasure.

Clear men they are of skin and hue, but of themselves careless and bestial. Their women are well favored, clear coloured, fair headed, big and large, suffered from their infancy to grow at will, nothing curious of their feature and proportion of body.[5]

According to Waugh, Campion's true superiority over his fellow countrymen at the time is demonstrated by contrasting his description with another anonymous history written about the same time:

And here you may see the nature and disposition of this wicked, effrenated, barbarous and unfaithful nation who (as Cambrensis writeth of them) they are a wicked and perverse generation, constant always in that they are inconstant, faithful in that they be unfaithful.[6]

---

[5]Edmund Campion, *A Historie of Ireland* (New York: Scholars Facsimiles & Reprints, 1940), 13; quoted in Evelyn Waugh's *Edmund Campion, Jesuit and Martyr* (Garden City, New York: Image Books, 1946), 43.

[6]Waugh, *Edmund Campion*, 44. Campion clearly spoke of the weaknesses of the "mere Irish", but clearly had a great respect especially for the history of medieval Ireland, which for him chronicles the

Despite the effort to portray the native Irish as unchristian and therefore uncivilized in an attempt to justify the conquest, a document from the 16th century which has survived gives a more balanced assessment. The document was written according to O'Dwyer by an Italian or Spaniard who had spent some time in Ireland and is descriptive of Irish customs and far more balanced.

1. The use of money is very rare in these regions, barter of goods is the common practice. 2. There are no guesthouses or hostels except perhaps in ports. Whoever is travelling receives everything *gratis* in whatever house he stays – not immediately but when the father of the family eats. 3. Normally they do not eat before evening time, but they do not refuse drink to travellers in the meantime. 4. There are 8 types of drink: beer made from barley and water, milk, whey, wine, soup . . . , wine sweetened with honey, whiskey and pure water. 5. Men cover their heads . . . with mantles, women with very wide linen tiaras. They use very long knives which could also serve as daggers. 6. The most honoured person sits in the middle, the second on his right, the third on his left, the fourth on his right and so on until the whole house is filled following the circuit of the walls. All face the door, no one has his back to it; the reason for this, they say, is so that nobody may be set upon, unprepared, by an enemy. 7. They hold the Catholic faith so firmly that they seem never to have given ear to heretics. They rise at midnight to pray and meditate, some give a whole hour, others a half-hour. They always light the fire at that time. 8. Their language is similar to Chaldaeic and Hebrew; they add aspirations to many letters, which has the effect that they seem to pronounce words different from what is written. 9. They rise to recite the Lord's prayer at Mass, and they hear it

---

story of many holy men and great monasteries. See Campion's *Historie of Ireland*, 30-47.

standing. 10. Wednesdays they abstain from meat and on Friday from milk products. 11. Both men and women kiss each other as soon as they meet. 12. Though they lack education in the humanities (*urbana educatione*), nonetheless they live peacefully and lovingly together so that I never saw them or any soldiers come to arms for six whole months. The same peace is found among horses and dogs so that I am led to attribute all this to the excellence of the region and the air. 13. Such is the temperateness of the sky that it varies little so that there is always grass for herds and flocks in the fields. 14. No poisonous animal is found in Ireland; no snake, viper or toad. 15. As they eat copiously when there is plenty, they also fast for two or even three days at a time. 16. They do not violate their oath to their lords and they observe peace or fight according to his wishes. 17. In battle the more courageous will leave his own ranks and penetrate the enemy lines, paying little attention to what his comrades are doing. 18. They are as fast on their feet as horses or even faster. 19. They sit quite freely on grass, turf or straw. They shun benches (stools) completely and also rocks and would choose rushes or straw instead. 20. They mount horses by catching their left ears and with no support for their legs. 21. They do not use metal or any other shin (foot) protection. 22. The more noble wear cloaks made of leather of varied inlaid colours. 23. They cultivate sacred poetry; they learn it without much study. They do not compose religious poems without preparatory prayer and fasting. When dealing with very serious business poets are their negotiators. 24. At supper before they give thanks, bishops and priests deliver a sermon to those present, which is heard with great attention.[7]

---

[7]Reginald Walsh OP, "Irish Manners and Customs in the 16th Century", *Archivium Hibernicum or Irish Historical Records* Vol. 4 (1917), 183. Quoted in Peter O'Dwyer O. Carm., *Towards a History of Irish Spirituality* (Blackrock: The Columba Press, 1995), 158-160.

Another source of embitterment to the Elizabethans, in addition to their personal loss, was the lack of clear national unity in Ireland. This caused them to view the country as being in a state of perpetual confusion lacking both law and order. Ireland, unlike England, never *developed* the idea of a strong centralized national state ruled by a sovereign.[8] The old high kings of Ireland (*Ard Righs*), although occasionally strong and dominant, were for the most part weak and ineffectual. The High Kingship in Ireland vanished with the advent of the Normans in the twelfth century. Although the bards often sang of "my dark Rosaleen," as an image of the nation, regionalism and the politics of the clan took precedence frequently over national interests. Among the Irish Celts, as among the ancient Greeks, the Italians of the Middle Ages and other European peoples, the basic desire for local autonomy usually prevailed over the policy of centralization. This was especially true of rural Ireland. This instinct for local freedom also affected the Anglo-Norman houses in Ireland to such a degree that they became in custom, dress and speech *Hibernis Hiberniores*, "more Irish than the Irish themselves." This primacy of clan politics as practiced by the Gaelic kings and petty chiefs in detriment to the national interest crippled the Irish efforts to attain national independence up to the seventeenth century. It was just this weakness that the Catholic Confederacy, established by Hugh O'Donnell and Hugh O'Neill, sought to cure. The Irish confederates hoped to initially stop the

---

[8]It should be noted that other European nations and peoples were also slow in this development. The untimely death of Brian Boru and his usurpation of the High Kingship certainly weakened the chances for this development in Ireland.

spread of the English colonial administration with its alien religion and defend the Gaelic order of things which had witnessed a strong, vibrant resurgence in the 14th and 15th centuries.[9]

The Nine Years War 1594-1602 was certainly a war of Gaelic independence but primarily and most importantly a war fought in defense of the Roman Catholic Faith. When negotiations were opened and terms discussed, inevitably the first article demanded by the Confederates was the free practice of the Catholic, Apostolic, Roman religion.

For nine years these heroic clansmen defeated every army sent against them by the English Protestants. O'Neill and O'Donnell were the first leaders to successfully interlock the hopes of Irish national resistance to the star of the Catholic Faith, thereby strengthening both.

Religious belief, when deep, is undoubtedly the strongest feeling in the soul of man. It can endow a nation steeped in it with a fiery, unconquerable strength. History has shown time and again that Catholicism can be for a nation a profound emotion, capable of uniting a people and transcending their previous limitations. For example, one can think of the impact which Catholicism has had on Spain and Poland.

It is during this war and the few years preceding it that Ireland once again entered into the mainstream of European thought. The Catholic Reformation was well under way. Men of courage possessed by a deep sense of mission

---

[9]G. A. Hayes-McCoy, "Gaelic Society in Ireland in the late Sixteenth Century" (*Historical Studies*, 4 [1963], 45-61.) and Nicholas Canny, "Hugh O'Neill, Earl of Tyrone, and the Changing Face of Gaelic Ulster" (*Studia Hibernica*, 10 [1970], 7-35.)

were winning back to the ancient Faith those nations which had fallen into heresy. Jesuits from Douai, with bishops and priests from the Irish colleges in Spain, France and Rome poured into Ireland during this period. These men, along with the native clergy, especially the mendicant friars who had witnessed the savage destruction of their churches, monasteries and sacred shrines, preached a crusade against the English heretics who sought to force Ireland into their national apostasy.[10] Sir William Cecil foresaw this danger in his illustrious work entitled *Device for the Alteration of Religion*:

> The Pope all that he may, will be incensed, but this will not go further than excommunication, interdicts, and intrigues with foreign princes, although *by reason of the clergy so addicted to Rome, the papal hostility will mean trouble in Ireland.* (Emphasis added.)[11]

The Desmonds and Kildares in the south, along with the O'Donnells, the Maguires and others in the north, soon showed themselves animated by the new spirit of ardent Catholicism in opposition to the new religious revolutionaries. O'Neill and O'Donnell drew from this force which had so inspired the people. Upon this new spirit they built a powerful Catholic Confederacy and laid the ground work

---

[10]John Watt, *The Church in Medieval Ireland* Vol. 5 of the *Gill History of Ireland* (Dublin: Gill & Macmillan Ltd., 1972), 216-217. The self-confidence of Gaelic Catholic culture can be seen especially in the remarkable mendicant expansion and reform 1400-1508. Gaelic princes established most of the new religious houses, which totaled over ninety (Watt, 193-202).

[11]Philip Hughes, *Rome and the Counter Reformation in England* (London: Burns Oates, 1944), 134.

for a new nation. This Confederacy nearly destroyed English power in Ireland and kept Elizabeth in constant agitation and fear during the closing years of her reign.

The importance of this war has never been fully appreciated by historians. Perhaps this is because most historians in the English national literary tradition have chosen to build up what Belloc has perceptively called the "Elizabethan myth."[12] The Nine Years War in Ireland was an international event whose outcome was of great importance for Christendom. This struggle should hold a far more prominent position in the history of late sixteenth century Europe. Virtually all of the great powers and key figures of the age were involved in the conflict: Hugh Roe O'Donnell, the Prince of Tirconnaill, Hugh O'Neill, the Earl of Tyrone and "the O'Neill", Hugh Maguire, the Lord of Fermanagh, Donal Gorm MacDonnell, James VI of Scotland, Henry IV of France, Philip II and Philip III of Spain, Gregory XIV, Clement VIII, Paul V, Robert Cecil, Elizabeth, Norris, Essex and Mountjoy. The finest of England's soldiers served in the Irish wars. Some have failed to see the military significance of this war as if it involved little military strategy save chasing wild, half naked Irish kearnes through the woods. This war demanded intricate and complex strate-

---

[12]Hilaire Belloc, *Characters of the Reformation* (Garden City, New York: Image Books, 1958), 101.

The mere mention of "rebellion" in Ireland was enough to make Elizabeth "sick and ill". John McGurk, *The Elizabethan Conquest of Ireland* (Manchester: Manchester University Press, 1997), 3. Efforts to reduce the scale and significance of this war by simply referring to it as "Tyrone's Rebellion" fail to grasp the scale and significance of this conflict, as if it was simply one man who acted in a "treasonable" fashion.

gies and included a number of significant battles and campaigns. Hugh O'Donnell and Hugh O'Neill both had well disciplined armies which fought with brilliance and distinction against a powerful and well equipped army for over a decade.

The continental impact of the war has never been adequately studied. It most certainly hurt the Protestant cause on Continental Europe. Elizabeth, "the champion of Protestantism," due to the instability of her own kingdom, was unable to render viable assistance to her Protestant allies.[13] Maurice of Nassau and the Union of Utrecht were seriously hampered in their efforts to reunite the Low Countries due to a lack of consistent English support. Charles Wilson, in his work *Queen Elizabeth and the Revolt in the Netherlands,* alludes to the fact that the maintenance of Belgium as a Catholic country was due in part to the Irish wars.[14] This work however touches only the surface. Far more serious research is necessary in this area which however lies beyond the range and purpose of this present work.

I hope to trace the religious, political and military aspects of the war which eventually ended in the moving pathos of the "Flight of the Earls." History involves a story and it should be told well. I have drawn from a number of sources and have tried to provide a popular and coherent account of this important war. It is only fair that the historian communicate openly his world view. I am writing in

---

[13]A new and excellent work which examines the tremendous importance and profound effect of the Nine Years War on England is John McGurk's *The Elizabethan Conquest of Ireland.*

[14]See Charles Wilson, *Queen Elizabeth and the Revolt in the Netherlands* (Berkeley: University of California Press, 1970).

what has been described by some as "the nationalist" tradition. In this age of deconstructionism and the cult of the anti-hero, I am well aware that such an approach will be out of favor in certain scholarly circles. Many have sought a reinterpretation of Irish historiography which often times has been described as too "patriotic" and too "clerical" i.e., too nationalistic and Catholic. Nationalism and Catholicism have been replaced by a number of contemporary fads, from feminism to socialism. Taking smaller details, these new doconstructionists have sought to build a new and allegedly "broader" view with varying degrees of success. Often times with this revisionist view there has been a rupture with a broader and stronger tradition of the development of Gaelic Irish nationalism. I also am writing as a Catholic historian which means that I accept the historic reality of the Incarnation and the fact that Jesus Christ established his Church upon the rock of Peter. This viewpoint is also very much out of style in today's secular world. It is often thought that a secular historian can be truly objective while a religious man cannot. On the contrary, I believe that a fuller grasp of reality is afforded to the man who can see more deeply into what Hilaire Belloc in *Europe and the Faith* referred to as "his own story," the story of Christendom.

One of the great tragedies of the history of Christendom has been its terrible religious division at the time of the Protestant revolt. This religious turmoil has certainly played a large role in Irish history. All true Christians will pray fervently for a healing of this tragic division. Nothing however, could be more injurious to true ecumenism than a false irenicism. These efforts in the past to force Catholic Ireland into a rejection of its traditional faith must be seen objectively as an unfortunate evil. If we are to understand history and modern Ireland, no secular effort to downplay the deeply religious motivations of the men and women of 16th and 17th century Ireland will do justice to the complex reality of that period. Happily today Christians are working more closely together as the specter of an even more hostile, secular and apostate culture seeks to dominate and destroy the remnants of Christian civilization.

At the end of the Nine Years War, Catholic and Gaelic Ireland emerged as a nation without a state. Despite the destruction of the old Gaelic order in the seventeenth century, the people's faith grew deeper and stronger. This is perhaps the greatest legacy of the war: that O'Neills, O'Tooles and MacSweeneys might pass away, but the Catholic faith of Ireland would not. It alone was to remain unmoved and even thrive despite one of the most severe and savage persecutions in history, helping to form a new nationalism. Certainly no greater tribute can be paid to the memory of these men and the depth and power of their vision.

one

tꞬe Setting

"The Irish have a foolish opinion that the Bishop
of Rome is the King of Ireland."
                    Sir Anthony St. Leger to Henry VIII

E ngland's claim to dominion in Ireland had always been
precarious. Pope Adrian IV's bull *Laudabiliter* (1155)
which granted Ireland to Henry II was conditional upon his
reform and protection of the Church:

> We therefore, meeting your pious and laudable desire
> with due favour and according a gracious assent to your pe-
> tition, do hereby declare our will and pleasure that, with a
> view to enlarging the boundaries of the Church, restraining
> the downward course of vice, correcting evil customs and
> planting virtue, and for the increase of the Christian religion,
> you shall enter that island and execute whatsoever may tend
> to the honour of God and the welfare of the land; and also
> that the people of that land shall receive you with honour
> and revere you as their lord: provided always that the rights
> of the churches remain whole and inviolate, and saving to
> the blessed Peter and the Holy Roman Church the annual
> tribute of one penny from every house.[1]

Needless to say the stipulations of the bull were never car-

---

[1] Edmund Curtis, ed., *Irish Historical Documents 1172-1922* (New
York: Barnes & Noble, 1968), 17.

ried out. This led to the Remonstrance of the Irish kings to Pope John XXII in 1317.[2] Fully accepting papal authority and its prerogatives, the kings argued that the English had broken faith with their treaties and promises. They had infringed upon the rights of the Church and pillaged her possessions. The Pope in response wrote to the dissolute Edward II calling upon him to do justice to the Irish and reminding him of the spirit and obligations demanded of him by the Bull.[3] The Irish often turned to the See of Peter for assistance as it was a common belief among them that the Pope was the king of Ireland.[4]

Ireland had never truly been conquered by England. Large portions of the Island had remained inviolate and outside the sphere of Anglo-Norman influence.[5] In fact, during the Gaelic resurgence of the fourteenth and fifteenth centuries, many of the leading Anglo-Norman families (such as the Desmonds) married the native Irish and became Gaelic in all things. The degree to which this was happening can be seen in the famous Statutes of Kilkenny drawn up in 1366.[6] These statutes lament the fact that Eng-

---

[2]*Ibid.*, 38.

[3]Charles-Marie Garnier, *A Popular History of Ireland* (Baltimore: Helicon Press, 1961), 33.

[4]*Ibid.*, 26.

[5]R. F. Foster gives a contemporary overview of the complex state of "pre-modern" Ireland in *Modern Ireland 1600-1972* (New York: Penguin Books, 1989), 2-45.

[6]M. F. Clare, *History of Ireland* (London: Longmands, Green, & Co., 1873), 359. Recent efforts such as Ellis' to break with the traditional understanding of the Gaelicization of the early Norman invaders has raised a number of fascinating questions concerning this cultural absorption which necessitated the famous Statutes of Kilkenny.

lish settlers were abandoning their native language, their customs, their style of horseback riding and their laws for the speech, mannerisms, dress and customs of the "enemy Irish."[7] After 192 years the statutes tacitly admit the failure of "the Conquest" and the effort to bring the whole nation under English feudal law. Those Irish princes who had remained independent were recognized as kings by the sovereigns of Scotland, France, Spain, Rome and even at times in England itself![8]

In the Annals of the Four Masters, under the year 1537, we read:

> A heresy and a new error broke out in England, the effect of pride, vainglory, avarice, sensual desire and the prevalence of a variety of scientific and philosophical speculations so that the people of England went in opposition to the Pope and to Rome.
>
> At the same time they followed a variety of opinions; and, adapting the old law of Moses, after the manner of the Jewish people, they gave the title of Head of the Church of God, during his reign, to the king. They ruined the Orders who were permitted to hold worldly possessions, namely, monks, canons regular, nuns and Brethren of the Cross, etc . . . They broke into the monasteries, they sold their roofs and bells so that there was not a monastery from Arran of the Saints to the Iccian Sea that was not broken and scattered, except only a few in Ireland.[9]

See Steven G. Ellis, *Ireland in the Age of the Tudors, 1447-1603: English expansion and the end of Gaelic rule* (New York: Longman, 1998).

[7]*Ibid.*, 361.

[8]A. J. Thebaud, S.J., *The Irish Race* (New York: P.J. Kennedy, 1883), 208-9.

[9]Four Masters, *Annals of the Kingdom of Ireland* Vol. 6 (Dublin:

With the Henrician Revolution, the principles by which Christendom had been ruled for centuries were beginning to break apart. New and divergent theories for the administration of modern nations were being put forward.

In the old order of Christendom the foundation stone of the political edifice had been the papacy. All Christian nations up to the sixteenth century had acknowledged the Sovereign Pontiff as the supreme arbiter of international disputes. If England did possess any authority in Ireland it was due to the previous decisions of popes. But with England's rebellion against Rome, even that claim was thrown away. When Pius V issued the Bull *Regnans in Excelsis* on February 25, 1570, Elizabeth was excommunicated and the Irish were freed from any lingering illusion of allegiance.[10]

> We declare the said Elizabeth to be a heretic and an abettor of heretics, and that those who adhere to her have incurred the sentence also and are cut off from the unity of Christ's body.
>
> And moreover we declare that she is deprived of her pretended right to the said kingdom; and that all her nobles,

Hodges, Smith, & Co., 1856), 1445-6.

[10]Waugh, *Edmund Campion*, 47. The saintly pope (Papa Ghislieri, 1566-1572) had spent a considerable period of time in prayer and fasting before signing the Bull. Elizabeth began her reign with a Catholic coronation ceremony in 1558. She had violated her sacred coronation oath, deposed Catholic bishops, promulgated a heretical prayer book and repudiated papal authority. For over a decade, Rome had made overtures to Elizabeth but she spurned them all and chose to destroy the Catholic Faith aided by her chief councilor William Cecil. See also Warren Carroll's *The Cleaving of Christendom*, Vol. 4 in the *History of Christendom* (Front Royal, VA: Christendom Press, 2000), Chapter Five.

subjects and peoples of the said kingdom, and all others who have in any way sworn allegiance to her, are absolved for ever from such oath, and from any obligation of lordship, fidelity and homage, as now by the authority of this bull we have absolved them.

We deprive the said Elizabeth of her alleged right to the kingdom and of all the rest aforesaid.

We command and we forbid all and singular her nobles, subjects, people and whomsoever else we have already named, to dare to give any obedience to her counsels, her commands or to her laws.

Whosoever shall act otherwise we bind with the sentence of like anathema.[11]

Roman Pontiffs, Emperors of Germany, Kings of France and Spain openly received the envoys of O'Neill, Desmond and O'Donnell and sent envoys, troops and fleets to assist the Irish in their efforts for their *de facto* independence. All these proceedings were in perfect accordance with the authority which the Catholic powers still recognized in the Sovereign Pontiff. The Irish wars, in defense of faith and fatherland during the reign of Elizabeth, were not acts of rebellious treason, but the actions of a people separate and distinct, upholding their ancient and revered religion against the usurpations of an apostate queen.

This new religious fervor of the Catholic Reformation which was to play such an important role during the Nine Years War in Ireland can first be seen dramatically in the efforts of James Fitzmaurice and the Desmond War in Munster.

---

[11]Hughes, *Rome and the Counter Reformation*, 187.

 19

The religious persecution initiated by Henry was ruthlessly continued whenever possible by Elizabeth.

> The English, in every place throughout Ireland where they established their power, persecuted and banished the nine religious orders and particularly they destroyed the monastery of Monaghan and beheaded the guardian and a number of friars.[12]

The destruction of the monasteries and the slaughter of the native Catholic clergy outraged popular feeling. Although the persecution was at times sporadic, it was severe, as bishops, priests and religious were hunted down and driven into remote mountains, glens and sheltered in caves in those parish churches and monastic chapels which had escaped the rapacity of Henry VIII.[13]

It was the Catholic religion which unified and strengthened the people during this difficult time. For this reason, the counsellors of Elizabeth urged the destruction of the monasteries and the Catholic clergy in Ireland whenever politically expedient as clear threats to English claims in the country.

Such was the condition of Ireland when James Fitzmaurice, "a belligerent Roman Catholic and a bitter opponent of English rule,"[14] landed in Ireland on July 17, 1579.[15] He

---

[12]Four Masters, *Annals,* 6:1455.

[13]Thebaud, *The Irish Race,* 222-8.

[14]Conyers Read, *Lord Burghley and Queen Elizabeth* (New York: Alfred A. Knopf, 1960), 241.

[15]James Fitzmaurice was a cousin of the Earl of Desmond and an intelligent, devout, Roman Catholic. He exiled himself from his native land in a six year effort on the continent to seek support for a

called for a crusade under papal auspices in defense of the Catholic religion "against a tyrant who refused to hear Christ speaking by His Vicar."[16] Four years previously Fitzmaurice, influenced by the Jesuit, David Wolf,[17] had left Ireland for France in order to seek foreign aid for an Irish uprising. His mission carried him to Spain and eventually to Rome where he was graciously received by Gregory XIII. With the aid of the Franciscan Bishop of Killaloe, Cornelius O'Mullrain, Fr. Nicholas Sanders, a priest and Oxford professor who had become papal nuncio to Spain, and Fr. Allen, S.J., Fitzmaurice obtained a papal bull which encouraged the Irish to fight for the recovery of religious freedom and for the liberation of their country.[18] An expedition was fitted out at the expense of the Holy See and maintained eventually by Philip II. Fitzmaurice was accompanied by his wife, two bishops, some friars and the newly appointed Papal legate, Fr. Nicholas Sanders, whose *De Visibille Monarchia Ecclesia*, published in the summer of 1571, justified Pius V's papal Bull of excommunication and the Rising of the North in England.[19] Fr. Sanders was an English Catholic zealot who was destined to become the pivotal figure in the

---

Catholic rising in Ireland which would start in the province of Munster. He had been well received at the royal courts in France and Spain but especially in Rome where he met other Catholic exiles such as Frs. Sanders and Allen and received spiritual, material and military support from Pope Gregory XIII.

[16]Edmund Curtis, *A History of Ireland* (New York: Barnes & Noble, 1936), 198.

[17]Read, *Lord Burghley*, 441.

[18]Clare, *History of Ireland*, 241.

[19]Read, *Lord Burghley*, 241.

upcoming invasion.

Three small ships with the cross of Christ emblazoned upon their sails set out for Ireland. Two English ships were captured on the way and the crews were taken prisoner. The major bulk of the expedition which was to follow was led by a Captain Stukeley, an English Catholic adventurer. This second group however, never followed Fitzmaurice as was planned. Due to the treachery of Stukeley, the force was diverted to assist King Sebastian of Portugal in his disastrous expedition against Morocco.[20] Fitzmaurice's selection of Stukeley proved a tragic mistake. Undaunted, thinking of the sad plight of the Catholics of Munster with its murdered priests and desecrated Churches, he continued the crusade.[21]

The expedition soon landed in Dingle and reports were circulated throughout the south how the friars had first stepped out, followed by a mitered bishop, then by the papal legate with a great banner, followed lastly by Fitzmaurice and a group of Spanish soldiers with English prisoners in chains. The invasion was numerically small and yet powerful. These men possessed the zeal of idealists. A

---

[20]William C. Atkinson, *History of Spain and Portugal* (Middlesex, England: Penguin Books Inc., 1960), 156-60.

[21]The savage persecution of the Catholic clergy can be seen in Deputy Drury's treatment of Bishop O'Herly of Mayo and Fr. O'Rourke O.F.M. who were captured at Kilmallock in August of 1579. They both admitted they were priests and in an effort to gain information on the movements of Fitzmaurice, Drury had these men racked, their arms and legs broken with hammers, needles thrust under their nails and finally hanged. (E. A. D'Alton, *History of Ireland* Vol. 3 [London: Gresham Publishing Co.], 102-103.)

banner blessed by the Pope himself was unfurled bearing the arms of Fitzmaurice, Christ crucified, and the great scroll, "*IN OMNIA TRIBULATIONE ET ANGUSTIA JESUS ET MARIA.*"[22] The cry of *Papa abu!* (the Pope to victory) was taken up by the crusaders. A letter from the Pope offering indulgences to all who would join the army was read.[23]

The papal crusade in Ireland and the "Jesuit invasion" of England in June of 1580 alarmed Elizabeth.[24] The Lord Chancellor and council of England ordered that all the fit

---

[22]O'Faolain, *The Great O'Neil,* 97.

[23]The Catholic spirit of the times can be seen in the correspondence of James Eustace the Viscount Baltinglas to the Earl of Ormond dated July 27, 1580: "I have received your letter. Whereas you hear that I assemble great companies of men together, you know I am not of such power, but whatsoever I can make it shall be to maintain truth. Injuries though I have received, yet I forget them. The highest power on earth commands us to take the sword. 'Questionless it is great want of knowledge, and more of grace, to think and believe, that a woman uncapax of all holy orders, should be the supreme governor of Christ's Church; a thing that Christ did not grant unto his own mother. If the Queen's pleasure be, as you allege, to minister justice, it were time to begin; for in this 20 years past of her reign we have seen more damnable doctrine maintained, more oppressing of poor subjects, under pretence of justice, within this land than ever we read or heard (since England first received the faith) done by Christian princes. You counsel me to remain quiet, and you will be occupied in persecuting the poor members of Christ. I would you should learn and consider by what means your predecessors came up to be Earl of Ormond. Truly you should find that if Thomas Beckett, Bishop of Canterbury, had never suffered death in the defence of the Church, Thomas Butler, *alias* Beckett, had never been Earl of Ormond.'" (J. S. Brewer, and William Butler, eds. *Calendar of the Carew Papers in the Lambeth Library* Vol. 2 [Nendeln/Liechtenstein: Kraus-Thompson Ltd., 1974], 289).

[24]Read, *Lord Burghley,* 244.

men of the Pale should gather and execute by martial law "all leaders of the blind folk, harpers, bards, rhymers, and loose and idle people."[25] The war was declared on these individuals by England for they stirred up the flames of the indigent Gaelic culture and nationalism. The rising spread through Munster but on August 18, scarcely a month after his arrival, Fitzmaurice was killed during a petty skirmish near Castleconnell. As James lay dying, he gave command of the Catholic army to John, the brother of the Earl of Desmond. John rallied the Catholic forces at *Gort-na-Tibrid* (Springfield near Limerick) where he decimated an English force led by the Deputy Drury, killing the two captains who led the force. Drury himself died several days after this defeat.

The death of Fitzmaurice, however, proved a fatal blow to the cause. The Earl of Desmond, the head of the Geraldine clan who initially hesitated in joining the war, now belatedly entered the conflict due to English suspicions and the promptings of Fr. Sanders. The Earl lacked both the vision and the character of his brother James yet he remained true to his cause until the end. On September 13, 1580 further assistance arrived from Spain. Colonel Sebastian San Jose landed with 700 men (and a large supply of arms) on the coast of Kerry and fortified themselves in the fort on Golden Island.[26] The English Lord Deputy Grey, whose fine army had been thoroughly routed earlier on August 25th

---

[25]Cyril Falls, *Elizabeth's Irish Wars*, (New York: Barnes & Noble, 1970), 127.

[26]A. M. Sullivan, *The Story of Ireland* (Dublin: M.H. Gill & Sons, 1861), 227.

by Fiach McHugh O'Byrne in the pass of Glenmalure in County Wicklow, realizing what was at stake for his sovereign, immediately assaulted them by land and sea but was unsuccessful in his efforts. With the approach of winter, Grey, a fierce Puritan, sent in a flag of truce and offered honorable terms to the Spanish commander. The Spanish commander accepted and ordered the men to lay down their arms. When all the supplies and weapons were confiscated, Grey sent in his soldiers and massacred all 700 men. A number of women who had taken shelter in the castle (fearing exposure to the wilderness), including several who were pregnant, were hung. Fr. Sanders also relates that his servant William Walsh, Father Lawrence Moore and Oliver Plunkett were kept for special execution. Sanders states of these last three that their arms and legs were broken in three places and were left that night in agony until they were hung, drawn and quartered the following day. The Lord Deputy's treachery was never forgotten in Ireland and became proverbial on the Continent as *Graia fides.*[27]

The Geraldine cause reached its lowest ebb following this horrible tragedy. The Earl of Desmond and his family

---

[27]Clare, *History of Ireland*, 444 and O'Faolain, *The Great O'Neil*, 7. The poet Edmund Spencer, who served as secretary to Grey, described him as "a bloody man who regarded not the life of the queen's subjects, no more than dogs." Cyril Falls commented, "Many more terrible acts have been committed in war, but the cold horror of this has continued to leave its mark upon the pages of history after over three centuries and a half." (Falls, *Elizabeth's Irish Wars*, 144.) See also a fine summary in Alfred O'Rahilly *The Massacre at Smerwick 1580* (Dublin: Cork University Press, 1938.)

 25

became fugitives in their own land. The English government offered a pardon to the Earl if he would hand over Fr.
Sanders, the papal legate. This, however, he stoutly refused
to do. Fr. Sanders continued his spiritual ministry until
worn out with sufferings and exhaustion; he died in 1581 in
the woods of Claenglass.[28] He was administered to by the
Bishop of Killaloe from whom he received the last rites of
the Church. One by one the Geraldine leaders were captured and killed.[29] The Earl himself was hunted down and
forced to fly from place to place. This cautious man was finally, tragically assassinated on the Feast of St. Martin, the
patron saint of soldiers, November 11, 1583. His head was
sent to Elizabeth and impaled on London Bridge. The now
hopeless struggle ended with his death.[30]

---

[28]Clare, *History of Ireland*, 445.

[29] In January of 1581, John of Desmond, who had nobly sought to
aid the Spaniards at Kerry, was killed in an ambush. His turquoise
set in gold was sent overseas to Queen Elizabeth, his *agnus dei* to the
Earl of Beford and his severed head was "gifted" to Grey.

[30]Cyril Falls gives the following reflection on the Earl's death, "In
viewing events in an age in which lineage and position are highly regarded, the tragedy overwhelming a great house in the person of a
great nobleman is not to be measured by his private virtues and accomplishments. It becomes a tragedy of the first order because it has
been felt to be that in so many breasts. Better men, with higher gifts
and nobler personalities than Desmond himself, died for Desmond.
They are forgotten and he is remembered, without injustice. If he was
deserted by all at the end, he was never betrayed for the reward upon
his head. The cynic may retort that this was because the would-be be-
trayer knew that he would be denied absolution if he ventured to
succumb to the lure of the reward; but there is no doubt that honour
was a powerful motive with the poorest. Desmond lives on in tradition and in legend. The great Anglo-Irish historian, visiting the
scenes of his revolt at a time within the memory of men who are still

The land was deliberately wasted by the English and the inhabitants mercilessly slaughtered by the Queen's soldiers. The slaughter was excessively bloody even by the standards of the sixteenth century.[31] We may accept the English Victorian historian James Froude's comment on all of this:

> The English nation was shuddering over the atrocities of the Duke of Alva. The children in the nurseries were being inflamed to patriotic rage and madness by tales of Spanish tyranny. Yet Alva's bloody sword never touched the young, the defenseless, or those whose sex even dogs can recognize and respect.[32]

---

alive, was told by countrymen near Holycross, in Limerick, that the ghost of the Earl, mounted on a ghostly horse shod with silver, sometimes rose by night from the neighbouring waters of Lough Gur. And when in winter a gale from the Atlantic swept up the valleys, the folk of Kerry still called upon the traveller to listen to the famous and intimidating howl of the Desmond gallowglasses born down the wind." (Falls, *Elizabeth's Irish Wars*, 151-152.)

[31] R. Trevor Davies, *The Golden Century of Spain* (New York: Harper & Row, 1961), 212.

[32] O'Faolain, *The Great O'Neil*, 77. Froude also states that Munster was so desolate "that the lowing of a cow was not to be heard from Valentia to the Rock of Cashel." As to the conduct of the Elizabethan soldiers, the English historian relates, "When sent to recover stolen cattle or punish a night foray, they came at last to regard the Irish peasants as unpossessed of the common rights of human beings, and shot and strangled them like foxes or jackals. More than once in the reports of officers employed on these services, we meet the sickening details of these performances related with a calmness more frightful than the atrocities themselves; young English gentlemen describing expeditions into the mountains 'to have some killing,' as if a forest was being driven for a battle." (James Anthony Froude, *The English in Ireland* 3 Vols. [New York: AMS Press, 1969], 56).

The war cost Elizabeth half a million pounds.[33] Munster was desolate. Those who escaped the ferocity of the soldiers could not escape the deadly embrace of the famine they induced as it swept over the land. The English poet Edmund Spenser (who received a few acres from Raleigh, who had seized forty thousand for himself) hauntingly described the ghastly scene in the winter cold and rain:

> Out of every corner of the woods and glens they came creeping forth, upon their hands, because their legs would not bear them; they looked like anatomies of death, they spoke like ghosts crying out of their graves; they did eat of the dead carrions, happy were they if they could find them yea, and one another soon after...and if they found a plot of watercresses or shamrocks, there they flocked as to a feast for the time, yet not being able to continue there withal; so that in short space there were none almost left, and a most populous and plentiful country suddenly made void of man and beast.[34]

The Desmond War in Munster left behind a horrific legacy of fear and hatred. To many of the Irish, the courageous lives of Fitzmaurice and Fr. Sanders served as a vivid reminder of their ancient Catholic Faith given to them by St. Patrick. Despite overwhelming odds and the untimely death of key leaders, Catholic Munster had risen to the war cry of *Papa abu*. Fitzmaurice showed that the old yet resurgent Gaelic world was capable of grasping what was at

---

[33]O'Faolain, *The Great O'Neil*, 108.

[34]Edmund Spenser, *A View of the State of Ireland*, eds. Andrew Hadfield and Willy Maley (Oxford: Blackwell Publishers Ltd., 1997), 101-102.

stake and acting on it. Hugh O'Neill, the Baron of Dungannon, although he fought with the English against the Desmonds, came to realize, along with other leaders in Ireland, the power of the religious issue and saw the need for national unity if the claims of England were to be successfully challenged. As O'Faolain observed, he undoubtedly caught something of the spirit of Fitzmaurice's ideas. Always cautious and prudent, O'Neill realized that there was little he could do to save the Desmonds, and therefore he made the best of a bad situation. The savage ugliness and coarse brutality of this new type of war awoke all of Gaelic Ulster from its lethargic slumber. The southern wars showed the tremendous power of the new system of centralization symbolized by the Crown. As the Gaelic chieftains saw the Desmond lands confiscated and sold to Protestant English settlers, they knew that they soon would be the next targets for this land speculation. Of all the provinces, Ulster had remained the least affected by English power. If there was to come any serious challenge to English power in Ireland it was to come from the Catholic, Gaelic kings of Ulster. Secretly, Hugh O'Neill and the elder Hugh Dubh O'Donnell prepared their people for the struggle ahead.

Hugh O'Neill, due to his service rendered during the Desmond War, was made Earl of Tyrone by Elizabeth. Upon his return from London, he was even permitted to keep a standing army of six companies "to preserve order in the north."[35]

---

[35]Clare, *History of Ireland*, 447.

The state of Ulster was now beginning to cause considerable anxiety to the English government. In 1586, over 1,000 English soldiers were withdrawn from Ireland and sent to aid the Protestant cause in the Spanish Netherlands. O'Neill began to manifest a degree of independence which alarmed English officials. He married Joan, a daughter of Hugh Dubh O'Donnell, and O'Donnell refused to allow an English sheriff into his country. In the North, the smoldering fire of war was to flame forth again. The English Protestants themselves, due to the policy of religious persecution and treachery, were to trigger the greatest alliance they were to ever face in Ireland. This alliance was eventually to shake English power in Ireland to its very foundations and even threaten England itself. It was to be a source of endless fear and anxiety for Elizabeth and William Cecil. Neither the Queen nor Lord Burghley were to live to see the submission of "The Northern Lucifer" or "Beelzebub" which the Queen had angrily nicknamed Tyrone. In Rome, the noble Pontiff Gregory XIII, when he heard of the tragic fate of Fitzmaurice, issued yet another Bull on May 13, 1580, praising the noble qualities of James Fitzmaurice "of happy memory" and granting once again the special indulgence, "as that which was imparted to those who fought against the Turks for the recovery of the Holy Land" to all those who would support the Catholic cause in Ireland.[36]

The heroic struggle of James Fitzmaurice and the Desmonds in defense of their faith and native land was not for-

---

[36]T. D. McGee, *History of Ireland* Vol. 8 (New York: D. & J. Sadlier and Co., 1863), 25.

gotten in Ireland and therefore was not fought in vain. A seed had been planted which ten years later was to bear fruit. Gaelic Ulster was to rise up in defense of the Catholic faith and national independence with profound consequences for all of Ireland and Christendom.

TWO

ħuGħ ROE
PRINCE OF TIRCONNAILL

Sacred the cause of Clan Connaill's defending,
The altars we kneel at the homes of our sires
Ruthless the ruin the foe is extending,
Midnight is red with the plunderers' fires.
On with O'Donnell then,
Fight the old fight again,
Sons of Tirconnell, all valiant and true.
Make the false Saxon feel
Erin's avenging steel!
Strike for your country, "O'Donnell Aboo!"[1]

I n 1586 Captain Humphrey Willis and 300 soldiers described as "the scum of the kingdom"[2] left Dundalk and
entered into O'Donnell's country, Tirconnaill, modern day
Donegal. If the O'Donnells had been prudent they would
have attacked these men at once. Willis soon declared himself a sheriff and when his soldiers ran out of money they
began to pillage and loot the country. The Englishman,
Captain Lee, left the following characterization of the soldiers' activity, "The rascals did rob and spoil the people,
ravished their wives and daughters, and made havoc of

---

[1]M.J. McCann, *The Clanconnell War Song* taken from, *Irish Poetry*
ed. Devin A. Garrity (New York: The New America Library, 1965),
236.

[2]O'Faolain, *The Great O'Neil*, 123.

all."[3] The people soon rose up in arms and Willis barely escaped with his life. This whole incident was slight and vulgar yet the English government in Dublin took serious note of it. Hugh Dubh O'Donnell, the son of Calvach O'Donnell and chief of the clan, was considered a dangerous man. He had been inaugurated as King of Tirconnaill in 1566. Accordingly, the new Lord Deputy, Sir John Perrot, who had taken office in 1584, entered into consultation with the Council in Dublin as to how the situation could best be handled. O'Donnell was a devout Catholic and the churches and monasteries in his country had remained untouched. Priests continued to celebrate the Mass in the remote and sheltered glens of Tirconnaill. The Desmond War was not long over and the Lord Deputy had grown weary of armed conflict and was short of money. In addition, many of the Queen's troops had been sent to the war in Flanders. Perrot pointed out to the Council that it would take at least an army of 3,000 men to subdue Hugh Dubh O'Donnell and the whole effort would be a treacherous and costly undertaking in the remote northwest.[4] In addition, the year was 1587, and the lofty, threatening sails of Philip II's invincible Spanish Armada could be seen at Corunna.

The situation was further complicated by Hugh Dubh O'Donnell's son, Hugh Roe, more popularly known as Red Hugh. Even before he reached manhood, the boy was famous throughout Ireland for his wisdom, eloquence, comeliness and noble deeds.[5] Hugh Roe's birth in 1572, his vir-

---

[3]Denis Murphy, S.J., historical introduction to *The Life of Hugh O'Donnell* by L. O'Cleary (Dublin: Fallon & Co., 1895), 33.
[4]*Ibid*.
[5]Seamus MacManus, *The Story of the Irish Race* (New York: The

tues, his strength, his charismatic ability to lead men and his future triumphs over the enemies of Ireland - all these things were firmly believed by the Irish to have been foretold by St. Columcille, who himself was a member of the same clan, the Cinel Conaill.[6]

> There will come a man glorious, pure, exalted,
> Who will cause mournful weeping in every territory
> He will be the god-like, prince
> And he will be king for nine years.[7]

As early as 1593 this prophecy and others had reached the ears of the then Lord Deputy Fitzwilliam. In the same year, the Lord Deputy wrote the following letter to Lord Burghley:

> An old devised prophecy flieth among them in no small request, importing that when two Hughs, lawfully, lineally, and immediately succeed each other as O'Donnells, being so formally and ceremoniously created according to the country's custom, the last Hugh forsooth shall be a monarch in Ireland, and banish thence all foreign nations and conquerors.[8]

It is a clear tribute to Tudor statecraft that the gout-ridden William Cecil, back at Hampton Court, was able to

---

Devin-Adair Co., 1944), 379.

The Four Masters relate that "the look of amiability on his countenance captivated everyone who beheld him," and emphasize "his great power of command."

[6]Murphy, introduction to *Life of Hugh Roe O'Donnell*, 31.

[7]L. O'Cleary, *The Life of Hugh Roe O'Donnell* with a historical introduction by Denis Murphy, S. J. (Dublin: Fallon & Co., 1895), 5.

[8]Murphy, introduction to *Life of Hugh Roe O'Donnell*, 32.

 35

maintain an intelligent policy in Ireland despite the veritable maze of Irish clans and their conflicting politics.

With effective military action in Ireland all but impossible, Lord Deputy Perrot resorted to a treacherous plan by which young Hugh O'Donnell was to be captured and held as hostage. This would certainly insure his father's good behavior. The dreaded fifteen year-old boy was being fostered according to the Gaelic custom by MacSwiney, Lord of Fanat along the Northern Sea in Ulster. The ancient tradition of fostering, whereby a child was temporarily raised by a neighboring clan was meant to strengthen ties of friendship and affection. Perrot, through bribes and threats, induced a sea captain named Skipper to take 50 armed men and a cargo of wine and beer and sail around Ireland into Donegal.[9] The captain was to feign that he had come from Spain with rare and excellent wines. The ship set out from Dublin on Michaelmas in 1587.[10]

Hugh Roe was only fifteen years of age when an innocent looking merchant ship entered Lough Swilly, approached Rathmullen with its Carmelite monastery near the shores (a well known resort for pilgrims from Innishowen and Tirconnaill), and anchored near the white stone Doe Castle of MacSwiney. Skipper invited the local lords aboard and MacSwiney with Hugh Roe and several friends entered the ship. O'Cleary relates that when they had feasted with a variety of food and drink they became relaxed. Suddenly their weapons were seized by the ship's officers and the soldiers imprisoned Hugh in the bowels of

---

[9]O'Faolain, *The Great O'Neil*, 124.
[10]O'Cleary, *Life of Hugh Roe O'Donnell*, 7.

the ship. MacSwiney was released and the ship set sail for Dublin with its prized possession. Perrot wrote his own account of the transaction in a letter to Queen Elizabeth dated September 26, 1587:

> Inasmuch as I found Sir Hugh O'Donnell to be one that would promise much for the delivery of his pledges and the yearly rent of beeves set upon that country and perform little, and that in respect he was married to a Scottish lady, the sister of Angus MacDonnell, by whom he had a son, Hugh Roe O'Donnell, who ruled that country very much, and thereby not only nourished Scots in those parts but also certain of the MacSwynes (a strong and disordered kind of people there), who have been ready to send aid to any that were evil disposed in your kingdom, as of late they did to Granye ne Male (Grace O'Malley) to see if they would make any new stir in Connaught, I devised to send a bark hence under the charge of one Nicholas Skipper of this city with certain wines, to allure the best of the country aboard, who had such good success as he took and brought hither yesterday in the said bark without any stir at all the said Hugh Roe O'Donnell, the eldest son of the galloglasse called Mac-Swyne Fana, the eldest son of the galloglasse called Mac-Swyne ne Doe, and the best pledge upon the O'Gallahores, all being the strongest septs of Tyrconnel. Whereby now you may have (in those parts) your pleasure always performed, and specially touching Sir John O'Doghertye, Hugh O'Donnell, and MacSwyne Bane, in whose behalf it pleased you and the Council to write unto me of late to show them favour, because they had served you well, and were therefore beaten down by the said MacSwynes and others. The having of Mr. Hugh Roe O'Donnell, in respect he is come of the Scots and matched in marriage with the greatest of Ulster, will serve you to good purpose.[11]

---

[11]Murphy, introduction to *Life of Hugh Roe O'Donnell*, 33-4.

The Queen was pleased with the efficient work of her Deputy. Gaelic Ireland burned with indignation at the outrage. Hugh was put in chains and upon his arrival in Dublin was examined by the Lord Deputy and imprisoned in Dublin Castle's Birmingham Tower. Here the young prince remained for three years, with other noble captives, half-starved and distressed in mind. During these three years young Hugh contemplated the fate of his country.[12] He saw first hand the effects of English law: the savage persecution of the Church, the seizure of Irish lands by the English colonist, and the government's efforts to destroy his family and Gaelic civilization. This made a deep impression on the mind of this young man who had grown up in the wild, free beauty of northwest Ulster. After three years Hugh made a daring escape from the castle on a December night. Hugh had successfully reached Wicklow and the territory of Felim O'Toole, but was retaken. He was brought back to Dublin and imprisoned again but with a more vigilant guard: "Iron fetters were bound on him as tightly as possible, and they watched and guarded him as closely as they could."[13] He was treated cruelly by the English guards who resented his escape. The bitter experiences in prison were the sources of Hugh's unending animosity toward the English.

In the meantime, Hugh Dubh O'Donnell had begged in vain for his son's release. The kidnapping had united the O'Donnells and O'Neills in their efforts to secure the boy's

---

[12]Four Masters, *Annals*, 6:1897.

[13]The Four Masters cited in Murphy, introduction to *Life of Hugh Roe O'Donnell*, 37-8.

release. Hugh O'Neill, the Earl of Tyrone, was married to Hugh Dubh's daughter Joan, and O'Neill's own daughter Rose was to have married Hugh Roe.[14] Tyrone offered a ransom of a thousand pounds and wrote the Earl of Leicester asking him to be "a mean for the enlargement of the prisoner upon security."[15] He also communicated with Lord Walsingham asking him to use his influence with Her Majesty for the same purpose:

> The Lord Deputy hath caused O'Donnell's son called Hugh O'Donnell to be taken, who now remaineth a prisoner in the Castle of Dublin. He is my son-in-law, and the only stay that O'Donnell hath for the quieting of his country and the detaining of him in prison is the most prejudiced which might happen to me. Your Honour is the only man next unto the Earl of Leicester on whom I can rely, and O'Donnell hath no friends but mine.[16]

All of O'Neill's efforts ended in frustration. Elizabeth was not to be moved. The Queen reacted in this way not so much because the elder Hugh O'Donnell was himself a man to be feared, as that his wife, Ineen Dubh (known as the Dark Lady), was one of the MacDonnells of the Isles. Ever since Walter Devereux, the Earl of Essex, had slaughtered over 500 of the people (men, women and children) of her uncle on Rathlin Island in July of 1575, the "Dark Lady" was one of the bitterest opponents of English rule in Ireland. The two were married in 1569 and she bore Hugh Dubh four sons, Hugh Roe, Rory, Manus and Caffar. The

---

[14]O'Faolain, *The Great O'Neil*, 125.
[15]Murphy, introduction to *Life of Hugh Roe O'Donnell*, 35.
[16]*Ibid.*, 35-6.

valiant woman was described by the Four Masters as a woman, "like the mother of the Macabees, who joined a man's heart to a woman's thought."[17] She was deeply devoted to her eldest son Red Hugh (born 1572), who was destined to succeed his father as Lord of Tirconnaill. Elizabeth sent the following order forbidding the release of the boy:

> And hereto we add the remembrance of one thing that being well ordered may breed quietness in those parts, viz., the continuancing in prison of O'Donnell's son and O'Gallagher's son, lately seized upon and remaining in our Castle in Dublin.[18]

When the ships from the Spanish Armada were wrecked along the northwestern coast of Ireland, Hugh Dubh O'Donnell and Hugh O'Neill fed and protected the refugees.[19] Acting as independent Catholic Lords they transported nearly 3,000 Spaniards safely away to Scotland.[20] Whether this was an act of charity and Catholic solidarity or an act of common humanity, it was undoubtedly an important action of high courage. A lesser nobleman named Brian O'Rourke, Lord of Leitrim, with equal

---

[17]Four Masters, *Annals*, 6.

[18]Murphy, introduction to *Life of Hugh Roe O'Donnell*, 36.

[19]Garrett Mattingly, *The Armada* (Cambridge, Massachusetts: The Riverside Press, 1951). Contrary to some claims, the Irish sought, whenever possible, to assist the shipwrecked Spaniards (Falls, *Elizabeth's Irish Wars*, 166). According to O'Sullivan, the Spaniards were sent to Scotland to the Earl Bothwell and transported to France or the Spanish Netherlands (Don Philip O'Sullivan Bear, *Ireland Under Elizabeth* [London: Kennikat Press, 1970], 61).

[20]O'Faolain, *The Great O'Neil*, 36. See also, Curtis, *History of Ireland*, 204.

humanity, clothed, armed and refurbished the 1,000 Spaniards in his territory and was savagely attacked by the notorious English governor of Connaught, Sir Richard Bingham. His land was burnt and O'Rourke had to flee to Scotland. James VI treacherously handed him over to Elizabeth however, and this just man was hanged in London as a common criminal in November of 1591.[21] O'Rourke was respected throughout Ireland and his cruel death further united the clansmen.

O'Donnell and O'Neill continued to secretly plot for the freedom of Hugh Roe. A file had been passed to him and he planned his escape with two fellow prisoners, Henry and Art O'Neill, the sons of Shane the Proud.

The Christmas Eve of 1591 was cold and dark with snow falling in flurries. Christmas merriment was celebrated by the castle guards with wine and strong ale. Now was the chance the boys had waited for. Working furiously with the file they cut through their fetters and made a rope from the hangings of their beds. When, as O'Donnell's chronicler relates, "it seemed to the Son of the Virgin full time that he should escape,"[22] Hugh and his companions let themselves down with a silken rope through the sewer into the icy moat which surrounded the castle. The boys climbed to the opposite bank and there met a guide sent by Fiach MacHugh O'Byrne outside the castle gate. In the cold darkness of night with the snow swirling about them, the small group hurried through the dark streets and alleys to the outer rampart of the city. Henry O'Neill had fallen be-

---

[21]O'Faolain, *The Great O'Neil*, 137.
[22]O'Cleary, *Life of Hugh Roe O'Donnell*, 19.

hind during the scramble and lost his way. There was no turning back now, for behind them was the dungeon and certain death.

Leaping over the rampart they scurried into the open country toward Glenmalure. The guide led the way and the boys pressed on past silent bogs glimmering white with snow. Art being rather corpulent due to his inactivity in prison began to slow down. Hugh fell back to support and cheer his friend. On into the night they continued to struggle into the highlands of Wicklow until eventually Art could no longer walk. The two carried their companion until dawn. Hugh's feet were blistering and his strength began to fail. The guide continued on to seek help from Fiach O'Byrne. The boys struggled up the side of a mountain and hid themselves under a rock between two loughs, Dan and Glendalough.[23]

Back in Dublin as the light of the new day broke and church bells rang in the birth of the Savior, the princes were discovered missing and soldiers were angrily sent out on Christmas Day to retake the valuable fugitives.

The boys slept deeply through the piercing cold of the night and awoke the next morning shivering and hungry. They had not eaten now for over 40 hours. The day passed and the biting cold of the night nearly killed the two boys. The shouts of English soldiers could now be heard around the white Wicklow mountains. When the morning of the third day arrived, Art was dying. Hugh gathered some leaves and grass and tried to get Art to eat: "Art, see how the brute beasts feed on grass and leaves. We, too, though

---

[23]MacManus, *Story of the Irish Race*, 381.

endowed with reason, are animals; why should we not support life as they do? We soon shall have food sent to us by our friend."[24] Hugh chewed the leaves and swallowed them. He could not however force Art to eat them. A frozen, white death was now beginning to numb his mind and body. As evening came the two boys embraced each other and were covered by snow. In the fading twilight O'Byrne's soldiers finally reached the boys. O'Cleary graphically describes their condition:

Alas! truly the state and position of these nobles was not happy or pleasant to the heroes who had come to seek for them. They had neither cloaks nor plaids, nor clothing for protection under their bodies, to save them from the cold and frost of the sharp winter season, but the bed clothes under their fair skins and the pillows under their heads were supports heaped up, white-bordered of hailstones freezing all around them, and attaching their light coats and shirts of fine linen thread to their bodies, and their large shoes and the fastenings to their legs and feet, so that they seemed to the men that had come not to be human beings at all, but just like sods of earth covered up by snow, because they did not perceive motion in their limbs, but just as if they were dead, and they were nearly so. Wherefore the heroes raised them from where they lay and bade them take some of the food and of the ale, and they did not succeed, for every drink they took they let it out of their mouths again. However, Art died at last and was buried in that place. As for Hugh he retained the beer after that, and his strength was on the increase after drinking, except his two feet, for they were like dead members without motion, owing to the swelling and blistering from the frost and snow. The men carried him to the valley of which we have spoken. He was put into a house hidden

---

[24]Murphy, introduction to *Life of Hugh Roe O'Donnell*, 40.

in a remote part of the thick wood. He had medical skill and care in every way he needed until the arrival of a messenger in secret to inquire and get news about him from his brother-in-law Hugh O'Neil.[25]

As soon as Hugh could ride, O'Byrne and O'Toole escorted him across the Liffy and Boyne Rivers.[26] After resting at the Old Melifont Abbey, the first Cistercian house in Ireland, founded by the great St. Malachy in 1133, Hugh brilliantly succeeded in avoiding all English ambushes and sentries, even riding openly in the city of Dundalk. They spent the night secretly in Armagh, eventually reaching Hugh O'Neill at Dungannon.

Red Hugh O'Donnnell's dramatic escape sent a thrill throughout all the length and breadth of Ireland. Joyfully, messengers rode to Ulster and Leinster and Munster and Connaught with the glad tidings. The successful escape deeply disturbed not only the Queen's government in Ireland but in her majesty's court in England. Elizabeth was furious at what she perceived to be the corrupt deportment of her officials in Ireland. In May of 1592, she wrote to the then Lord Deputy Borough strictly charging him to take severe measures to find out and punish the offenders:

> O'Donnell escaped by the practice of money bestowed on somebody. Call to you the Chancellor, Chief Justice Gar-

---

[25]O'Cleary, *Life of Hugh Roe O'Donnell*, 24-5. MacManus states that Hugh was so grief stricken at the death of Art that he wept "passionately" and refused to eat or drink for some time. (MacManus, *Story of the Irish Race*.)

[26]T. W. H. Fitzgerald, *Ireland and Her People* (Chicago: Fitzgerald Book Co., 1909), 350.

diner, and the Treasurer, and inquire who they are that have been touched by it.[27]

O'Donnell and Hugh O'Neill conferred secretly in a private chamber in Tyrone's castle at Dungannon. Only O'Neill's most trustworthy people were allowed to visit Red Hugh as the Earl was still considered submissive and loyal by the English government in Dublin.[28] After remaining at the castle for four days and nights, O'Donnell prepared to leave O'Neill and Red Hugh gave him his blessing. O'Neill sent a body of troops with the prince until he entered the territory of Hugh Maguire, Lord of Fermanagh, who was a close friend and relative of Red Hugh (a first cousin) on his mother's side.[29] Hugh Maguire was tall, young, handsome and a brilliant and courageous leader. He graciously received him and the young prince was royally entertained to the general joy of the country. Hugh Roe was carried in Maguire's state barge in a triumphal procession down the Erne River. On the western bank his own kinsmen from Tirconnaill joyously greeted him and they journeyed with him to his family's castle at Ballyshannon. There were high spirits in the castle as the jubilant noblemen feasted, with the sound of war pipes filling the great hall. His presence and noble spirit renewed their courage as men now vowed to follow him. Hugh did not remain long at Ballyshannon. Donegal was in disarray. His father was now quite old and unable to effectively govern the country. Captain Willis and a body of English Protestants

---

[27]Murphy, introduction to *Life of Hugh Roe O'Donnell*, 41.
[28]O'Cleary, *Life of Hugh Roe O'Donnell*, 31.
[29]*Ibid.*, 33.

had reentered the country, taking possession of the beautiful Franciscan monastery with its priceless library in Donegal Town, and were besieging his father and mother in Donegal Castle. Hugh was especially angered that the Franciscan monastery built by his family should be profaned by heretics.[30]

The religious monasteries and convents of Tirconnaill and Tyrone had been granted to the King of England by the "Irish Parliament" in 1538.[31] The Commissioners who had been appointed to suppress them did not proceed to hold their normal appraisals on their possessions, to take inventory of their chapel adornments or to expel their peaceful religious, for the simple reason that the Irish kings held sway there and the piety of the people would not permit it. Myler Magrath, in his work *The State of Ireland* distressfully related that in Ulster, Connaught and even within the Pale itself, "divers friaries of divers sorts remained and were standing."[32] He went on to state that in Ulster alone there were at least 16 monasteries in the hands of Franciscans, Augustinians, Cistercians and other religious orders.

Hugh gathered his people in arms and led them to Donegal to drive out the English forces then inhabiting the

---

[30]O'Cleary, *Life of Hugh Roe O'Donnell*, 37. Willis had been sent into the territory by Bingham, the English Governor of Connaught. Donegal Castle itself recently restored, was described thus by Lord Deputy, Sir Henry Sidney, during his visit to Donegal in 1566: "It is the greatest I ever saw in Ireland in an Irishman's hands and would appear to be in good keeping; one of the fairest situated in good soil and so nigh a portable water as a boat on ten tons could come within twenty yards of it."

[31]Thebaud, *The Irish Race*, 180-1.

[32]Murphy, introduction to *Life of Hugh Roe O'Donnell*, 42.

monastery. Upon his arrival Hugh liberated the castle, freeing his devoted mother and father and summoned the English garrison to depart immediately and not to further profane the church. Hugh Roe displayed remarkable clemency allowing them to flee by whatever road they wished, but he sternly ordered them not to take any of the property they had plundered during their sojourn. Despite the fact that they had been reinforced by a body of 200 men sent by the English in Dublin,

> when news came to them that O'Donnell had reached Donegal in safety, quaking fear and great terror seized on them. They resolved to leave the country, and they went away as they were ordered to do, glad to go away alive, and returned to Connaught whence they had come.[33]

Chief Justice Gardiner wrote the following letter to Lord Burghley on February 27, 1592:

> Hugh O'Donnell is returned to his own country and has freed the pledges of that country out of the Abbey of Donegal, and has expelled Captain Willis and the Sheriff with his band of 100 soldiers.[34]

---

[33]Four Masters, *Annals*, 6:1927. O'Sullivan Bear relates that Red Hugh gave "an injunction to remember his words that the Queen and her officers were dealing unjustly by the Irish; that the Catholic religion was contaminated by impiety; that holy bishops and priests were inhumanly and barbarously tortured; that Catholic noblemen were cruelly imprisoned and ruined; that wrong was deemed right; that he himself had been treacherously and perfidiously kidnapped; and that for these reasons he would neither give tribute nor allegiance to the English." (O'Sullivan Bear, *Ireland Under Elizabeth*, 68.) The Franciscans returned and resumed chanting their psalms and saying their Masses especially for young Red Hugh.

[34]Murphy, introduction to *Life of Hugh Roe O'Donnell*, 42.

 47

Young Hugh O'Donnell's actions fired the imagination of his fellow countrymen and he became the hero of Gaelic Ireland. His father, being advanced in years, was no longer able to control the dissension among his people. In the face of these domestic problems and the growing dangers of an English attack, the elder O'Donnell prudently decided to resign his authority to his son. The nobles and soldiers, along with the chiefs of the various districts under his sway, held council together and unanimously agreed to Hugh Dubh's proposal. He had now grown tired of the troubles and treacheries of the world and, devout man that he was, decided to seek the rest and shelter of a prayerful monastery. His mother, who had, "the heart of a hero and the soul of a soldier" now had the joy of seeing her son's position secured.

The inauguration of the O'Donnell as King of Tirconnaill was both civil and religious in nature.[35] The ceremony took place on the great Rock of Doone which is one mile west of Kilmacrenan, from which one is given a breathtaking view of the surrounding country. It began with the religious rites in the church of the nearby monastery and holy well singing psalms and hymns in honor of Christ and St. Columba for the success of the prince's sovereignty. Standing on the rock surrounded by nobles and his clansmen, the Prince received an oath in which he promised to preserve the Church and the laws of the land. The Prince also vowed to deliver the succession of the realm peacefully to his *Tanist* (his successor). O'Ferghil, the hereditary warden and abbot of Kilmacrenan, performed the religious cere-

---

[35]*Ibid.*, 43.

mony of the inauguration of the O'Donnell. O'Gallagher was the Prince's marshal and O'Clery was the *ollamh* or scholarly lawyer who presented to him the book containing the laws and customs of the land and the straight, white wand symbolizing the moral rectitude demanded of his judgments and rule.

Accordingly, on May 3, 1592, having received his father's blessing, Hugh Roe O'Donnell, now scarcely twenty years old, "the boy with gifts of mind and body that made men look to him as the hope of Ireland" stood on the Rock of Doone and was inaugurated as "The O'Donnell." The white wand was placed in his hand symbolizing his authority and the faith and veracity demanded of him.[36] After turning thrice from left to right and thrice from right to left, in honor of the Holy Trinity, he surveyed every point of his kingdom from that spectacular, rocky height. While Red Hugh stood, "still, erect and kingly", O'Ferghil then proclaimed "O'Donnell!" and each of the nobles, according to their rank, reechoed the name as the countless voices of jubilant clansmen reverberated the name far into the distance. Hugh Roe O'Donnell, "the son of prophecy", was now King of Tirconnaill and the Nine Years War had begun.

---

[36]MacManus, *Story of the Irish Race*, 383.

τhree

τyROnE and the CaτhOLIC COnfEOERaCy

O'Donnell is deceased whose place Manus, his son,
has obtained by the assent of the country and the
favor of O'Neill, whose two strengths joined is a
great power, and to be feared by your subjects.
George Carew to Henry VIII, 1537[1]

after his inauguration, Hugh O'Donnell gathered a small force to attack Turlough O'Neill. During O'Donnell's imprisonment, Turlough O'Neill, with his English allies, had plundered Tirconnaill. O'Neill's country, adjacent to Donegal, was also being used as a base for English spies who kept Dublin informed of his movements and the condition of his country. Turlough was in addition, "The O'Neill" (head of the O'Neill clan) and the chief rival of the Earl Hugh O'Neill of Tyrone who was a close friend of the O'Donnell's. Hugh Roe now led his clan, the Cinel Conaill, deep into Turlough O'Neill's country, plundering and laying waste to his territory.[2] This initial action caught the O'Neill's by complete surprise, and the Cinel Conaill returned to Donegal with great spoils. That very same week, O'Donnell returned to attack the inhabitants of the country

---

[1]Murphy, introduction to *Life of Hugh Roe O'Donnell*, 18.
[2]*Ibid.*, 19.

for a second time. This time, O'Neill and his force of both English and Irish troops awaited his arrival. When O'Donnell heard of this he called his forces together and addressed them saying:

> I have heard it for certain from persons of knowledge and experience that the well-known saying has always proved true: every army which does not attack will be attacked. Wherefore it seems to me if we abandon the territory now and turn our backs on our enemies, they will follow on our track and on our footsteps to attack us boldly on our rear, and they will feel sure that weakness and fear is our reason for not attacking them at all. But if we first make the attack now boldly, obstinately, fear and deadly terror will not allow them or the foreign tribe that is with them to follow us again.[3]

Accordingly, at mid-day the Cinel Conaill made a "resolute attack and angry advance"[4] on the enemy. O'Neill's lines broke and his forces sought shelter in the nearby castle of Limavaddy on the banks of the river Roe. The fortress was impregnable and O'Neill's forces remained secure behind its walls. O'Donnell remained in the region for three days plundering and wasting the land. Upon returning to Donegal Castle, he rested his army and had his physicians examine his feet. As a result of the hardships he had endured during his escape from Dublin Castle, part of his two large toes which had been severely frostbitten were amputated.

After two months of preparation, O'Donnell again set off to attack O'Neill's stronghold of Strabane where Tur-

---

[3]O'Cleary, *Life of Hugh Roe O'Donnell*, 47.
[4]*Ibid.*

lough and the English had remained in the castle. No defense was given the town and the Cinel Conaill burnt and plundered the four quarters of the town on July 18, 1592.[5] As the English did not sally forth from the castle in an effort to avenge the destruction of the town, the Cinel Conaill returned to their homes.

Earl O'Neill, perceiving the growing hostility of his own clan against O'Donnell and the growing concern of the English in Dublin, journeyed to Donegal to visit O'Donnell. O'Neill was politically astute and deeply cautious. He felt that O'Donnell had initiated the conflict prematurely. O'Neill was still considered by the English as loyal to the Queen's cause. He had promised the Lord Deputy William Fitzwilliam that he would try to reconcile O'Donnell with the English government. When O'Neill arrived at Donegal there was great rejoicing.[6] Into the wee hours of the morning the two men discussed their hopes and dreams as well as their strategy for O'Donnell's reconciliation with the English. Although Red Hugh certainly did not wish to go and seek peace from the English, he acquiesced for the sake of his friendship with Hugh O'Neill.

On the following day the two set out with a troop of men for Dundalk. There they met the Lord Deputy who welcomed O'Donnell and forgave him for escaping from Dublin. Hugh made his formal submission to Fitzwilliam. That Hugh O'Donnell was entirely lacking in sincerity can hardly be doubted. This maneuver accomplished two things: first, it appeased the English government thereby

---

[5]*Ibid.*, 51.
[6]*Ibid.*

gaining more time for the Irish princes to prepare for the struggle ahead; secondly, it solidified O'Donnell's hold on Tirconnaill by ending all possible opposition to him among his own clan.[7]

O'Donnell and O'Neill returned together to the Earl's castle at Dungannon where they celebrated and feasted together for several days. When O'Donnell thought it time to return to Donegal he prepared to depart. The two men had become such close, good friends that "it was painful to both to be separated from each other."[8]

Hugh O'Donnell, upon his return to Donegal, did not begin acting as one submissive to England's Protestant Sovereign. The Irish princes knew that without foreign assistance they lacked the strength to oppose the might of England. Accordingly they sought aid from other countries especially those united with them in the common bond of religion. O'Donnell sent messengers such as MacGauran, the Archbishop of Armagh, in 1592 and letters to Spain. Spain was the leading power in Europe during the late sixteenth century and the hope of the Catholic world. Philip II of Spain was the self-ordained champion of Catholicism during the Catholic Reformation. He lavishly poured a vast quantity of gold, which was flowing into Spain from the New World in the 16th century, into an effort to arrest the spread of the new Protestant heresies in Europe.[9] From his

---

[7]*Ibid.*, 53. Neale Garve, the eldest son of Red Hugh's Uncle Calvagh, had married Red Hugh's sister Nuala and thought he had a claim to the chieftaincy. English policy frequently sought to set up rivals against a prince who would not do the government's bidding.

[8]O'Cleary, *Life of Hugh Roe O'Donnell*, 53.

[9]Davies, *Golden Century of Spain*, 297-8.

magnificent palace, El Escorial, that monumental structure which catches the spirit of Spain's unwavering orthodoxy in granite, Philip directed the political course of the Catholic Reform.

> Philip, King of Spain, the firmest bulwark of the Christian religion and of the Catholic Church, moved with compassion on account of the calamities that had befallen the church of Ireland, provided and made a most generous provision for the faith of the Island almost rooted out, by establishing and endowing seminaries.[10]

O'Donnell also sought the aid of the Irish in foreign lands. He especially exhorted Irish officers in the service of European princes to aid the Catholic Irish cause. The following letter he addressed to Maurice Fitzgerald, Fitzmaurice and the other Irish gentlemen in Spain from Donegal, April 8, 1593:

> You will have heard, my beloved friends, how I found a means of escaping from the prison in which I was, and how after much labour and hardship I reached my own territory. There I found an Englishman, agent of the Queen, and with him many soldiers; all of whom, with the help of God's grace, I slew or drove out in a very short time, and never since have the English returned here, though not for want of will and desire to destroy me and do me all the harm they could. This is why I and the other chiefs who have united with me and are striving to defend ourselves, cannot hold out long against the power of the Crown of England without the aid of his Grace, the Catholic King. Wherefore, by common consent, we have thought it well to send the Archbishop of Tuam, though his presence is very necessary

---

[10]O'Sullivan Bear, quoted in Murphy's introduction to *Life of Hugh Roe O'Donnell*, 48.

here, to treat of this matter with his Majesty, and to give you, gentlemen, who are there, our letters, that you may all speak to his Majesty and beg of him immediate aid to assist us in fighting and combating for the service of God, and to protect and get back our lands, for it is right that we should be all of one mind, and that we should help each other in this undertaking. This I will do for my part till death, with the aid which I hope for from his Grace and with your presence and help. I will say no more, but pray God may be with you, and enable the Lord Archbishop to return with this favour.[11]

Fitzmaurice, in response, addressed a letter to Philip in his own name, on behalf of his fellow countrymen. He sought aid for his companions in arms and begged the king's approval that he might partake in any military expedition set to succor the country:

> Sire,—Maurice Fitzmaurice, heir of the Earl of Desmond, and the other Irish gentlemen in your Majesty's service have received, through the Archbishop of Cashel, at present at Court, letters from the principal Catholic gentry now united. They write that they are agreed to carry on war against the Queen of England, and they have asked us to implore your Majesty to send them aid in all possible haste. We know that these Lords are Catholics, and among the strongest and most powerful in Ireland, and uniting thus of their own free will, they risk their lives and estates to serve God and your Majesty. We have thought it right to implore your Majesty, for the love of God, to be pleased to take their needs to heart, and to send the aid you will think fit; and with it to send us to defend and uphold the said undertaking, for we hope, with God's help, your Majesty will be vic-

---

[11]*Ibid.*, 50. Cyril Falls observes that Red Hugh never deviated from the firm resolve expressed in this letter. (Falls, *Elizabeth's Irish Wars*, 175.)

torious and conquer and hold as your own the kingdom of Ireland, and obtain thereby an entrance into England, for it would be a great pity that these lords should be lost for want of aid, as was the Earl of Desmond, who rose in arms in the same way. We trust in God that your Majesty and the Council will weigh well the advantages that will ensue to Christendom from this enterprise, and since the opportunity is so good, the cause so just and weighty, and the undertaking so easily completed, your Majesty will do what is best for the service of God and of your Majesty; seeing that by so doing the Queen of England will be compelled to withdraw the forces she is accustomed to send to Flanders and France, and cannot employ English on the coast of Spain. This is what we can say and beg of your Majesty, on this subject; we are ready to do whatever your Majesty may command. May our Lord preserve your royal person, as Christendom requires.

In Lisbon, 4th of September, 1593.

Don Mauricio Geraldino[12]

James O'Hely, the Archbishop of Tuam, had also been sent to Spain by Red Hugh to inform Philip of the needs of the newly formed Catholic Confederacy.[13] Writing from Ferrol on April 4, 1593, the Archbishop sent a letter to the king. In the letter, O'Hely relates to his Majesty that in his recent journeys through Ireland he found the nobility as well as the bishops of the country resolute and of one mind: the Catholic Faith must be defended in Ireland. In this undertaking, aid from Catholic Spain was essential.

The Archbishop's petition appears to have been warmly received by the Spanish Court. The following document was presented to King Philip by the Court:

---

[12]Murphy, introduction to *Life of Hugh Roe O'Donnell*, 51.
[13]*Ibid.*

The Archbishop of Tuam in Ireland says that for years past he has been anxious, and has laboured much both in public and private, to unite and combine in a league and in friendship the Catholics of Ireland, for the purpose of making them take up arms on behalf of the Catholic faith and of your Majesty's service against the English heretics. In this he has been successful, for the most powerful Lords of the Catholic party in the northern part of the kingdom have united and risen against the Queen with great unanimity, and many other Catholics mean to do the like. Wherefore, the said Archbishop, on behalf and in the name of all these, as is evident from the letters which they wrote to your Grace, has come to ask your Grace to help, on such a favourable opportunity as this of making war on the Queen at home, the said Lords and their people; and the Irish gentlemen who are now serving your Majesty in this kingdom, will give very great help in this undertaking, especially Maurice Fitzmaurice and the Viscount Bartinglas. Wherefore, the said Archbishop humbly beseeches your Grace to order some aid both of men and arms for this purpose, and that they should be given so that he may be able to return with an answer suitable to the good-will and earnestness with which they offer to serve your Majesty. He says it will be of much importance for the success of the confederation if your Majesty will order a friendly letter to be written to the Earl of Tyrone, called O'Neill, that he may enter into the confederation publicly, seeing that he belongs to it already in secret, assuring him that your Majesty's aid will not be wanting.[14]

Exiled Irish clergy such as Cornelius O'Mulrain, the bishop of Killaloe, eagerly took up the Irish Catholic cause. From Lisbon the bishop addressed the following letter to Philip dated September 3, 1593:

---

[14]*Ibid.*, 52.

Sire, —By letters from Ireland I have learned that many very powerful gentlemen have risen in the north of Ireland against the Queen of England, as your Majesty has learned from the Archbishop of Tuam, who has come on their behalf to beseech your Majesty to be pleased to send them aid in all haste, as it is evident that these powerful gentlemen, with the others in Ireland, mean to put themselves under your Majesty, and for this they have taken up arms with such spirit and Catholic zeal in defense of the faith, trusting in the aid that will be supplied by your Majesty, and ready to subject the kingdom to you. I beg of you, most mighty King, by the Blood of Jesus, to enter on this task with a lively faith and courageous mind. By sending this force to Ireland your Majesty will acquire everlasting renown and a vast and very fertile kingdom. There you will be at the door of England, and no English will further molest the coast of Spain or oppose your Majesty in Flanders or in France. I trust your Majesty will consider all this. I now conclude, and beg to offer myself to bear a part in this expedition, for the service of God and of your Majesty. May God in his infinite mercy preserve and prosper us, and grant you a long life, as is needed by all the Christian people.

Your servant and chaplain,
Cornelius, bishop of Killaloe.[15]

While these diplomatic efforts continued in Spain, Hugh O'Donnell also sent letters to Scotland inviting additional forces of soldiers, warriors and mercenaries which he hoped to employ. Back in Ireland more of the northern chieftains decided to join the Catholic Confederacy. When Hugh Maguire, the Lord of Fermanagh, "heard of the great attempt which O'Donnell intended"[16] he hoped to be the

---

[15]*Ibid.*, 53.
[16]O'Cleary, *Life of Hugh Roe O'Donnell*, 61.

first to enter into the war. Maguire was a skillful, courageous soldier and an excellent horseman who was to put
his heart and soul into the war. His acquisition greatly
strengthened the Confederacy.

O'Donnell's strategic efforts against Turlough O'Neill
and his English auxiliaries paid off as Turlough, now an old
man, was forced to resign the leadership of his clan to
Hugh O'Neill, the Earl of Tyrone:

> Whilst he was staying in his princely seat and his chief
> residence at Lifford (24 January, 1593), confronting his en-
> emy Turlough Luineach O'Neil, he proceeded to wreak his
> vengeance and his enmity on him by driving him from his
> principality and weakening him, in the hope that Hugh
> O'Neil might be inaugurated in his place. The foresight
> which he used proved of advantage to him, for the chief-
> tancy fell in the end to Hugh O'Neil, and Turlough Luineach
> gave his consent and yielded to him as to the title that he
> should be styled The O'Neil. He was proclaimed after that
> and Turlough sent away the English who were with him,
> since he entered into peace and friendship with O'Donnell.
> In the month of May exactly, in the year of our Lord 1593, he
> did this.
>
> Since O'Donnell was at peace with him the two Hughs
> brought the province of Conor Mac Nessa under their
> friendly peaceful sway immediately.[17]

This action greatly increased O'Neill's strength and
made him the most powerful lord in Ulster. He was inaugurated as the O'Neill at the great stone chair at Tullaghoe
eight miles north of Dungannon. As Camden rightly observed in his history of Elizabeth, even the title of Caesar

---

[17] *Ibid.*, 59.

was contemptible to the Irish when compared to the title of "O'Neill".[18] Hugh O'Neill, although realizing that a fight was imminent, preferred to follow a policy of hesitation and delay rather than the fiery, zealous course followed by young Hugh O'Donnell. The Englishman, Fynes Moryson, left the following description of O'Neill:

> He was of mean stature but of strong body, able to endure labors, watching, and hard fare, being withal industrious and active, valiant, affable, and apt to manage great affairs, and of a high, dissembling, subtle, and profound wit.[19]

Camden also supports this description:

> His industry was very great, his soul large and fit for the weightiest business. He had much knowledge in military affairs, and a profound dissembling heart.[20]

Hugh's grandfather was Conn Bacagh O'Neill who had been the Earl of Tyrone. His father, Matthew O'Neill, was made Baron of Dunganon but was murdered by his brother Shane O'Neill (the Proud), who was "The O'Neill" and the arch-enemy of the English in Ireland.[21] For the safety and proper upbringing of young Hugh, then only a boy of nine, the Lord Deputy Sir Henry Sidney sent him in September of 1559 to his castle at Ludlow in England.[22] The young boy

---

[18]Murphy, introduction to *Life of Hugh Roe O'Donnell*, 45.

[19]Fynes Moryson, *The Itinerary of Fynes Moryson* Vol. 2 (Glasgow: James MacLehose & Sons, 1907), 178-9.

[20]Murphy, introduction to *Life of Hugh Roe O'Donnell*, 45.

[21]MacManus, *Story of the Irish Race*, 369-71.

[22]O'Faolain, *The Great O'Neil*, 49. Hiram Morgan, although acknowledging O'Neill's visits to London denies the historical tradition of his early stay in England. (Hiram Morgan *Tyrone's Rebellion; The Outbreak of the Nine Years War in Tudor Ireland* [Woodbridge, England:

became friends with Leicester who he later referred to as "my honorable patron who from my youth had a special care of my bringing up and well doing."[23] While in London the future Earl learned the ways of the court as well as the customs and habits of the Elizabethans. How utterly different and bewildering it must have been for the boy who had spent the first nine years of his life at Dungannon in the hills of Ulster! It is believed that for eight years Hugh O'Neill remained in England. It certainly does not take much imagination to contemplate what a profound effect this had on the boy. As a boy of nine he had left Ireland in August, 1559, and did not return until June of 1567.[24] Hugh had grown up in the powerful, courtly houses in England in the city of London itself. He was exposed to the ideas of the new religion with its Puritan infusion so common at the time.[25]

Upon Hugh's return to Ireland as the Baron of Dungannon, Lord Burghley and the English had high hopes for this young man who had tasted first hand the fruits of Elizabethan civilization. The dissolute but courageous Shane O'Neill, who had murdered Hugh's father, was himself murdered by the Scots of Ulster in 1567.[26] A diplomatic struggle ensued between Turlough and the young baron as to who was to be made the Earl of Tyrone. Hugh O'Neill,

Boyall Press 1993].)

[23]O'Faolain, *The Great O'Neil*, 51.

[24]*Ibid.*

[25]*Ibid.*, 52.

[26]MacManus, *Story of the Irish Race*, 371. He had taken refuge with them after being completely routed near Lough Swilly by Hugh Dubh and the O'Donnells at the Battle of Farsetmore in 1567 for his cruel treatment of Calvagh O'Donnell.

still under the protection of Lord Deputy Sydney, began to maneuver for his own personal advancement. As baron of Dungannon he received 1,000 marks a year from the royal treasury. He served with the English Protestants against the Earl of Desmond in the Munster war of the 1580's. Here he gained valuable experience in warfare. The young man saw first hand the ugliness of war and the savage barbarity with which the government could prosecute a war. He also witnessed the persecution of the Church, and the spirit of Fitzmaurice's religious idealism.[27] In addition, the Baron saw the vast confiscations of Irish lands in Munster and their subsequent distribution to English colonists. O'Neill, a man of great intellect, could read the signs of the times but in his present state could do little to change things. He assisted Sir John Perrot against the Scots of Ulster in 1584 which strengthened his own position and in the following year was made the Earl of Tyrone for his loyalty and service. O'Neill had married the Catholic daughter of Hugh Dubh O'Donnell, Joan. Joan died in 1591 and later that year O'Neill fell in love with the beautiful Mabel Bagnal (who later became Catholic). She was the sister of Sir Henry Bagnal who served as Marshal of the English Army from 1590-1598 and had received a gold chain from O'Neill as a token of his love. O'Neill and Mabel eloped in August after a dinner party at Turvey Manor outside Dublin. The romance of the event had no effect on Sir Henry, who strongly objected to the Earl's action and became his bitterest enemy.

---

[27]O'Faolain, *The Great O'Neil*, 63.

It is difficult to ascertain with certainty when O'Neill first began to seek the overthrow of English power in Ireland.[28] As he continued to observe the government's policy of confiscating the lands of the native Irish, he knew that the greed of the colonist would one day turn upon his own territory. O'Neill and the other Irish clansmen could not respect English law. They knew that according to that law they had no title to their ancestral lands and that their chieftancy was based upon the native Brehon law which was not recognized by English law.

Elizabeth herself had shown contempt for Irish titles by granting in 1572 the peninsula of Ards to Sir Thomas Smith. She also granted to Sir Walter Devereaux, the Earl of Essex, a vast track of land in the Northeast between Coleraine and Belfast. In addition, many of Elizabeth's chosen representatives in Ireland created a spirit of distrust and fear.

The clansmen still remembered the English attempts to poison Shane O'Neill, the elder Earl of Essex' slaughter of the Scots on Rathlin Island and Ardmaree, Lord Deputy Perrot's kidnapping of Red Hugh and Sir Richard Bingham's treachery and cruelty in Connaught. The cruel execution of noble figures such as O'Rourke of Breifne at Tyburn, MacMahon of Monahan and the shocking, brutal murder of Brian O'Neill of Clandeboye along with his wife and forty kinsmen by the same Essex, who had invited them to a Christmas feast in 1574, had burned deep into the Irish memory.[29]

---

[28]Richard Bagwell, *Ireland Under the Tudors* Vol. 3 (London: The Holland Press, 1963), 245.

[29]Lord Deputy Perrot's savage execution of Donogh O'Brien, a relative of the Earl of Thomond, was shocking even by 16th century

On the religious question, the new English religion not only appeared foreign but also as a harsh force of violence and injustice. In the wake of the Henrician revolution perpetuated by Edward and Elizabeth, Catholic Ireland found itself under persecution for the first time in its long and glorious history, not by pagan Vikings, but sadly by a Christian nation.

One of the most distressing examples was the cruel martyrdom of Dermot O'Hurley, the Archbishop of Cashel in 1584.[30] After ministering to his flock he was accused of treason and yet he courageously returned to Dublin to protest his innocence.[31] The government, thinking he was hiding valuable information, subjected him to terrible torture.[32]

---

standards. According to the account in the Four Masters he was arrested for "disturbing the peace in Clare" and was, "led forth, hanged from a car, then taken down alive, his bones broken with the back of a heavy axe, and in this mangled condition, though he still lived, he was tied with ropes at the top of the steeple of Quin church, and left there to die." (D'Alton *History of Ireland*, 3:106.) One can easily see how actions such as this would lead to little trust or confidence in English law.

[30]He had been born near Emly in County Limerick in 1530. He was sent to Louvain to study law and eventually became dean of the law school. After a brief stay in Rheims from 1567 until 1570, he went to Rome. Pope Gregory, in the summer of 1581, told him he was to be made Archbishop of Cashel and sent to Ireland. He was ordained on August 13th and appointed to his See on September 11, 1581.

[31]At the execution site he proclaimed his innocence, "I am a priest anointed and also a bishop, although unworthy of such sacred dignities, and no cause could they find against me that might in the least degree deserve the pains of death, but merely my function of priesthood wherein they have proceeded against me in all points cruelly contrary to their own laws." (O'Dwyer, *Irish Spirituality*, 162.)

[32]His legs were inserted into boots filled with oil and held over a fire until the flesh fell of his bones.

They sought to force him to take the Oath of Supremacy, but the courageous martyr stoutly refused. Having no case against him, they had sought to have him secretly executed very early in the morning of June 19th. He was hanged at Hoggen Green (now College Green). A number of Catholics however, gathered to see him and hear his final words.[33]

The destruction of sacred images of the Mother of God and the saints long venerated in Ireland shocked the faithful. The Protestant Archbishop Browne publicly burned the *Baculum Jesu*. This priceless relic, thought to be the "staff of Christ", had been venerated for centuries as St. Patrick's crosier. The Mass and the sacraments touched the common people deeply. When the Crown appointed Adam Loftus Archbishop of Dublin 1567-1605, he destroyed the altar at the east end of St. Patrick's Cathedral in Dublin, and set up a table in the center of the church. He also changed the service from Latin, the ancient language of the Church, into English. Many Irishmen knew instinctively that this was not the traditional faith established by Christ, entrusted to Peter and planted in Ireland by St. Patrick.[34]

---

[33]The following account of his burial was recorded in a Catholic paper, "And when the report of the execution was spread about the city, certain devout women went forth and had his body brought down which they carried with great respect unto a little church without the city called St. Kevin's, where he was buried and his clothes which he did wear were kept among them, as relics of his martyrdom." (P.J. Cornish, *The Irish Martyrs* [Dublin, 1989], 11-13; quoted in O'Dwyer, *Irish Spirituality*, 162.)

[34]For a good treatment of Loftus' mindset see Brendan Bradshaw, "Sword, Word and Strategy in the Reformation in Ireland", *Historical Journal*, 21(1978), 475-502.

Bale, the Protestant Bishop of Kilkenny, began destroying images of the saints in his diocese. When he turned his efforts toward destroying the great Market Cross in the center of the town, the town folk rioted, killing five of his guards and nearly the bishop himself who had to flee and barricade himself in his episcopal residence. English garrisons, stationed in the country, enforced the Protestant revolution where they were able to do so. The destruction of the abbeys and monasteries also deeply shocked the common people. These monastic institutions were vital to the welfare of the country as centers of civilization and hospitality. They were chiefly responsible for cultivating learning and religious devotion in rural Ireland.[35]

---

[35]See John Watt, *The Church in Medieval Ireland*, Vol. 5 of *The Gill History of Ireland* (Dublin: Gill and Macmillan Ltd., 1972.) 202-214. McGee related the horrific destruction of ancient Clonmacnoise in 1552, "But the most lamentable scene of spoliation, and that which excited the profoundest emotions of pity and anger in the public mind, was the violation of the churches of St. Kieran—the renowned Clonmacnoise. This city of schools had cast its cross-crowned shade upon the gentle current of the Upper Shannon for a thousand years. Danish fury, civil storm, and Norman hostility had passed over it, leaving traces of their power in the midst of the evidence of its recuperation. The great Church to which pilgrims flocked from every tribe of Erin, on the 8th of September—St. Kieran's Day; the numerous chapels erected by the chiefs of all the neighbouring clans; the halls, hospitals, book-houses, nunneries, cemeteries, granaries—all still stood, awaiting from Christian hands the last fatal blow. In the neighbouring town of Athlone—seven or eight miles distant—the Treasurer, Brabazon, had lately erected a strong 'Court' or Castle, from which, in the year 1552, the garrison sallied forth to attack 'the place of the sons of the nobles'—which is the meaning of the name. In executing this task they exhibited a fury surpassing that of Turgesius and his Danes. The pictured glass was torn from the window frames, and the revered images from their niches; altars were overthrown; sacred vessels polluted. 'The left not,' say the Four Masters,

Ulster was the most untouched by the effects of the English invasion and the new religious revolution. This bastion of the ancient Gaelic order was also filled with bards, poets, brehons and chroniclers who bitterly opposed this foreign intrusion into the national tradition. In 1541, the first members of the Society of Jesus had arrived in Ireland. Dispossessed bishops appointed by the Pope in Rome also entered the country. Irish colleges committed to defending the traditional Faith in Ireland sprang up in the Low Countries, Spain, Portugal and Italy. The new found zeal of the Catholic Reformation epitomized in the Council of Trent inspired the Irish abroad to work closely with leaders at home with a crusading ideal to save the Catholic Faith in their country.[36]

For some time now O'Neill had been training his countrymen in the use of modern weaponry and organizing them into regiments so that they became disciplined soldiers. Spanish gold circulated in Tyrone and there were reports gun powder was being made with imported sulfur.

'a book or a gem, nor anything to show what Clonmacnoise had been, save the bare walls of the temples, the mighty shaft of the round tower, and the monuments in the cemeteries, with their inscriptions in Irish, in Hebrew, and in Latin. The Shannon re-echoed with their profane songs and laughter, as laden with chalices and crucifixes, brandishing croziers, and flaunting vestments in the air, their barges returned to the walls of Athlone.'

In all the Gaelic speaking regions of Ireland, the new religion now began to be known by those fruits which it had so abundantly produced." (McGee *History of Ireland* , 2:348.)

[36] A fine list of Irish martyrs and confessors during the reign of Elizabeth can be found in Myles O'Reilly *Lives of the Irish Martyrs and Confessors* (New York: James Sheehy, 1878).

He received permission from the government to import large quantities of lead for the roofing of his house at Dungannon which he promptly fashioned into bullets.[37] Jesuits and Irish seminary priests were traveling throughout Ireland during this period. The rise in popular emotion which followed the efforts of Hugh O'Donnell were drawing O'Neill directly through friendship, marriage and alliance into the heart of a fight which he outwardly hoped to avoid and postpone. The events in Ulster and the rumored actions of O'Neill alarmed the English government in London and Dublin. Yet O'Neill apparently continued to work in the Queen's service. Hugh O'Donnell knew the Northern Confederacy needed O'Neill's strength and he constantly urged him to openly join the cause. O'Neill, not believing the time ripe for open conflict, continued his policy of procrastination. Yet the flow of events was soon to force him into action.

Hugh Maguire, with the consent of O'Donnell, attacked the English governor of Connaught, Sir Richard Bingham, who had been cruelly preying on Maguire's territory and killing his people.[38] Maguire had sent letters to the Lord Deputy and the Council in Dublin demanding that Bingham make restitutions but to no avail. Maguire now demanded that his people be left free to practice their Catholic Faith and that no garrison be placed in Fermanagh. Maguire's attack upon the English under Bingham near Tulsh in County Roscommon was a small skirmish and neither

---

[37]P. W. Joyce, *History of Ireland* (London: Longmans, Green, & Co., 1923), 241.

[38]Murphy, introduction to *Life of Hugh Roe O'Donnell*, 53.

ther side could claim victory. [39] Maguire succeeded in carrying off some booty but the primate Archbishop MacGauran (who had been sent back by the King of Spain to exhort the Irish to continue the war), while administering the sacraments to the wounded, was killed by the English forces "out of hatred for his calling."[40] Bingham left the following account of the skirmish:

> Upon our first intelligence that the rebels were come in, we sent out twenty principal horsemen to discover them, who falling in amongst all their strength of horsemen unawares were forced to retire, and there we lost a tall gentleman William Clifford and one of the Rullidges, all the morning being so foggy and misty as the like was not this year. The darkness of the weather hindered us much, for if the morning had been clear that we might have discovered still where the footmen had been, we had not left them one horseman to carry the news home. The primate MacGauran lost his life, a man of more worth in respect of the villainy and combinations which he hath wrought with the ill Irishry than the overthrow of divers hundreds of the other beggars, and so generally is his death lamented as if the same were their utter overthrow. And assuredly, right honourable, he was the only stirrer and the sole combiner of all their mischiefs towards in Ulster, and the primer of MacGuire to come forward in their two journeys, making the Irishry full of belief that they should have the aid this summer of Spaniards, and another champion of the Pope, like Doctor Allen, the notable traitor, but God be thanked he has left his dead carcass on the Maugherie, only the said rebels carried his

---

[39]*Ibid.* This engagement became known as "the Battle of the Erne Fords".

[40]Murphy, introduction to *Life of Hugh Roe O'Donnell*, 54.

head away with them that they might universally bemoan him at home.[41]

The English government in Dublin was incensed at the assault made on the Governor's forces. The Lord Justice gathered a large force to attack Maguire and gave the command of the army to Sir Henry Bagnal and Hugh O'Neill. O'Neill had to not only take up arms against his secret ally, but also was ordered to share the command with his taunting enemy Bagnal, who was still resentful of O'Neill's marriage to his sister. The Four Masters relate: "It was not pleasing to the Earl of Tyrone to go on that expedition; however he had such dread of the English that he was obliged to obey."[42]

The English army marched north in October of 1593 and met Maguire's forces near Belleek across a ford of the river Erne. The English attempted to cross the ford but were initially checked by the Irish defenders. Eventually, due to their superiority in numbers and arms, (Maguire's men lacked guns), they forced passage killing over 340 of Maguire's men.[43] Hugh O'Neill was wounded, having been struck by an Irish javelin in the thigh during the engagement, "and was pleased thereat, so that the English should not have any suspicion of him."[44]

Most of Maguire's men escaped into the woods after the battle and were sheltered by O'Donnell. Maguire had previously sent his cattle and flocks to Tirconnaill in the north

---

[41]*Ibid.*
[42]Four Masters, *Annals*, 6:1940.
[43]Murphy, introduction to *Life of Hugh Roe O'Donnell*, 55.
[44]O'Cleary, *The Life of Hugh Roe O'Donnell*, 65.

that they might not be plundered. The English army, not finding any spoil after the victory, disbanded and returned home. The Lord Deputy and Council rebuked O'Neill "for lingering the service."[45] The Lord Deputy in addition informed Lord Burghley that the Earl "had made earnest motion to be gone the day before the conflict with Maguire." The Deputy also took note of "the suspicious manner of his horsemen sitting all night on horseback, close to Marshal Bagnel's camp."[46] O'Neill protested, proclaiming his innocence and offering his wound as evidence of his valor and service. O'Donnell protected Maguire in the north and did not attack the English as O'Neill secretly assured him that the English troops would not remain in the country.[47]

Hostilities ceased for the three months of the winter till the early spring of 1594. The Lord Justice assembled a large force and set out to capture Enniskillen castle which was Maguire's stronghold. It was thought that this would drive Maguire out of Fermanagh as Bingham had successfully driven Brian O'Rourke out of Breifne. The castle was situated on an Island in Lough Erne in the middle of the territory of Fermanagh. The English army, moving with speed and determination, arrived so quickly that the garrison (of 36 men with equal numbers of women and children) was unable to make provisions for itself. The castle was strong and the Lord Justice besieged the fortress without success. Eventually, a member of the garrison was bribed and the castle was handed over to the Lord Justice.[48] Having

---

[45]Murphy, introduction to *Life of Hugh Roe O'Donnell*, 55.
[46]*Ibid.*
[47]Sullivan, *Story of Ireland*, 255.
[48]Bagwell, *Ireland Under the Tudors*, 3:235. Falls states that the

achieved his purpose, Fitzwilliam garrisoned the castle with 30 soldiers who could adequately defend the fortress. He supplied the garrison with stores of food and arms and returned to Dublin. O'Donnell, who had been awaiting the arrival of soldiers from Scotland grew impatient and gathered his clan, the Cinel Conaill, and set off for Enniskillen. He laid siege to the castle from June to August in an effort to starve out the garrison within. Due to the closeness of the watch, the English began to run short of food supplies.[49] The government in Dublin knew of the condition of its troops in the castle. A large force, totaling 2,500 foot and 400 horse men, was sent to relieve the castle.[50] The army was placed under the command of Sir Henry Duke, the English governor of Offaly, who was a capable officer. The army took with them large quantities of salt, meat, cheese and biscuits with which they hoped to resupply the garrison. As these preparations were going on, O'Donnell received several letters at Enniskillen informing him that Donnell Gorm and MacLeod of Aran had arrived in Lough Teabhall[51] with a large fleet and over 3,000 Scots were now awaiting him at Derry.[52] Fearing that the English would attack in his absence, he left his army with Maguire and hastened to the north with a small body of men. He welcomed

---

English, under able command of Captain Dowdall, had procured the surrender of the castle (See Falls, *Elizabeth's Irish Wars,* 177-178). O'Sullivan Bear relates that all the defenders including the old men, women and children were thrown down headlong from the top of the castle bridge. (O'Sullivan Bear, *Ireland Under Elizabeth,* 73.)

[49]Murphy, introduction to *Life of Hugh Roe O'Donnell,* 57.
[50]*Ibid.*
[51]O'Cleary, *Life of Hugh Roe O'Donnell,* 71.
[52]Bagwell, *Ireland Under the Tudors,* 3:244.

the Scots and they were attended to and entertained for three days and nights "with strong drink and every sort of food that was best in the country."[53] The English, hearing of O'Donnell's departure to the north, hastened to relieve the castle. Red Hugh was informed of their plans and he sent word to O'Neill that, "the Protestants were coming to relieve Enniskillen, that he was determined to prevent them at all hazards, and that he would no longer consider the Earl his friend if he did not give his aid in such a straight."[54]

O'Neill now found himself caught on the horns of a serious dilemma. The cause of the Catholics was in danger even if they received his aid. On the other hand, if the Earl chose not to assist them he would still be suspected by the English and treated as an enemy by both sides. Even in this predicament he did not take the final step. His brother, Cormac O'Neill, arrived at the Catholic camp at Enniskillen with a hundred horse and three hundred light foot armed with guns. It was not openly known whether he came of his own accord or at the direction of the Earl.

Maguire and Cormac O'Neill set off with 1,000 men to keep the English army from destroying the countryside and to harass them in order that they might not be rested for their encounter with Hugh O'Donnell, who was now moving south with his Scottish gallowglasses.[55]

---

[53]O'Cleary, *Life of Hugh Roe O'Donnell*, 71.

[54]Murphy, introduction to *Life of Hugh Roe O'Donnell*, 57. See also O'Sullivan Bear, *Ireland Under Elizabeth*, 79.

[55]MacManus, *Story of the Irish Race*, 387. The gallowglasses were men of "mighty body", great warriors who wore mail and wielded broadswords and battle-axes.

Sir Henry Duke halted his march for the night on a ford near the river Farney, five miles south of Enniskillen. As soon as darkness fell, the Catholic Irish forces opened fire on the camp with "a discharge of leaden bullets."[56] Duke sent out his men to repel the attack and the fighting continued through the night, depriving the English forces of rest. O'Sullivan gives the following vivid description of the battle known as "The Ford of the Biscuits":

> Early the next morning Duke formed his forces into three bodies, and protected them on the flank by troops of cavalry and musketeers. He divided the beasts of burthen, which were carrying large supplies of provisions, and the camp-followers into two parts, and put one between the two first divisions of the army, the other part between the second and third. The army, wearied in consequence of their want of sleep during the preceding night, was set on from time to time by the Catholics during the march and forced to halt. About eleven o'clock in the day he reached the ford. He bade the horsemen dismount. as the place was ill suited to the movements of cavalry. Here Maguire and Cormac, with their full force of 1,000 men, attacked them, and their sharp-shooters pressed on the first body, while the rear was assailed not only by the musketeers but by the spearsmen. But the enemy's first body made a passage for itself by the sword, and beating the Catholics off both sides, entered the ford. Meantime the Catholics, who were attacking the rear, forced the enemy's sharpshooters in among the main body, and by a continuous fire caused confusion among them; and as the ranks were broken, the Catholic spearsmen rushed in and drove the first body in among the camp-followers and beasts of burthen. The middle body was engaged in a two-fold task, supporting those in the rear and resisting the

---

[56]Murphy, introduction to *Life of Hugh Roe O'Donnell*, 57.

Catholics; but these by their onset increased the disorder and drove the middle and rear in among the front lines. The whole army rushed pell-mell into the river, leaving behind the supplies, taking with them only their horses.

Duke asked those around him what he should do. George Oge Bingham recommended him to return and attempt to save the supplies; if not, they would die of hunger, as well as the garrison which they were going to relieve; now they could not help them. Fool the marshal protested loudly against such a course, and besought him to go to the relief of the castle. The place where they halted was very soft, and the horses sunk in the ooze and could not be of any help to them. Hence the Catholics continued their fire with impunity. Wherefore Fool ordered a body of sharp-shooters to advance against them in order to drive them off while the ranks were forming. Immediately after he was pierced by a javelin and slain. The consequence was that the whole army in terror left their horses, broke their ranks, and of themselves returned to the ford which they had crossed shortly before. But the Catholics, some of whom were plundering the supplies, while others were defending the ford, prevented them. Not knowing what to do, they set off for another ford which was near at hand, and crossed it in all haste before the Catholics could come to defend it. They rushed into it in such confusion and terror that one hundred of them were drowned; the rest crossed over on the dead bodies. Few of the Irish followed them across, despising the smallness of their number. Duke and the other officers of his army halting, threw away their arms, and stripped to their shirts; yet this did not help him to escape, for he was seized by four Irish soldiers and dragged away from his own men.[57]

The Catholic army allowed the remainder to flee as they turned back to plunder. Over 400 of the English army had

---

[57]*Ibid.*, 58.

been killed. The horses, baggage and large quantity of supplies and arms were captured. The garrison, hearing of the defeat of the army sent to aid them, surrendered the castle to Maguire. The victory was complete. News of the battle and defeat of the English army circulated throughout England, Scotland and even reached Spain.[58] The battle's stirring moral impact far exceeded its military importance.

The English government in Dublin and London now feared the worst, for during this disaster Hugh O'Neill, the Earl of Tyrone, had done absolutely nothing to aid the Queen's cause. An exhausted Sir William Fitzwilliam had been replaced by Sir William Russell in May, 1594. Elizabeth had given the following instructions to the new Lord Deputy:

> After he had received the sword he should, in the place of Council, require to be informed of the causes in Ulster, both touching the rebels Maguire, young O'Rourke, and certain of the MacMahons, and the behaviour of O'Donnell, of the Earl of Tyrone's proceedings since last he was at Dundalk with the Commissioners, and what opinion they had of his disposition to behave himself like a loyal subject, and to serve the Queen by subduing Maguire and the other rebels and containing O'Donnell in his duty. . . . She did not hear of any public disturbance in any other part of the realm than Ulster, which should be taken in and without delay.[59]

Russell stoutly refused to take the office unless Fitzwilliam first gave him a report on the condition of the kingdom. Fitzwilliam prepared the report and informed Russell that,

---

[58] O'Faolain, *The Great O'Neil*, 189.
[59] Murphy, introduction to *Life of Hugh Roe O'Donnell*, 59.

all the rebels in Fermanagh and Monaghan had been aided
and countenanced by O'Donnell in person and the principal
forces of Tirconnell, who were combined with the rebels and
had openly shown themselves with them at the siege at Enniskillen and the preying of Monaghan.[60]

Just six days after hearing of the English defeat, O'Neill
without even asking for safe conduct, boldly hastened
down to Dublin and presented himself before Council. The
Earl's speed and daring shocked the Council which had
hoped to seize him.[61] O'Neill proclaimed that he was innocent of any wrongdoing and pointed out that for over 16
years he had labored in the service of the Queen. There
were rumors that he was to be taken and imprisoned. Bagnal bitterly made numerous accusations against him. He
was defended in the Council however by Secretary Fenton
and his close friend Thomas Butler, the Earl of Ormond. A
tribute to O'Neill's ability can be seen in the fact that he so
impressed the Council that they decided to let him go on
August 19. They ordered him to control his people, restrain
O'Donnell and Maguire, expel the Scots and send his son to
Dublin as a pledge. When Elizabeth heard of his release
she was enraged! She blamed Russell and the Council for
their negligence in a letter dated October 1594:

> We can no longer forbear to let you know what great
> mischief the remiss and weak proceedings of late have
> wrought in that kingdom. We do not impute it to you our
> Deputy, who are but lately come to the helm, but to you our
> Council. . . . It is gross to find that such a man, so laid open
> to you all and made so suspicious by his own actions, hath

---

[60]*Ibid*.
[61]Sullivan, *Story of Ireland*, 256.

been suffered to grow to this head. . . . When voluntarily he came to you the Deputy, it was overruled by you the Council to dismiss him, though dangerous accusations were offered against him. This was as foul an oversight as was ever committed in that kingdom. . . . Command him, without any respite or excuse of business or sickness, to make his present repair to you, to answer wherein he is justly charged, and to submit to our estate there; which if he do not we are determined to proclaim him a traitor.[62]

Elizabeth was so rankled that even three years later when Russell approached her with a present (a basket filled with the heads of some unfortunate Gaelic captains) she ridiculed him and scornfully ordered him from the court.[63]

Once safely back in the north at Dungannon, O'Neill refused to send his son to Dublin as a pledge, claiming that his foster parents had taken him away. He also declared that his people had sworn fealty to O'Donnell. Lord Deputy Russell irefully responded that these were "undutiful and loose answers."[64] All of Ireland was now filled with rumors from Spain. The English heard rumors of secret landings in the northwest of ducats, arms, powder and men.

The government in London, now thoroughly alarmed, withdrew 3,000 of England's best veteran troops from Bretagne and Flanders and prepared to send them into Ireland.[65] Sir John Norris, the most experienced general of Elizabeth, who Charles Wilson describes as the "ablest

---

[62]Murphy, introduction to *Life of Hugh Roe O'Donnell*, 62.
[63]O'Faolain, *The Great O'Neil*, 191.
[64]*Ibid.*, 192.
[65]Joyce, *History of Ireland*, 243.

commander in the Netherlands,"[66] was selected to command this force. A capable commander he certainly was, for at the battle of Rymenant in the Netherlands he defeated the Spanish forces under Don Juan and Farnese.

O'Neill foresaw this action to be the beginning of the government's subjugation and eventual plantation of Ulster with Protestant English colonists. Remembering the horrors which had befallen Munster, O'Neill took immediate action. He sent his men under the command of his brother Art to attack the English fort in the Blackwater. The crucial fort fell to O'Neill's men and now prevented easy passage from Louth into Tyrone, the heart of O'Neill's country. By the middle of 1595, O'Neill had cast in his lot with O'Donnell and openly joined the Northern Catholic Confederacy.[67] From shore to shore, all of Ulster stood united prepared to fight for their Faith and country in order that a dream might become a reality.

---

[66]Wilson, *Revolt of the Netherlands*, 85.

[67]Fynes Moryson in his *Itinerary* gives the following reasons for the rebellion after discussing Hugh Maguire's grievances: "Thus the fire of this dangerous Rebellion is now kindled, by the above named causes, to which may be added, the hatred of the conquered against the Conquerors, the difference of Religion, the love of the Irish to Spain (whence some of them are descended), the extortions of Sheriffs and sub-Sheriffs buying these places, the ill government of the Church among ourselves, and the admitting Popish Priests among the Irish, and many such like. And this fire of rebellion now kindled shall be found hereafter to be increased to a devouring flame..." (Moryson *Itinerary*, 2:191.)

FOUR

FIGHT AND PARLEY
THE WAR: 1595–1598

But those wars also are just, without doubt which
are ordained by God Himself, in Whom is no in-
iquity and Who knows every man's merits. The
leader of the army in such wars, or the people itself, are not so much the authors of the war as the
instruments.

St. Augustine, *Quaestiones in Heptateuchum*

O'Neill united his forces with those of Maguire and
MacMahon and openly took the field against the English. O'Neill drove into Cavan plundering the settlements
of the colonists and driving them back into the Pale, the
English stronghold around Dublin. A strong garrison of
English troops had reoccupied Monaghan and taken possession of the Franciscan monastery. In response, the Confederates laid siege to the city and soon put the garrison in
great distress. The capable veteran, Sir John Norris, had
now arrived in Ireland and was appointed Lord General.[1]
Bagnal, Norris and his brother Sir Thomas marched north
with a large force to raise the siege of Monaghan.[2] O'Neill,

---

[1]Bagwell, *Ireland Under the Tudors*, 3:252.

[2]This army consisted of nineteen companies of foot and six troops
of horse. G. A. Hayes-McCoy, in his excellent work *Irish Battles*, gives
a fine account of the Battle of Clontibret. He disagrees with Bagwell,
however, and states that Sir John Norris was not present at Clontibret

hearing that Norris was marching north, allowed the English to re-supply the garrison and withdrew his army six miles from Monaghan, to Clontibret. Tyrone knew that the English would pass Clontibret on their return march to Newry. On the far bank of a small stream he positioned his forces and awaited the English. Bagnal and Norris soon arrived with the English army and saw O'Neill's army across the river barring his passage. The Lord General was an officer of great ability and experience. Twice the English infantry charged and twice they were beaten back. Norris and his brother personally led the charge and were met with a veteran firmness which astonished them.[3] Both were severely wounded during the main attack on the Irish battle line. With the Lord General and Sir Thomas wounded, the Irish began to cheer, counting the victory won. Suddenly an enormous English officer named Segrave led a body of 40 English cavalry in a fierce charge across the river. Segrave sought out O'Neill himself and the two leaders met in deadly hand to hand combat. Both armies lowered their weapons and silently awaited the outcome with breathless expectation. Segrave drove his horse against O'Neill's and hurled his enormous frame upon Tyrone in an effort to unhorse and crush him. O'Neill grabbed his arm and the two men fell to the ground. For several tense moments, which seemed an eternity, the warriors fought and wrestled in the

---

in May but fought O'Neill at Mullaghbrack just north of Newry in a separate engagement in September of the same year with similar results. (G.A. Hayes-McCoy *Irish Battles: A Military History of Ireland* [Belfast: The Appletree press Ltd., 1990], 87-105.)

[3]John F. Finnerty, *Ireland* Vol. 1 (New York: P.F. Collier & Sons, 1904), 138.

embrace of death. Then there was a loud groan and death claimed its victim. O'Neill had thrust his sword in the Englishman's groin under his coat of mail.

When O'Neill rose, a thunderous shout of joyous triumph echoed through the hills. The Irish cavalry charged across the river and furiously assaulted the stunned English ranks. Norris quickly retreated south and Monaghan was again surrendered to the Irish. O'Neill's men continued to harass the English till they reached Newry. Bagnal was so depressed by the defeat that he took a boat down the river and sailed around the sea to Dundalk.[4] His lands near Newry were burnt and his tenants dispersed by O'Neill. Bagnal claimed that he lost only 140 men in the battle. Sir Ralph Lane wrote privately to Lord Burghley, however, that there were "more hurt men in the late service than was convenient to declare."[5] O'Sullivan states that the English lost nearly 700 men.[6] Sir John Norris wrote in dismay concerning the numbers, arms and skill of the Irish. The battle of Clontibret was a great moral victory which had a strong psychological impact on the Irish, increasing their hope and confidence. The colonists, however, were gripped by a general feeling of panic and division. Lord Deputy Russell and Sir John Norris fought and bickered with each other over the handling of the war. Elizabeth professed her "grief at the loss and death of so many good soldiers."[7] The English now appeared vulnerable and news of the victory spread

[4]O'Faolain, *The Great O'Neil*, 211.
[5]*Ibid.*
[6]O'Sullivan Bear, *Ireland Under Elizabeth*, 87.
[7]O'Faolain, *The Great O'Neil*, 211.

like wildfire. When news reached the Iberian peninsula, there were public processions and *Te Deums* sung in Lisbon thanking God for this initial rebuff to the English heretics.[8]

In the West, Red Hugh O'Donnell, "the son of prophecy", excited the country with a stunning and brilliant raid deep into the heart of the ancient province of Connaught. Sir Richard Bingham was the English governor of Connaught. Together with his brother George he mercilessly drove the Irish and Norman Irish off their lands. Many of these nobles and common people came to O'Donnell and complained of their bitter sufferings and unjust persecution. O'Cleary gives the following description of Red Hugh's compassion for these exiles:

> He was their pillar of support, their bush of shelter and their shield of protection for all those that were weak. Moreover he kept their nobles and chiefs in his company and society. Besides, he gave entertainment throughout his territory in his farmhouses and castles to the wretched poor people, to the houseless and to the weak and feeble. At the time he received them into his territory he ordered his people generally to distribute aid in herds and flocks, young cattle and corn to them.[9]

O'Donnell, seizing the historic moment, promised to free them from their slavery and bondage if he could, and restore them to their patrimonies. He gathered his forces and on May 3, 1595 "he crossed the Saimear's green vale" and burst into Connaught. The English were taken completely

---

[8]*Ibid.*, 212. Te Deums were sung in many of the great cathedrals of Spain when news arrived of Irish Catholic victories over Elizabeth and the English.

[9]O'Cleary, *Life of Hugh Roe O'Donnell*, 109.

by surprise and could offer little resistance. O'Donnell swept through the province with an avenging sword ravaging the lands of the colonists and driving them into the shelter of fortified towns. O'Sullivan gives the following account of O'Donnell's drive into the province:

> 1595. O'Donnell remembering the cruelty with which the English had thrown women, old men, and children from the Bridge of Enniskillen, with all his forces invaded Connacht, which Richard Bingham was holding oppressed under heretical tyranny. In his raids extending far and wide he destroyed the English colonists and settlers, put them to flight, and slew them, sparing no male between 15 and 50 years old who was unable to speak Irish.
>
> He burnt the village of Longford in Annaly, which Browne, an English heretic had taken from O'Farrell. He then returned to Tyrconnell laden with spoils of the Protestants. After this invasion not a single farmer, settler or Englishman remained except those who were defended by the walls of castles and fortified towns, for those who had not been destroyed by fire or sword, or despoiled of their goods, left for England, heaping curses upon those who had brought them into Ireland.[10]

---

[10]O'Sullivan Bear, *Ireland Under Elizabeth*, 81-2. Red Hugh's raids sought to punish the colonists and their Irish supporters by bringing the wealth of the province north to help support the war effort. Church lands and schools of the learned were exempted from these attacks. During one such excursion, cattle was inadvertently taken from a poet in Thomond's land, named Mailin Oge, by some of Red Hugh's soldiers. The poet followed them back to Red Hugh's camp. He revealed his knowledge and ability and composed a hymn in honor of the prince. Red Hugh was delighted and returned all his herds and flocks and gave him even more, whereupon Mailin blessed him and took his leave. (O'Cleary, *Life of Hugh Roe O'Donnell*, 193-99.)

 85

O'Donnell and his army returned home exuberant with vast treasures to help the war effort. O'Donnell and O'Neill, as well as several other leading members of the Confederacy, were increasingly being possessed by the fire of religious idealism. All religious zealots see things in a radiant, supernatural light which often leads them to be highly optimistic and pray that "God's will be done whether in victory or defeat." The role which was played by Jesuits and seminary priests in assisting and encouraging the war will perhaps never be fully recorded. For example, there were reports that by the end of 1594, O'Neill was surrounded by priests and Jesuits, such as Fr. Francis Montfort.[11] The clergy of the Catholic reformation were most certainly having a profound effect on the country which had continued to remain true to the traditional Faith of their fathers. The ancient Faith was also being strengthened among the Anglo-Irish, or old English, in the towns. The Protestant Archbishop of Cork complained that the mayors of the town refused to attend Protestant services, that four men declined to become mayors on religious grounds, and that priests had become so influential that they succeeded in persuading doctors not to serve apostate clergy.[12] In June of 1595, at the direction of William Cecil, Lord Burghley, the English government issued a proclamation against the leaders of the Catholic Confederacy: Tyrone, O'Donnell, O'Rourke, Maguire, and MacMahon, de-

---

[11]O'Faolain, *The Great O'Neil*, 225-6. Fr. Montfort, although listed in English State papers as a Jesuit, was not a religious, but secular priest. See R. Dudley Edwards' *Ireland in the Age of the Tudors* (London: Croom Helm, 1977), 284.

[12]*Ibid.*, 226.

claring them traitors. In this document O'Neill is portrayed as having "allured" O'Donnell into the Confederacy when in reality quite the opposite was true. This was done by Elizabeth in the hope she might "recover" O'Donnell. She informed the Lord Justice to deal with him secretly and tell him that she had "a disposition to serve him."[13] The efforts of the Lord Justice in his sovereign's behalf utterly failed to create any disunion between O'Donnell and O'Neill which became one of the true, great friendships in Irish history. The following is the text of the proclamation:

> Aspiring to live like a tyrant over a great number of good subjects in Ulster, he has lately allured O'Donnell, the chieftain of Tyrconnell, by matching with him in marriage, whose father and predecessors have always been loyal, to enter into rebellion; and has in like manner comforted and provoked, with the aid of his brethren and bastards, certain other disobedient subjects, as Maguire, chieftain of Fermanagh, the traitor O'Rourke's son, and sundry of the MacMahons of Monaghan, to invade divers counties in and near the English Pale. In order to become Prince of Ulster, he has also, partly by force, partly by false persuasions, allured and drawn to concur with him in rebellion a great part of the chieftains of Ulster. For these causes her Majesty doth now, upon the preparation of her army, notify to all her good subjects, both English and Irish, the said Earl to be accepted the principal traitor and chief author of this rebellion, and a known practiser with Spain and other of her Majesty's enemies; commanding all her subjects that have aided and accompanied him, and yet shall now desire to live peaceably in her favour, to withdraw themselves from him and his complices. And when her army shall enter Ulster, if they come to the Lord Deputy, they shall, upon their submission,

---

[13]Murphy, introduction to *Life of Hugh Roe O'Donnell*, 65.

have pardon of their lives and lands. If those who were the servants or followers of Turough Luineach, her very loyal subject, return from the said Earl to the said Turough Luineach, and join him in withstanding the said traitors, they also shall have like pardons.[14]

The Lord Justice Russell again prepared an army to march north against the Confederates. The English army reached Dundalk on June 18, 1595. O'Neill hastily sent messengers to O'Donnell informing him of the movements of the Lord Justice. O'Donnell "could not suffer to hear the news"[15] and immediately gathered his forces and marched to O'Neill's aid. Russell had hoped to recapture Portmore which was an English fort on the Blackwater. When news reached Russell of the arrival of O'Donnell, he knew they were prepared for him and so he personally remained in Dublin. The combined Irish forces prevented any further advancement of the English army which remained in Dundalk under the command of Norris.

While O'Donnell was away from his territory, aiding O'Neill, the brother of Sir Richard Bingham, George Oge, sought to revenge himself against O'Donnell by plundering Tirconnaill. Bingham left Ulick Burke in charge of strategic Sligo castle and with a body of men sailed along the northwest and entered into Lough Swilly. He plundered the Carmelite monastery on the shore at Rathmullen which was built "in honor and reverence of holy Mary, Mother of the Lord,"[16] seizing the priestly vestments, the sacred vessels

---

[14]*Ibid.*

[15]O'Cleary, *Life of Hugh Roe O'Donnell*, 91.

[16]*Ibid.* The haunting ruins of this famous pilgrimage site can still be visited today.

and destroying the church. The Island of Tory, "a place which Columba blessed,"[17] was also devastated by the English who returned safely to Sligo. O'Donnell was enraged when he heard reports of the sacrileges and marched into his territory to avenge these wrongs. Russell and Norris now decided to march against O'Neill. The Earl again sent messengers to Red Hugh and once again the Prince returned to aid his ally. O'Neill rejoiced at O'Donnell's return and "his soul was stirred on seeing him."[18] Russell and Norris set out from Newry to seize Armagh but the Irish forces successfully halted their advance and they were forced to fall back into Newry. The Irish lost 200 men and the English had nearly 600 killed in this engagement. Soon some unexpected good news reached the Confederate camp from the West. Ulick Burke had killed George Bingham, seized Sligo castle and confederated with O'Donnell. Both Red Hugh and O'Neill were delighted with the providential news. Sir Richard Bingham, hearing of the capture of Sligo, wrote to Lord Deputy Russell saying: "This is the worst news that ever happened in Connaught in my time."[19] Bingham summoned the Irish earls of Thomand and Clanrickarde and with his Anglo-Irish forces attacked and blockaded Sligo. The castle was valiantly defended by Burke. O'Donnell moved rapidly and soon arrived with 300 horse and 500 foot and rescued the besieged, forcing Bingham to flee. O'Donnell took the guns and stores of the castle and then eventually demolished it, that it might

---

[17] *Ibid.*
[18] *Ibid.*, 93.
[19] Bagwell, *Ireland Under the Tudors*, 3:253.

 89

never again be used by the English as a base to attack the north. Many of the exiled Connaughtmen now returned to their province and openly confederated with O'Donnell.[20] Sir Richard Bingham fled the province and journeyed to see Russell where he reported that four-fifths of the province was out of control.[21] O'Donnell left some of his forces in Sligo and then retired to his castle in Donegal with his mind at ease.

In July of 1595, O'Neill received an encouraging letter from the Bishop of Killaloe in Lisbon promising the Catholics immediate aid:

> In the beginning of March in the past year, the Archbishop of Tuam, Thomas FitzJohn, son of John of Desmond, and Mr. John Lacie, with a certain captain of his Catholic Majesty Philip II, set out from hence to cross over to you in Ireland, whose return we have awaited with the utmost anxiety. But it now appears evident that they are nowhere in existence either there in Ireland or elsewhere, but rather it is thought that they must have been swallowed up in the vast ocean. If they had come back Philip II would doubtless have sent you help. Now however we have just learned with great satisfaction that you the Earl of Tyrone have openly taken up arms and joined with the other chieftains of Ulster against the Queen, and I have every confidence you will be successful. I have earnestly, but with great caution, persuaded the King to send you a fleet with which to oppose the enemy and subjugate the English government, and that you may free yourself and all your people from the oppressive yoke of the English forever. Furthermore, I find the King's mind most ready and willing to send you assistance, and that immediately. Wherefore you must

---

[20] *Ibid.*, 260.
[21] O'Faolain, *The Great O'Neil*, 213.

manfully and bravely and vigorously resist, without making
any peace or treaty with the enemies of the faith, for King
Philip has seen these letters and requested me to write to
you that you shall be helped immediately, and be assured
that I shall be with you very shortly, so that you may crush
the enemy and regain your liberty. Resist therefore like a
brave nobleman and an uncompromising warrior, and I
promise that instant succour shall not be wanting. I would
freely unfold to you everything, only I fear my letters might
fall into enemy's hands. The one thing I ask and beg of you
is that you will not make peace with the enemy till I come to
you.[22]

The English, due to their lack of success against the
united forces of O'Donnell and O'Neill, hoped for a respite.
The Lord Deputy sought a parley with the Catholic leaders
whereby he hoped to negotiate a truce. That the English
government was compelled to seek a truce from the Confederates seriously hurt their image in Ireland. It con-
versely boosted the prestige of O'Neill and O'Donnell
among the Irish. The English commissioners, Henry Wallop, Treasurer of Ireland, and Robert Gardiner, Chief Justice, invited O'Donnell and O'Neill to enter Dundalk for
negotiations offering to them her Majesty's protection. The
Irish leaders resolutely refused to enter the city fearing
treachery. Both sides were now jockeying for more time;
the Lord Deputy, in the hope of receiving more troops from
England, the Irish in the hope of additional Spanish aid.

The parleys finally took place in a field one mile outside
Dundalk. When Elizabeth heard the details of the conference, she was infuriated that the terms "war" and "peace"

---

[22]Murphy, introduction to *Life of Hugh Roe O'Donnell*, 68.

were used rather than "rebellion" and "pardon." Her commissioners, Wallop and Gardiner, had actually addressed the "traitors" as "your loving friends" and "our very good Lord."[23] The Queen was so angered that when Commissioner Gardiner returned to England and sought to visit Elizabeth at her palace in Richmond, in a vain effort to explain the proceedings in Ireland, she would not even admit him to her presence.

The chief demand of the Confederates was that all the Catholics of Ireland should have full liberty to practice their faith. On January 20th the Commissioners wrote to the Deputy and Council:

> Yesterday by your messenger we received such insolent demands, with no dutiful offer of his and their parts, only copy of them which we have thought meet to send unto your Lordship: 1) That all persons might have free liberty of conscience. 2) That the Earl and all the inhabitants of Tyrone should have pardon and be restored to their blood; and all the chieftains and others who had taken the Earl's part should have like pardon. 3) That O'Donnell should have pardon for himself and his followers and all those of Connaught that had taken O'Donnell's part; that O'Donnell should have such right in Connaught as his ancestors had. 4) That Feagh MacHugh be pardoned. 5) That no garrison, sheriff, or other officer shall remain in Tyrconnell, Tyrone or any of the inhabitants' countries before named, except Newry and Carrickfergus. 6) The Earl, O'Donnell, and the rest (if these requests be granted) will remain dutiful; and after a while, when the great fear which they conceived is lessened, they will draw themselves to a more nearness of loyalty to her Highness.[24]

---

[23]O'Faolain, *The Great O'Neil*, 230.
[24]Murphy, introduction to *Life of Hugh Roe O'Donnell*, 69.

These meetings continued until the end of January 1596. The truce was renewed an additional two weeks longer but there was little progress. The chief point of contention for the Commissioners was the Catholics' demand for liberty of conscience "which, besides the dishonour to God, is most dangerous, and being contrary to the laws, may not be granted."[25] These demands reveal not only a desire to defend the ancient traditional Gaelic order but also the desire to defend the Faith throughout the Kingdom of Ireland. The hope of reaching an agreement dimmed with each passing day. Gardiner left for England to inform the Queen concerning the proceedings. In reply she wrote to the Lord Deputy and Council as follows:

> You have at length in writing described the particular disorders almost in every part of the realm, an advertisement very uncomfortable from you who hath had the authority otherwise to govern the realm, than, for lack of regard in times convenient, now to present unto us so broken an estate of so great a part of our realm, as to have all Ulster wholly, saving two or three places, and all Connaught, saving as few places, wholly possessed with rebels, and likewise some of the counties next our English Pale in like danger. You propose remedies which rest altogether upon great preparations of forces and treasure without offering any reformation of the Government there.[26]

Elizabeth instructed the Council in Dublin to prepare separate answers to O'Neill, O'Donnell and the other chiefs. When O'Donnell demanded that the persecution of the

---

[25]*Ibid.*, 72.
[26]*Ibid.*, 75.

Catholic Faith be halted he received the same response from the Queen that O'Neill had:

> He may be sharply told that the request for free liberty of conscience was unreasonable and disloyal, it being a request to have liberty to break laws which her Majesty will never grant to any subject of any degree.[27]

The Commissioners knew full well that the Irish demands were insolent but there was little that they could do. With O'Neill and O'Donnell mounted on horseback these meetings appeared far more like the beginnings of a decorous battle than negotiations for a possible peace. The two armies were separated by only ¼ of a mile with two Irish soldiers standing guard between the Commissioners and the English Army and two English soldiers between the Irish princes and their armies. The Earl, as usual, was courteous and diplomatic in an effort to buy time. O'Donnell on the other hand remained resolute and haughty. The Commissioners themselves wrote the Lord Deputy concerning O'Donnell's firmness observing that he continued "insolent and arrogant as formerly."[28] The Commissioners also wrote that Red Hugh was very influential with the clansmen stating that "O'Donnell carrieth great rule among them."[29] After a day of negotiations, the Irish leaders withdrew. Red Hugh reminded the chieftains of the treachery and false promises of the English since the day they had first set foot in Ireland:

---

[27] *Ibid.*
[28] *Ibid.*, 72.
[29] *Ibid.*, 71.

It was thus that they acted towards you when implements of war and conflict were few and your battle ranks thin. . . . The English tell you lies now and they will attack you when they find you unprepared, not ready, with scantiness of arms and armour, of soldiers and champions, if peace is made with them and if securities or hostages not given by them for fulfilling to you what they promised you. Another thing, too; you will give up the friendship of the King of Spain if peace is made, and it will be disgraceful and shameful for you to practice a deceit on him who never tells a lie and who will perform what he has promised; and it would be dishonest also for you to entertain any suspicion of him; and besides you will never again be helped by him when you will need him after going over to the English.[30]

After this O'Donnell, true to his nature, withdrew and took no further part in the negotiations. When O'Neill resumed the negotiations with the English a year later, O'Donnell wrote to him protesting any peace. The fiery Prince vowed that he would break the peace even if he had left only one horse-boy to ride at his side![31] During these negotiations the Irish continued writing to Spain seeking further assistance. On September 25, 1595 O'Donnell and O'Neill sent the following letter through their envoy, the Archbishop of Tuam, to Philip II:

Our only hope of re-establishing the Catholic religion rests on your assistance. Now or never our Church must be succoured. By the timidity or negligence of the messengers our former letters have not reached you. We therefore again beseech you to send us 2,000 or 3,000 soldiers with money and arms before the feast of SS. Philip and James. With such aid

---

[30]O'Cleary, *Life of Hugh Roe O'Donnell*, 125.
[31]O'Faolain, *The Great O'Neil*, 250.

we hope to restore the faith of the Church, and to secure you a kingdom.[32]

O'Neill also wrote to the King's son, Don Carolo, on the same day:

> I have been informed by the bearer of this that you have written to me, but your letter has not yet reached my hands. I was confident that I should not appeal to you for aid in vain. The faith might be re-established in Ireland within one year if the King of Spain would only send 3,000 soldiers. All the heretics would disappear, and no other sovereign would be recognised than the Catholic King. Both I and O'Donnell have besought him to succour the Church. Pray, second our petition. If we obtain positive assurance of succour from the King, we will make no peace with the heretics. We have written frequently, but are afraid none of our letters has reached the King as he has returned us no answer. The bearer, a man of pious zeal, has undertaken this perilous mission.[33]

The English for their part withdrew 1000 men from the war in the Spanish Netherlands during the negotiations and sent them into the Irish wars. With these additional forces to strengthen the army, Russell and Norris marched quickly into Ulster and seized Armagh "the holiest metropolitan city of Ireland."[34] The monks, priests, and nuns were driven from the city. The churches were profaned (they were used as stables), and the images of the saints were destroyed.

---

[32]Murphy, introduction to *Life of Hugh Roe O'Donnell*, 76.

[33]*Ibid.*, 77. Murphy refers to Don Carolo as King Philip's son. McGurk citing Maxwell states that Don Carolo was likely Don Luis de Carillo, the Governor of Corunna. cf C. Maxwell, ed. *Irish History from Contemporary Sources* (London, 1923), 187 n.2.

[34]O'Sullivan Bear, *Ireland Under Elizabeth*, 90.

The Viceroy's army was composed of both English and Anglo-Irish royalists. The army, having taken the city, had high hopes of defeating O'Neill. They left the city on the following day but the Catholic forces furiously assaulted them and they were thrown into confusion. The army was forced to retreat back into the city. The English left 500 men under the able command of Francis Stafford to maintain the city. The bulk of the English army then fell back to Dundalk. Russell himself returned to Dublin and left Norris in command of the army.

The garrison soon began to suffer from a great swarm of lice.[35] O'Neill began to lay siege to the city. Norris sent three companies of foot and a body of cavalry with provisions for Stafford and his men. O'Neill, with eight companies of foot and some horse, surprised these troops in a night attack at Mount Bued and captured the English with all their stores. He then attempted a stratagem: the English were stripped of their uniforms and he had an equal number of his own men put them on; the same evening a body of his men under his son, Con O'Neill, were hidden behind the walls of a ruined monastery just east of the city. The following morning the garrison saw what appeared to be a strong force of their countrymen in full march to relieve them with food and provisions. They then saw O'Neill's men rush to attack them with guns firing, spears flying and men falling as if wounded. A deadly conflict seemed to ensue. Stafford dutifully sent out half the garrison to assist their comrades. This strong sallying party poured out from the city but upon their arrival on the field of battle the com-

---

[35]*Ibid.*, 77.

batants on all sides turned upon them. The English, realizing that they had been tricked, turned and fled back toward the wall of the city. Con O'Neill and the Irish in the monastery now charged and blocked the path of their retreat. The English fought bravely but were slaughtered. Following this debacle, Armagh was surrendered by Stafford and his men, who once disarmed, were allowed by O'Neill to return to Dundalk. O'Neill, in the hope of preventing the English from using the town as a power base in Ulster, dismantled the fortifications and burnt the entire town save for the cathedral.

Norris, having failed in his efforts against O'Neill, marched with his veterans to Athlone to crush Red Hugh. He was joined at Athlone by the Earls of Thomond and Clanrickarde and other Irish chiefs of the English party. Many of the Anglo-Irish also joined forces with Norris. His reputation in France and the Spanish Netherlands had earned him a great name even though, as McManus states, his "laurels" had been "draggled" by his recent efforts against O'Neill. Nearly 10,000 horse and foot were gathered: men in scarlet tunics, puffed sleeves, iron breast-plates, carrying excellent weapons, colorful pennants and the banner of St. George.[36] O'Donnell, assisted by Mac-Sweeney, O'Doherty and Maguire, mustered 5,000 horse and foot to oppose this large army. He was also assisted by the clans from Connaught: O'Rourke, MacWilliam, O'Kelly, MacDermott, O'Connor Roe and O'Dowd. O'Donnell took up a defensive position on the north side of the river Robe.[37]

---

[36]MacManus, *Story of the Irish Race*, 386.

[37]MacManus gives the following description of Red Hugh's forces

On the first day the two armies met and a heavy fire was maintained by both sides. On the following day, Norris beat a parley and O'Donnell agreed to meet the English general in an effort to buy time. Every day, under the flag of truce, peace terms were discussed. At night however both sides would fiercely attack each other's camp and bitter hand-to-hand combat would ensue. On one night, during a surprise raid on an English camp, over 300 Royalists were killed.[38] Some of the Irish, seeing that Norris was not making any headway against the Catholic army, left the English general and joined O'Donnell. Raymond O'Gallagher, the Bishop of Derry and Vice-Primate of Ireland, was with Red Hugh. He absolved from the ban of excommunication all those who went over from the Protestant army to the Catholics. While this confrontation continued, a messenger reached the Irish camp and informed O'Donnell that Spanish ships had sailed into Donegal Bay! When Norris received word of this news and saw his forces

---

gathered on the banks of the Robe: "On the other bank are the Irish horse and foot, about five thousand men. The boy who had broken England's gyves from his wrists is there; the army is his; everywhere he has led it to victory. His cavalry are armed with head pieces, shirts of mail, a sword, a skian, a spear. Very skilful horsemen, who ride upon saddles without stirrups, and who carry the lances not under the arm when riding to the charge, but by the middle, above the arm. And his infantry—those picked and selected men of mighty bodies, the 'greatest force of the battle'—they are the gall-oglach (gallowglasses), 'great scorners of death,' men choosing to die rather than yield, 'so that when it came to handy blows they are quickly slain or win the field.' And his light infantry, the ceitherne (Kernes), with targets of wood, barbed darts and muskets: and the horse-boys, 'not less serviceable in the meating and dressing of horses, than hurtful to the enemy with their darts.'". (MacManus, *Story of the Irish Race*, 387.)

[38]O'Sullivan Bear, *Ireland Under Elizabeth*, 95.

weakening daily, he prepared to shift his camp. O'Donnell closely pursued, "seriously harassing his rear ranks and outside wings with missiles."[39] Norris, withholding help from his rearguard, hoped to entice the Irish over a high hedge and then entrap the eager pursuers. O'Donnell, perceiving the danger and "being mounted on a fleet horse,"[40] galloped up to the front and held his men back allowing none to cross. Norris, his plan frustrated, angrily continued his retreat haranguing horrid imprecations against fate which had condemned him "to lose in Ireland, the smallest speck of the wide world, that fame which his valor and military skill had earned for him in France and the Spanish Netherlands."[41]

Philip II had sent Alonso Cobos to Ireland as his envoy. Cobos came with three Spanish frigates and put in at the harbor of Killybegs in May of 1596. From this port he journeyed to O'Donnell's princely residence at Lifford[42] where

---

[39] *Ibid.*, 96.

[40] *Ibid.*

[41] MacManus, *Story of the Irish Race*, 387.

[42] The beautiful tower house at Lifford was built by cultured and traveled Manus O'Donnell in 1527. Quinn quotes the following description of the residence by the poet Tadhg Dall O'Huiginn,

"A beloved dwelling is the castle of Lifford, homstead of wealth-abounding encampment; forge of hospitality for the men of Ulster, a dwelling it is hard to leave. . . .

Beloved the delightful, lofty buildings, its tables, its coverlets, its cupboard; its wonderous, handsome, firm walls, its smooth marble arches.

Beloved is the castle in which we used to spend a while at chess playing, a while with the daughters of the men of Bregia, a while with the fair books of the poets.

The fortress of smooth-lawned Lifford—no one in the world can leave it once it is found." (Quinn, *The Elizabethans and the Irish*, 74-5.)

he was royally entertained. Each Spanish ship carried sixty musketeers along with supplies of guns, powder and munitions.[43] Cobos also brought beads, stones and relics sent by Pope Clement VIII in Rome.[44] The Pontiff also gave Cobos an indulgence for the Irish allowing them to eat meat every day in war time. The Irish had for some time now been fasting and practicing abstinence, limiting themselves to fish, butter and eggs on Fridays and Saturdays.[45] The envoy brought a letter from Philip addressed to O'Neill:

> I have been informed that you are defending the Catholic cause against the English. That this is acceptable to God is proved by the signal victories which you have obtained. I hope you will continue to prosper, and you need not doubt but I will render you any assistance you may require.[46]

By the same envoy Philip also wrote to Brian O'Rourke:

> The noble and greatly beloved O'Rourke:
> Seeing it is so notable a work to fight for the Catholic faith when the enemies thereof endeavour so mightily to trample the same underfoot. I may not doubt but that you as hitherto (as we hear) in the defense of God's cause have laboured so well, will now with might and main give yourself to the same cause. For mine own part I would be your guide that you would prosecute the same hereafter, lest the obdu-

---

[43]Murphy, introduction to *Life of Hugh Roe O'Donnell*, 77.

[44]Pope Clement (Aldobrandini) vigorously promoted the ideals of the Catholic reform. He was deeply pious and practiced great austerity in his personal life. He fasted, spent considerable time in prayer and made frequent use of the sacrament of penance. He was good friends with St. Philip Neri the founder of the Oratory and the Caesar Baronius, the father of Church history. He was pontiff from 1592-1605.

[45]Bagwell, *Ireland Under the Tudors*, 3:268.

[46]Murphy, introduction to *Life of Hugh Roe O'Donnell*, 77.

rate enemies of the true religion damnify it all, but rather they be repulsed. The which if you perform, you shall do me a most grateful work and always find the same favour wherewith I am wont to grace the true defenders of the Catholic religion.[47]

O'Donnell sent messengers to O'Neill informing him of Cobos' arrival. O'Neill hastened to Lifford where he was greeted by Red Hugh and Cobos. The Catholics dined together and the trio talked eagerly over wine far into the night. What an illustrious threesome: the suave, aristocratic Spaniard who had fought at Lepanto; the proud, passionate young Gael who had captured the imagination and hearts of his countrymen; and the profoundly dissembling, "imperious" Anglo-Gael. Cobos eventually retired but the other two carried their own discussions into the wee hours of the morning. O'Donnell and O'Neill replied to Philip II as follows:

> We have received most opportunely your majesty's letters so much wished for, full of clemency and almost fatherly love, shortly after we had been discussing about entering into a treaty with those who represented the person of the Queen of England, on account of the long delay in sending the aid expected from your Majesty, and the sufferings and complaints of our subjects and people worn out by the continuous wars and hardships. The terms were indeed honourable and very favourable, so far as they related to the liberty of the Catholics and the security of our country and friends. We did not however conclude it, though some of our pledges have been placed in the hands of our enemies. But as your letters, mighty King, clearly testify your feelings and kindly disposition, we shall not in future take into reck-

---

[47] *Ibid.*

oning comfort or discomfort but, supported by the hope of your favour next after God, we will again enter on the conflict and we will gladly renew the war, which has ceased for some time, though the forces of the enemy by sea and land are increasing daily. You, most merciful King, will in the meantime supply us with all that is needed to take the business in hand and to carry on the war, six thousand soldiers and arms for ten thousand. And we consider it most desirable that as soon as this letter reaches you, you would send some quick-sailing light-armed vessels of the fleet with lead, powder, and engines of war, and about a thousand soldiers, in order to increase the courage of our people and lessen that of the enemy. But in as much as we have felt to our great and indescribable harm the evil doings and crimes of those whom the Queen of England is in the habit of sending amongst us, we beg and beseech your Majesty to send someone well known to you and perfectly fit to be the King of this island, for his own welfare, ours, and that of the Christian state, who will not be unwilling to rule over and live amongst us, and to direct and guide our nation well and wisely; he will obtain much advantage and glory by so-doing, as it is quite certain that we are willing to encounter the risks of war through our great affection and love for you, caring little for the temporal advantages offered to us by the enemy; and would that your Majesty would appoint the Archduke of Austria, now Governor of Flanders, a famous man and worthy of all praise, than whom none would be more acceptable. Your Highness should know that we have given information about all to your Envoy. This declaration of our sentiments will suffice for all the other noblemen, and he can return to Spain all the sooner. May the great and good God long keep your Majesty safe for the spreading of the Catholic faith in all parts of the world.

Given in Lifford, the 16th day of May, in the year of our salvation, 1596. We wish in fine that your Majesty should give implicit credit to the bearer Alonso Cobos in all that relates to the present business.

Your Majesty's most humble servants,
Hugh O'Neill
Hugh O'Donnell[48]

O'Neill and O'Donnell at the same time wrote a letter to Don Carolo:

Most Serene Prince,

We have written to your father, the mighty King, as well as haste would allow us, what we thought most necessary for us and our country. In this business we beseech your Highness to respond generously to the hopes which we entertain of his generous qualities, and set us down in the number of his clients, and help us mercifully, as is his wont in a cause so pious and just, namely the asserting of Catholic liberty and the delivering our country from the yoke of wicked tyrants; and in this way obeying the majesty of God, he will save an infinite number of souls from the jaws of hell, gain them over to Christ, and either crush utterly the agents of Satan's wrath and the wicked disturbers of the Christian republic or compel them to return to wiser counsels. We beg God to grant your most serene Highness every blessing.

From Lifford, May 16th, in the year of 1596.
Hugh O'Neill
Hugh O'Donnell[49]

Other Irish chiefs, such as Maguire and MacWilliam Burke, also wrote to the King from Donegal espousing the same cause. Niall O'Boyle, the Bishop of Raphoe, wrote to Philip "from his manor of Killybegs, thanking him for the aid he was about to send especially on behalf of the Church, which was spoiled by the English heretics."[50] O'Neill and

---

[48]*Ibid.*, 78.
[49]*Ibid.*, 79.
[50]*Ibid.*, 80.

O'Donnell sent a joint letter to Don Juan de Idiaquez, the Spanish Councilor of State, from Donegal on May 25, 1596 requesting him to press their cause with the King:

> Having opened our minds by letter to his Catholic Majesty, and set briefly before him our wants, it remains for us to address you, who have always shown singular kindness to us. Therefore we beseech you earnestly to remember our ancient and remote descent, and as is your custom, to take means to inform his Majesty carefully and exactly of the state of this kingdom, which we have undertaken to defend as best we can, an honourable and holy undertaking, and persuade the King not to allow this excellent opportunity to pass unheeded; we can hardly hope that such another will ever again occur, and to send us aid as soon as possible. We leave to the care and fidelity of Thaddeus, bishop of Clonfer, and Bernard O'Donnell much more, in which we trust you will not fail to aid us.[51]

O'Donnell, O'Neill and all the other Catholic confederated chieftains greatly desired to send a joint letter signed by all to the Catholic King. However, the Irish Catholics hope for speedy relief from Spain and Cobos' fear that English ships would be sent to intercept him if news of his arrival reached Dublin, compelled him to leave prematurely before all the chieftains could arrive in Tirconnaill. This is borne out by a document given to the envoy by O'Neill and O'Donnell:

> We, the Lords O'Neill and O'Donnell, testify by this letter that it was by our persuasion Don Alonso Cobos, the Envoy of his Catholic Majesty, was impelled and moved to hasten his return to Spain before the arrival here of the rest of

---

[51]*Ibid.*, 80-1.

our nobility who live far away from this place. We are of one mind with these, and therefore can speak for all of them. Our chief reason is that he may take our letters with all possible haste to the Catholic King, and set before him our wishes.

Given at Lifford, 16th May, 1596.[52]

Cobos for his part bore witness that it was the unanimous desire of the Irish chiefs to cast off their allegiance to the heretical Queen and submit to King Philip:

> I, Alonso Cobos, say and certify to all who may see this, that I came to Ireland when all the Irish Lords had almost concluded peace with the Queen on terms favourable to them, and that solely through the conscientious motives, and for the great love they bear to his Majesty, they have declined to bring it to a conclusion, and have taken up arms against the Queen, and turned their hearts in all sincerity to God and the King, whose vassals they are, until his Majesty orders otherwise, as most suitable to his service. And to show that I am sure of what I state, I have set down at foot my name and seal.
>
> Lifford, 15th of May, 1596.[53]

Messengers between the two Catholic countries crossed and recrossed the sea. Another letter was sent by Philip and received by O'Donnell and O'Neill who sent the following reply:

> We welcome with much joy your Majesty's second letter, breathing the fragrance of sweetness and mercy, and in our inmost hearts we embrace it.

---

[52]*Ibid.*, 81.
[53]*Ibid.*

We have answered it not only with the same feelings but almost in the same words as we did your first. About the time we received your first letter from the hands of your Majesty's Envoy we were very urgently asked by those who governed here on behalf of the Queen of England to make a truce and accept terms of peace; just and very favourable terms were offered and laid before us, which guaranteed liberty and peace to the Catholic faith, and security of our possessions to us from the heretics. Some pledges of ours have passed to the enemy, for we were induced to accept their terms owing to the complaints of our suffering subjects, worn out by the hardships of the war continued up to the present, and most of all to the great delay in the coming of the succour we expected. But since we are asked piously and affectionately by your Majesty's letters, setting at nought the hellish devices of the English, and relying on God's mercy and yours, we have not hesitated to renew this war, which was interrupted for some time, even though the forces of the enemy both by land and sea are increasing day by day. It will be your duty, most merciful King, in the meantime to supply what is needed for bringing the business to an end, and to send the war supplies—six thousand soldiers and arms for ten thousand.[54]

O'Neill, O'Donnell, O'Rourke and MacWilliam sought to stir up the war in Munster. The Northern chieftains, in letters sent in July to members of leading families in the province, vowed that anyone who from the highest to the lowest "shall assist Christ's Catholic religion, and join in confederacy"[55] would receive their unflinching support. The war had now truly become one of national and international interest. The Catholic Confederates sought the full

---

[54]*Ibid.*, 82.
[55]Bagwell, *Ireland Under the Tudors*, 3:273.

support of the Anglo-Irish Catholics in the towns and Catholic Irish support abroad.[56]

As this diplomacy was vigorously continued, the war was again renewed. Lord Deputy Sir William Russell like so many of the English Viceroys, grew increasingly weary of his burdensome office. In October of 1596, Russell sent a lamentable petition to the English Privy Council in which he described his vexations and difficulties in great detail and pleadingly begged for his recall. The Lord Deputy also referred to the often bitter disagreements which took place between himself and Lord General Norris. Elizabeth realized the differences between these two strong men and the damage that their wranglings were causing. She prudently agreed to recall Russell in the beginning of 1597.

On April 18, 1597, the Queen appointed Thomas Lord Borough to be the new Lord Deputy. He set sail from England and landed in Ireland on May 15th. He entered Dublin and received the sword of office a week later. As Lord Deputy he held supreme authority in civil as well as military affairs. Borough, who had served with distinction in the Netherlands, ordered Norris to return to Munster in an effort to avoid the internal dissent which had injured the Queen's interests during the previous Viceroyalty. This humiliation, along with his unsuccessful efforts against the rebels, proved too much for the General who died two months later in Cork.[57]

---

[56]It was the early hope evidenced by these letters that perhaps a foreign leader from Catholic Spain might be able to eventually unite the entire Catholic nation, including the Anglo-Irish, many whom had remained aloof despite their common faith.

[57]Bagwell, *Ireland Under the Tudors*, 288.

Borough, upon accepting his new office, received the customary report on "the state of the realm" which was prepared by Russell and the Council. In the report he was given the following description of the Kingdom:

> Ulster was universally revolted, no part of it being free from hostility to her Majesty and adherence to the capital traitors of Tyrone, the only places left her beyond Dundalk being the Newry, Knockfergus, Carlingford, the Green Castle, Dundrum, and Oldrifleete. At the Earl's first entrance into rebellion there were several counties in Ulster which held for her Majesty, and some of the lords thereof paid rents, compositions, and risings out. Now they are all in Confederacy with the Earl. . . . In Connaught not one of the six shires was free from revolt, but each had its particular disturbers. Sir Conyers Clifford, Chief Commissioner there with twenty-one companies of foot and a half besides horse, was not strong enough to reduce the rebels to obedience, for his companies are weak, and O'Donnell tyrannized over most of these people at his pleasure, having drawn to his side the whole country of Leitrim whereof the O'Rourkes have usurped rule and are at his direction, and, in effect, the whole country of Mayo, where he set up a supposed MacWilliam, who is the most notorious traitor in Connaught, and altogether at his commandment only. . . . In county Sligo the O'Harryes, the O'Hartes, and divers others are overawed by O'Donnell and combined with MacWilliam.[58]

O'Neill continued to harass the English by sending his marauding bands into the Pale itself. In Connaught, Sir Richard Bingham, whose cruelty had caused many of the Irish in the province to join the Confederacy, was finally

---

[58]Murphy. introduction to *Life of Hugh Roe O'Donnell*, 86-7.

withdrawn by Elizabeth. In January of 1597 he was replaced by Sir Conyers Clifford who had won himself a
reputation for his display of courage against the Spanish at
Cadiz in June 1596. Although Clifford was far more prudent and reasonable than Bingham, his appointment as
governor came too late. From the Queen's point of view
the condition of the province grew worse with each passing
day. The war in the west blazed up more fiercely than ever.
At the end of January, O'Donnell again took the offensive
and marched into Connaught with an army of over 3,000
men. He assaulted the fortress and town of Athenry which
was held by the English.[59] The wooden gates were set on
fire and the Irish, using very large and long ladders,
stormed the walls and ramparts of the town. The city was
burnt and the Irish army seized a large quantity of wealth.
After this successful siege and assault, the Irish, now aided
by Spaniards, journeyed south to Galway, the city of the
tribes, the great port and trading center of the west. The
army threatened the city and burned the suburbs.
O'Donnell bargained with the people of the city and then
decided to turn back north carrying supplies and provisions into Donegal. This entire campaign was accomplished by O'Donnell's forces without any anxiety or apprehension as the English and their allies could give no serious opposition. Bingham, seeing these disasters befalling
the English, angrily complained saying, "It was plain that
his removal would not quiet Connaught nor any other alteration in the government there, but rather the expelling of

---

[59]O'Cleary, *Life of Hugh Roe O'Donnell*, 131.

all English, which is generally required throughout Ireland."[60]

The new Lord Deputy was determined to carry the war into the heart of Ulster. In "A Brief Discourse declaring how the service, against the northern rebels might be advanced,"[61] Lord Borough set forth his plan. He hoped to establish a firm defensive line on the south side of the Erne river. Borough began preparation for a united attack on Ulster from three different points: he would personally lead one army from Dublin to Portmore against Tyrone; Sir Conyers Clifford was to march from Galway to Ballyshannon against O'Donnell; and Barnewell, the son of Lord Trimleston, was to march north from Mullingar. All three armies were to unite near Ballyshannon. If this was accomplished the English army from that vantage point "will defend Connaught and the south side of the Pale, and so annoy O'Donnell that he will be forced to disunite himself for his own defense from the Earl."[62]

All three English armies set out early in the summer of 1597. Young Barnewell marched north with an army of 1,000 Palesmen. O'Neill dispatched 400 men under Captain Richard Tyrell and O'Conor of Offaly to ambush and destroy the force. The Catholic troops hastened south into the county of Westmeath, several miles outside Mullingar. Along a narrow pass Tyrell stationed his men and awaited the English advance. As the Palesmen entered the narrow pass, wooded on both sides, the Irish furiously fell upon the

---

[60]Bagwell, *Ireland Under the Tudors*, 3:273.
[61]Murphy, introduction to *Life of Hugh Roe O'Donnell*, 87.
[62]*Ibid*.

column. O'Conor attacked the rear with the bagpipes playing *Tyrell's March,* as Tyrell himself assaulted the front of the column. The army was utterly destroyed.[63] Of the 1,000 who entered "Tyrell's Pass" only Barnewell and one soldier survived. Barnewell himself was taken prisoner and sent to O'Neill who held him as a hostage. The lone soldier carried the frightening news back to Mullingar. The Lord Deputy and the Earl of Kildare however were already in full march for Ulster with their united forces, while Clifford, the new Governor in the West, marched north from Connaught to their prized objective at Ballyshannon.

After several hotly contested skirmishes, the Lord Deputy advanced to Armagh.[64] On the Blackwater was a high bank and deep ditch which was defended by 40 of O'Neill's men. Borough knew that if he was to get a foothold on the Irish side of the Blackwater he would have to move quickly. The Lord Deputy led a brilliant surprise attack with 1,200 foot and 300 horse the following morning. His men wavered but he courageously led them on himself and they swarmed over the defenses. The Irish defenders fled before reinforcements could arrive. This initial success appears to be due solely to the gallant efforts of Lord Borough. The fort on the Blackwater (Portmore) was fortified and strengthened by the Lord Deputy who hoped to use it as a base from which he might invade Tyrone. On the following morning, while the English army assembled "to hear a sermon and pray to God,"[65] O'Neill half surprised the army

---

[63]Finnerty, *Ireland*, 1:141-2.
[64]McGee, *History of Ireland*, 2:426.
[65]Bagwell, *Ireland Under the Tudors*, 3:283.

with a vigorous counter attack. The English confusedly managed to beat back the first wave of attackers. They then charged, following the retreating Irish into the woods. O'Neill succeeded in drawing the enemy into an engagement on very disadvantageous ground. As the English proceeded into the woods the Catholics then attacked with their full force. The Earl of Kildare was mortally wounded and over sixty royalist gentlemen were killed, including Francis Vaughan, the viceroy's brother-in-law, Captain Turner and Thomas Walen.[66] All further efforts to invade Tyrone were halted. After the battle of Drumfluich (2 miles west of Portmore) the English army retreated and the Irish counted the battle won. In spite of this victory, an English force of 300 men under the brave and capable leadership of the Welshman, Captain Williams, remained behind to defend Portmore.[67] Lord Deputy Borough, after resupplying Portmore, suddenly grew ill. He was carried on a stretcher to Armagh and then to Newry where he died a few days later. His viceroyalty was the shortest during Elizabeth's reign. Before his death the Deputy angrily wrote O'Neill saying: "All your popish shaven priests shall never absolve you, God destroying the counsels of the wicked against his anointed."[68]

Another envoy from the King of Spain arrived in Ireland carrying letters from his sovereign. Philip gave a golden chain to Hugh O'Donnell as a token of his high es-

[66]Joyce, *History of Ireland*, 244-5.
[67]O'Sullivan Bear, *Ireland Under Elizabeth*, 99.
[68]Bagwell, *Ireland Under the Tudors*, 3:286.

teem. O'Neill and O'Donnell wrote him a joint letter from the Franciscan monastery in Donegal dated October 16th:

> Most merciful King, —We cannot express in words the intense joy and delight which the letter of your Catholic Majesty, full of extreme kindness and mercy, has caused us. Since the former Envoys left us we have used every means in our power, as we promised we should do, to gain time and procrastinate from one day to another, without causing any bloodshed or allowing our countrymen to be plundered or oppressed. But how could we impose on so clever an enemy, so skilled in every kind of cunning and cheating, if we did not use much dissimulation, and especially if we did not pretend we were anxious for peace? We will keep firm and unshaken the promises which we made to your majesty to our last breath; if we do not, we shall incur at once the wrath of God and the contempt of men.[69]

In the west Clifford's advance was delayed due to a lack of supplies. He finally arrived at the ford of the Erne opposite O'Donnell's castle at Ballyshannon on July 29th.[70] O'Donnell had only a small force gathered on the opposite side of the river with which he hoped to prevent the Governor from crossing. Clifford, with a forced march, succeeded in crossing the river about one-half mile below Belleek but only after fierce fighting. Clifford's Irish auxiliaries included Donough O'Brien; the Earl of Thomond who had abandoned his Catholic faith and embraced Protestantism; the Baron of Inchiquin; Ulick, the Earl of Clanrickarde; O'Conor of Sligo; and Tibbot na long, the son of Grace O'Malley. Lord Inchiquin and O'Conor of Sligo vied with

---

[69]Murphy, introduction to *Life of Hugh Roe O'Donnell*, 83.
[70]O'Faolain, *The Great O'Neil*, 242-3.

each other to see who would first reach the opposite side. Inchiquin was shot under the arm by one of O'Donnell's marksmen and fell from his horse. Because of the weight of his armor he was unable to rise and was swept away by the power of the current and drowned.[71]

The following day an English ship sailed up from Galway and unloaded four large artillery pieces. Turning these guns upon the castle, Clifford began his assault. O'Donnell's garrison consisted of 80 men, six of whom were Spaniards and the rest were Irish under the command of a Scotsman named Hugh Crawford. Clifford attacked boldly with a force of 700 men but was beaten back with heavy losses, "for there were poured from the castle on them showers of bright fiery balls from the well planted straight-firing guns and from the costly muskets, and missiles of rough pointed, sharp rocks, heavy, massive stones, with beams and blocks which happened to be on the battlements of the castle."[72]

Red Hugh with his small force attempted to relieve the garrison but to no avail. He continued to harass them day and night so that their horse and cattle could not graze outside their camp. The English continued their courageous assault and made a breach in the lower part of the castle. They effected an entrance into the castle but were driven out by the fierce counter attack of the heroic defenders. The

---

[71]Bagwell, *Ireland Under the Tudors*, 3:285. The Baron of Inchiquin's body was recovered by the Irish and given a Catholic burial by the Franciscan friars of Donegal with the permission of Red Hugh and Bishops O'Boyle of Raphoe and O'Gallager of Derry. See Murphy, introduction to *Life of Hugh Roe O'Donnell*, 78-79.

[72]O'Cleary, *Life of Hugh Roe O'Donnell*, 147.

following day Clifford attempted to widen the breach but the Irish hurled down stones from the battlements crushing his machines and the soldiers within them. The Governor's army was now growing discouraged. For five days and nights there had been heavy fighting with little success. Now their supply of food was running out. Hugh Maguire and Brian O'Rourke, who had just come to O'Donnell's aid, were passing southward over the Erne to Clifford's rear, exuberantly cheering. The horrifying news of Borough's failure to advance beyond the Blackwater had reached the camp. O'Neill was presently on his way to join forces with O'Donnell and decimate their enemy. Clifford knew his position was desperate. Just above the fall of the Erne was a passage not guarded by the Irish because of its difficulty. At daybreak Clifford, having made his preparations the night before, crossed the river unperceived by the Irish. Many of his men were swept over the fall and out to sea. The English were forced to leave three of their four field pieces behind. When the garrison of the castle saw the army escaping they sallied forth from the castle and opened fire on the rear of the army. Those who had successfully crossed the river returned the fire and defended the rear as they crossed. O'Donnell, hearing the shooting, ran from his tent and led his clan in pursuit with such haste that they left behind "cloaks, long stocking and shoes, and other parts of their dress."[73] Clifford's efforts had been truly gallant but he now had to pay the price. During this retreat across the Erne, through the Curlew mountains, O'Donnell attacked fiercely and continuously. The Governor courageously

---

[73]*Ibid.*, 153.

held his people in order and marched on. O'Donnell accompanied him each step of the way, attacking furiously as the day wore torturously on. In six hellish hours the English army had marched only eight miles. Torrents of rain began to fall by the middle of the day and muskets could no longer be fired. The fighting became a fierce hand-to-hand struggle. O'Donnell's infantry were eventually called off due to the inclement weather and their lack of clothing. His horsemen however continued the attacks for another six hours. It must be a genuine credit to Clifford's generalship that his disciplined army was not entirely destroyed. The English returned to their homes in sorrow and confusion. There could be no doubt that the general expedition had been a humiliating failure.

Following this engagement, another envoy, Don Roderigo de Vayen, was sent by Philip II to confer with and assist the Irish. He landed at Killybegs and journeyed to Donegal Castle to meet O'Donnell. There he was most bountifully entertained. Upon his departure, Red Hugh gave presents of fine hunting dogs and excellent horses for King Philip. O'Donnell wrote the King on behalf of the other Irish chiefs:

> We have received your Highness's letter by Don Roderigo de Vayen this last March, in which you informed us that we should go forward in our enterprise, and that your Majesty would send us aid. We returned answer by the said Don Roderigo. Believe no news from England of any agreement in this country. Great offers have been made by the Queen of England, but we will not break our oath and promise to you. We are compassed round on all sides in such a way that except God keep us we shall be undone. But as yet we have defeated our foes. We skirmish with them

very often, and they come off the worst, and lately I was present at the killing of the Sergeant-Major of the Queen's army, and of the Lord Deputy's brother-in-law, with many others. The Earl of Kildare was hurt and died of his wound. The Governor of Connaught came into the country where O'Donnell was, with a great army, nearly as great as the Deputy's was, and laid siege to one of his castles; but after a while he was forced to steal away with the loss of a nobleman and many officers and soldiers, and driven to leave the Queen's great ordinance behind, with all their victuals and carriages. Hence at present we are so situated we must humbly crave your immediate aid.[74]

The Irish Confederates had begun the war with a series of brilliant victories. For the English at the close of 1597, things looked rather bleak indeed.[75] Elizabeth found herself without a Lord Deputy, a general, a plan and virtually without an army. Out of weakness she was once more forced to seek peace, in an effort to buy time.

The Earl of Ormond and the Protestant Bishop of Meath, Thomas Jones (the son-in-law of Adam Loftus), represented the Queen and parleyed with O'Neill; O'Donnell also joined in the negotiations only after a great display of unwillingness. The two Irishmen spoke on behalf of the rights of their comrades in arms and for all the Catholics of Ireland. They reiterated their fundamental demands: 1) Complete cessation of attempts to disturb the Catholic Church in Ireland. 2) No more garrisons—no more sheriffs or English officials of any sort whatsoever to be allowed into the Irish territories, which should be unrestrictedly

---

[74]Murphy, introduction to *Life of Hugh Roe O'Donnell*, 89.
[75]Garnier, *Popular History of Ireland*, 55-6.

under the jurisdiction of their lawfully elected native chiefs.

3) Payment by Marshal Bagnal to O'Neill of 1,000 pounds of silver "as a marriage portion with the lady whom he had raised to the dignity of an O'Neill's bride."[76]

Ormond sent a copy of the demands to London and cautiously marked it "Suppressed."[77] Elizabeth was again infuriated at the indignity of the demands and insolence of the rebels. The Irish War was truly the labors of Sisyphus for the aging Queen and her ministers. Something had to be done.

---

[76]Sullivan, *Story of Ireland*, 260.
[77]O'Faolain, *The Great O'Neil*, 250.

FIVE

Che Battle of Yellowford
Beal an acha Buīdhe

In the battle of the Yellowford
It is by him the foreigners shall fall.
After the destruction of the foreigners
The men from Tory will be glad. —St. Berchan[1]

Following the death of Lord Borough, Sir Thomas Norris, the President of Munster, was provisionally appointed Lord Justice. Sir Thomas, however, was so grieved over the loss of his brother, Sir John, that he requested to be relieved of the burdensome office. Acting upon this request the government was handed over to the Protestant Archbishop of Dublin, Adam Loftus and Sir Robert Gardiner. Thomas Butler, the Earl of Ormond, was appointed Lieutenant-General and Captain of the army.

In the spring of 1598, O'Neill sought to capture the fort on the Blackwater which had been taken and garrisoned with 300 men by Lord Borough.[2] His initial assault with 30 scaling ladders was repulsed with severe losses. The English defenders had two *robinets*, light field guns filled with shot, and also two *arquebuses en-croc*, a type of heavy wall mounted gun, which they used with great effectiveness.

---

[1]O'Cleary, *Life of Hugh Roe O'Donnell*, 171.
[2]Bagwell, *Ireland Under the Tudors*, 3:295.

The Irish made two additional assaults in an effort to take the walls but failed. When O'Neill learned that the defenders were short of supplies, he was determined to continue a close and constant siege in order to reduce the fort by starvation. Captain Thomas Williams, the commander of the English garrison, was an excellent soldier and a man of great courage. His leadership was of the highest order. William's dauntless bravery and fighting spirit inspired the garrison to defend the fort at all costs. As the siege continued, the supplies ran out and the English slaughtered the few horses they had in their possession for food. Eventually they were constrained to live on the grass which grew in the ditches and crevices in the wall.[3] They had to even fight for drinking water and wood for their fires as supplies within the fort were exhausted.

When this distressing news reached Dublin, the Council was thoroughly alarmed. Sir Henry Bagnal, the Queen's Marshal, undoubtedly motivated by his personal hatred of Tyrone, (his sister who eloped with O'Neill had become a Roman Catholic, but was now dead), volunteered and was sent by the government with the finest English troops to raise the siege and resupply the fort. He lived in Newry and knew the terrain well. Elizabeth sent over 2,000 additional troops which landed in Dublin on July 22.[4] The Earl of Ormond, who was Commander-in-Chief of the Queen's forces, was off "protecting his own estates"[5] and trying to maintain control in the province of Lenister.

---

[3]O'Faolain, *The Great O'Neil*, 254.
[4]*Ibid.*
[5]*Ibid.* The Kavanaghs, O'Byrnes, O'Moores and O'Connor's had stirred up hostilities in Lenister to aid the Catholic cause.

PLATE I. An Irish Lord with His Attendants

IRELAND
The Principal Clans and
Great Lordships
❧ 16th Century ❧
Miles
0   20   40   60

FANAD
INISHOWEN
O'Dherty
Doe
MacSweeny
TIRCONAILL
Derry
O'Cahan
MacQuillan
Glens
of
Antrim
Mac
Donnell
LORDSHIP
OF
O'NEILL
THE
ARDS
Carrickfergus
THE
EARLDOM
OF
ULSTER
BANAGH
MacSweeny
Donegal
O'DONNELL
Lough
Neagh
O'Neill
Ballyshannon
Dungannon
FERMANAGH
Enniskillen
Maguire
OF
TYRONE
O'Hanlon
Armagh
Magennis
INVEAGH
Newry
Sligo
O'ROURKE
OF
W BREFNI
THE
FEWS
O'Connor
MacMahon
Dundalk
MacWilliam
MacDonagh
Carlingford
MacDermot
O'REILLY
OF
E BREFNI
THE
Costello
O'Connor Don
O'Farrell
of
Annaly
LIBERTY
OF TRIM
ENGLISH
O'Malley
Tuam
Trim
IAR
CONNACHT
O'Flaherty
CLAN
O'Kelly
Athlone
O'Connor
Faly
Dublin
PALE
Galway
BURKE
O'Molloy
CARLDOM
OF
Naas
O'Loghlin
O'Carroll
of Ely
Kildare
KILDARE
O'Toole
Bray
Newcastle
THOMOND
O'Kennedy
of Ormond
LORDSHIP
O'Moore
OF LIEX
Wicklow
LORDSHIP
OF O'BRIEN
MacNamara
Limerick
SUPREMACY
O'Byrne
OF
Arklow
Glin
Burke
Carlow
EARLDOM
White Knight
EARLDOM
AND
MACMURROUGH
Gorey
Lord of
Kerry
Kilmallock
Thurles
Kilkenny
LORDSHIP
Cashel
OF ORMOND
KAVANAGH
Tralee
Roche
FITZGERALD
Clonmel
Enniscorthy
Smerwick
Dingle
AND
LORDSHIP
OF
DECIES
Dungarvan
Waterford
LORDSHIP
OF
Wexford
Wexford
OF DESMOND
MACCARTHY MORE
MacCarthy
of Muskerry
Roche
Barry
More
Youghal
O'Sullivan
More
Cork
O'Sullivan
Beare
MacCarthy
Reagh
Carbery
O'Driscol

N
W   E
S

PLATE II.

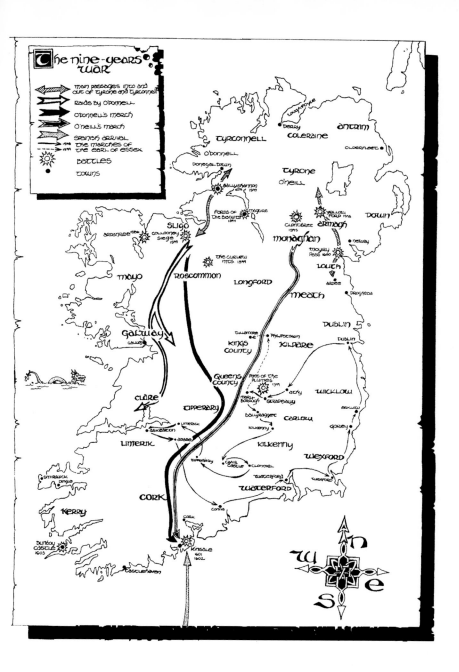

PLATE III.

PLATE IV. Hugh O'Neill

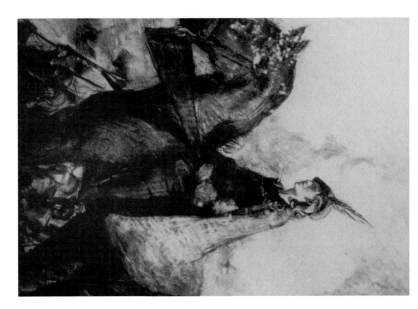

PLATE V. Red Hugh O'Donnell

PLATE VI. The Lord MacSweeny Dines in the Open Air

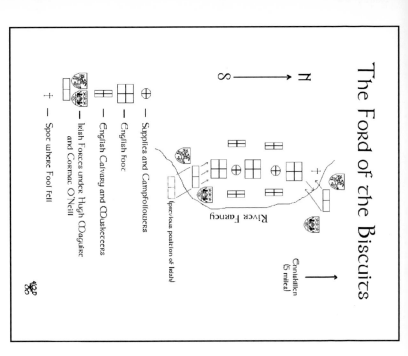

The Ford of the Biscuits

N

S

⊕ — Supplies and Campfollowers

▦ — English Foot

⊞ — English Calvary and Musketeers

— Irish Forces under Hugh Maguire and Cormac O'Neill

† — Spot where Fool Fell

River Farney

(perilous position of Irish)

Enniskillen (5 miles)

PLATE VII.

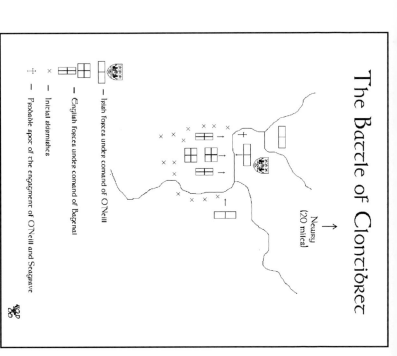

The Battle of Clontibret

— Irish Forces under command of O'Neill

▦ — English Forces under command of Bagenal

× — Initial skirmishes

† — Probable spot of the engagement of O'Neill and Seagrave

Newry (20 miles)

PLATE VIII.

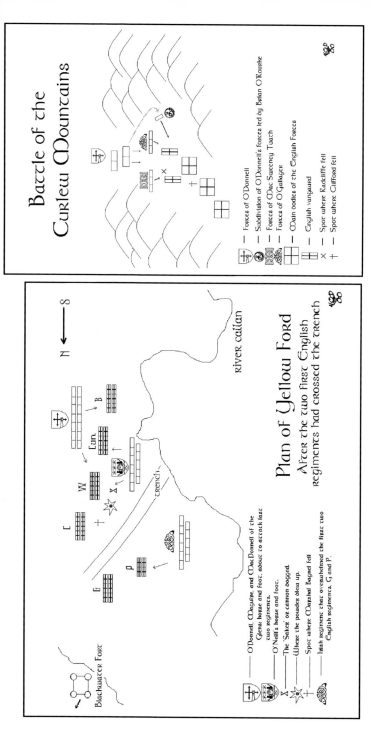

Battle of the Curlew Mountains

— Forces of O'Donnell
— Subdivision of O'Donnell's forces led by Brian O'Rourke
— Forces of Mac Sweeney Tuath
— Forces of O'Gallagher
— Main bodies of the English Forces
— English vanguard
× — Spot where Radcliffe fell
† — Spot where Clifford fell

PLATE X.

Blackwater Fort

N

S

river callan

Plan of Yellow Ford

After the two first English regiments had crossed the trench

G   p   L   W   Lun.   B

trench

— O'Donnell, Maguire, and MacDonnell of the Glens; horse and foot, about to attack last two regiments.
— O'Neill's horse and foot.
× — The 'Saker' or cannon bogged.
✶ — Where the powder blew up.
† — Spot where Marshal Bagnal fell
— Irish regiment that overwhelmed the first two English regiments, G and P.

PLATE IX.

PLATE XI. Battle of Kinsale

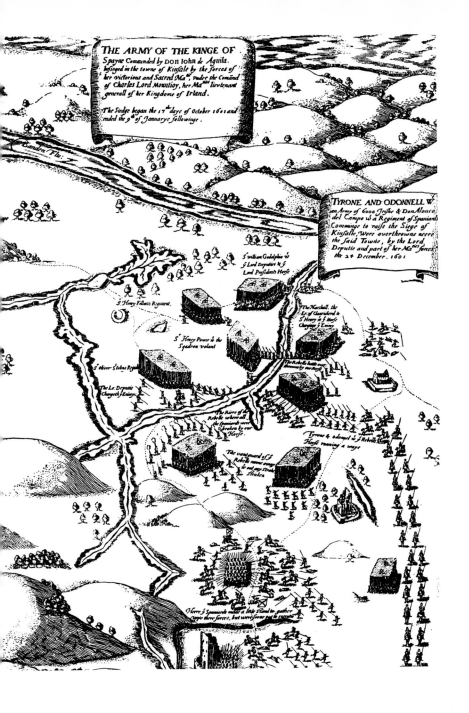

THE ARMY OF THE KINGE OF
Spayne Commanded by DON Iohn de Aguila.
besieged in the towne of Kinsale by the forces of
her victorious and Sacred Ma.tie, vnder the Comãnd
of Charles Lord Mountioy, her Ma.ties lieutenant
generall of her Kingdome of Irland.

The Siedge began the 17th daye of October 1601 and
ended the 9th of Jannarye followinge.

TYRONE AND ODONNELL W
an Army of 6000 Jesshe & DonAlonco
del Campo w.th a Regiment of Spaniards
Comãnge to raise the Siege of
Kinsale, Were overthrowne neere
the said Towne, by the Lord
Deputie and part of her Ma.ties forces
the 24 December. 1601

PLATE XII. A Raid by Irish Kern

PLATE XIII. The Return of an English Army after a Victory

PLATE XIV. English Army on the March

PLATE XV. Attack on Cahir Castle

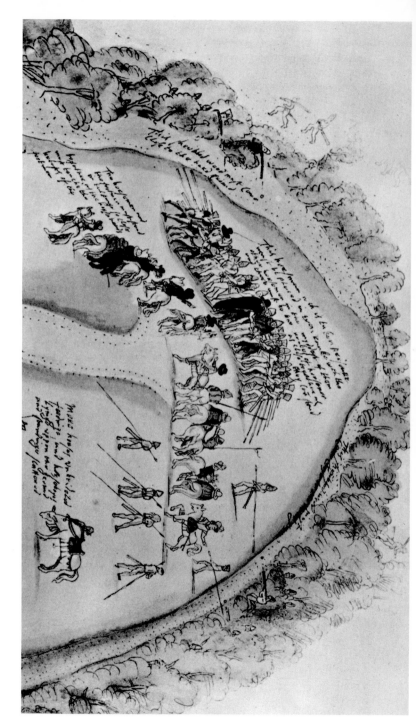

PLATE XVI. The Capture of the Earl of Ormond by Irish Forces

The 7 of Iune the
Army lodged here
Oppoſit to Dvnboy

betweene Page. 310 &. 311
Part of the great
Iland where ỹ Erle
of Thomond ſpake
wᵗ Richard Mˢ Geghape

The Caſtle of Dvnboy taken
by aſſault, the 17 and 18.
of Iune 1602 blowne vppe
wᵗ powder the 22 of the
monthe aſore Said.

THE SEIDGE OF DVNBOY

The Marlin

The Spaniſh Boy

The Hoye and
Boates tranſpor-
tinge of the
ordinance.

Here were two
Mounes planted

The Batterey plā
ted the 16 of Iune

The 10 Iune ỹ Campe
was quartred and
entrenched on the 11

A Smal Sconce
betwene the Campe
and the Brudge

PART

Here ỹ Ordia
ance Landed ỹ
10 of Iune

The Brudge

OF

THE

CONTRYE

OF   BEARE

THE MAYNE OCEAN

PLATE XVII. English Forces Assaulting Dunboy Castle

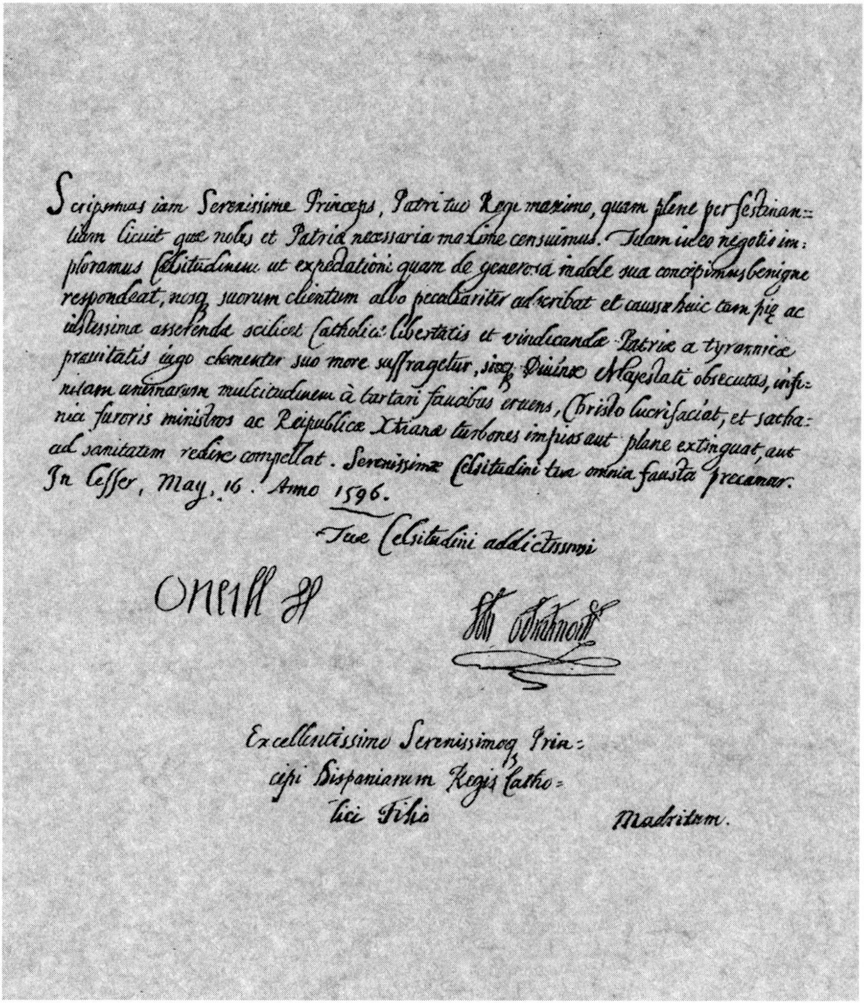

Scripsimus iam Serenissime Princeps, Patri tuo Regi maximo, quam plene per festinan=
tiam licuit quae nobis et Patriae necessaria maxime censuimus. Idem ideo negotiis im:
ploramus Celsitudinem ut expectationi quam de generosa indole sua concepimus benigne
respondeat, nosq suorum clientum albo peculiariter adscribat et caussae huic tam piae ac
iustissimae asserendae scilicet Catholicae libertatis et vindicandae Patriae a tyrannicae
pravitatis iugo clementer suo more suffragetur, sicq Divinae Maiestati obsecutus, infi=
nitam animarum multitudinem à tartari faucibus eruens, Christo lucrifaciat, et satha:
nici furoris ministros ac Reipublicae Xtianae turbones impios aut plane extinguat, aut
ad sanitatem redire compellat. Serenissimae Celsitudini tuae omnia fausta precamur.
In Cesser, May. 16. Anno 1596.

Tuae Celsitudini addictissimi

Oneill

Ho odonnell

Excellentissimo Serenissimoq Prin=
cipi Hispaniarum Regis Catho=
lici Filio

Madritum.

PLATE XVIII. Letter of Hugh O'Neill and Hugh O'Donnell

Bagnal, a man of experience "skilled in the art of war... both brave and prudent,"[6] began his march to the north on the 7th of August. The English army consisted of over 4,500 foot and 500 horse.[7] All these soldiers were well trained and many of them were seasoned veterans who had fought under Sir John Norris in France and included also a number of Irish soldiers of the Queen's party. The army was equipped with artillery and well armed with both heavy and light guns. They carried a large supply of gunpowder, iron and leaden balls as well as salt, meat, cheese and biscuits with which they hoped to relieve the fort.[8] They also carried four ordinance, the largest was a saker drawn by a team of oxen which was about a "six pounder." This powerful army, the finest yet Elizabeth had put in the field, reached Armagh and prepared for the final march against Tyrone.

The Irish received reports of the magnificent army which was marching north to rescue the fort and invade Ulster. The Catholic Confederates rushed to meet the threat and aid the forces of O'Neill. Hugh O'Donnell arrived with over 3,000 men from Tirconnaill and Connaught.[9] The united Catholic forces consisted of at least 4,500 foot and approximately 600 horse. The Irish had taken their position approximately two miles north of Armagh near the Callan River. The tower of Armagh Cathedral could be seen to the south and the hills of Benburb five miles to the west.

---

[6]Murphy, introduction to *Life of Hugh Roe O'Donnell*, 93.

[7]Joyce, *History of Ireland*, 246. D'Alton in the *History of Ireland* Vol. 3, page 141, gives the English numbers as 4,000 foot, 350 horse.

[8]Murphy, introduction to *Life of Hugh Roe O'Donnell*, 92.

[9]*Ibid.*

The impending battle was destined to be the biggest of the war in the North. Both sides were fully aware that a defeat would lead to disastrous consequences. The night before the battle the Irish chieftains took council discussing their battle plans. O'Neill, O'Donnell, Maguire, MacWilliam and Angus MacDonnell, Red Hugh's cousin, were all present when O'Donnell's hereditary historian, Feareasa O'Cleary, rose to speak. [10] He told the chieftains that over 900 years ago St. Berchan[11] was given a vision of a battle as he walked by the Yellow Ford. In this vision the saint heard the cries of battle and the sound of a stupefying, ineffable thunder. The spirit of prophecy came upon him and he wrote down that one day Ireland would defeat her foes in a great battle. O'Cleary read the prophecy to the spellbound princes:

> In the battle of the Yellowford it is by him the foreigners shall fall. After the destruction of the foreigners the men from Tory will be glad.

Whether the saint actually wrote down this prophecy is open to dispute. Nevertheless the Irish were inclined to believe in prophecies and O'Donnell and O'Neill had it read to their troops.[12] The prophecy had a profound effect on the men and raised their excitement and courage to a fevered

---

[10]MacManus, *Story of the Irish Race*, 390-1.

[11]St. Berchan was a bishop and is considered one of the "four prophets of the Gael." His feast day is December 4th according to the *Martyrology of Donegal*, 327.

[12]Murphy, introduction to *Life of Hugh Roe O'Donnell*, 30. The reference to the gladness of the "men from Tory" in the prophecy would have had special significance since the island off the Donegal coast had been recently plundered by George Bingham.

pitch. The soldiers were wild with enthusiasm and none doubted that their hopes would be fulfilled tomorrow. That night the Catholics sent out five hundred kearnes—light, fast moving, infantry men—armed with muskets, to harass the enemy on their march to relieve the Blackwater.[13] O'Neill reminded his men that, "Victory lies not in senseless armour, nor the vain din of cannon, but in living and courageous souls."[14]

The following morning, as the rays of the beautiful newborn day broke over the countryside, Bagnal rose and his mighty army with him. At exactly 8:00 on the morning of August 14, the eve of the Assumption of Mary, the English army proudly raised their standards, beat the Diana drum and marched out of Armagh with music and drums.[15] The army advanced in six regiments which were grouped in three divisions. The two regiments which made up the first division were commanded by Colonel Percy. Bagnal, who was Commander-in-Chief, rode in the second regiment. The second division, composed of the third and fourth regiments, was commanded by Sir Thomas Maria Wingfield and Colonel Cosby. The third and final division was entrusted to Captain Cuin and Captain Billing. These six infantry regiments were placed behind each other "at intervals of 600 or 700 paces."[16] The English horse under Captain Sir Calisthenes Brooke and Captains Montague and Fleming formed two separate divisions on both sides of the army's wings. The 500 Irish kearnes, whose Parthian war-

---

[13]O'Sullivan Bear, *Ireland Under Elizabeth*, 109.
[14]*Ibid.*, 107.
[15]O'Faolain, *The Great O'Neil*, 255.
[16]Joyce, *History of Ireland*, 247.

fare was proverbial, soon commenced firing.[17] They darted from tree to tree firing repeatedly from snaphance and matchlock. The English returned the fire but were unable to charge or dislodge them; Bagnal and his veterans angrily pressed on. The Irish hoped this would demoralize and weaken the enemy. The General knew however that soon he would meet his personal enemy Tyrone and the popish Confederates. Bagnal earlier that morning had offered over L1000 in gold to any man who brought to him the head of either O'Neill or O'Donnell that evening.[18] Through fire, bogs, fallen trees and pitfalls, Bagnal and the English marched on with pounding drums and carrying their heavy cannon. All through the morning the English army fought with courage and firm resolve. There were skirmishes, re-tirements, advances and charges. O'Neill's men attacked on the left while O'Donnell assailed the right. It was not until noon, nearly four hours since the English forces began the march, that they arrived in front of the main body of Catholic troops. The English soldiers in the fort at the Blackwater could now see the English army in the distance and began to cheer "and throw up their hats"[19] in the air at the sight of the long awaited relief.

O'Donnell and O'Neill exhorted their soldiers to fight courageously, saying:

> Brave men be not dismayed or frightened by the English on account of their strange weapons, their unusual armour and arms, and the thundering sound of their trumpets and

---

[17] MacManus, *Story of the Irish Race*, 391.

[18] O'Sullivan Bear, *Ireland Under Elizabeth*, 106.

[19] Falls, *Elizabeth's Irish Wars*, 216.

tabours and war instruments, and of their own great numbers, for it is absolutely certain that they shall be defeated
over this day's fight. Of this in truth we are convinced, for
you are on the side of truth and the others on the side of
falsehood, confining you in prisons and beheading you in
order to rob you of your patrimonies. Moreover we are
quite sure that this day will distinguish between truth and
falsehood.[20]

The historian Mitchel gives the following graphic ac-
count of the great battle which came to be known to the
English as the Blackwater and to the Irish as *Beal Atha
Buidhe*, the Yellow Ford:

> The sun was glancing on the corslets and spears of their
> glittering cavalry, their banners waved proudly, and their
> bugles rung clear in the morning air, when, suddenly, from
> the thickets on both sides of their path, a deadly volley of
> musketry swept through the foremost ranks. O'Neill had
> stationed here five hundred light armed troops to guard the
> defiles, and in the shelter of thick groves of fir trees they had
> silently waited for the enemy. Now they poured in their
> shot, volley after volley, and killed great numbers of the
> English; but the first division, led by Bagnal in person, after
> some hard fighting, carried the pass, dislodged the marks-
> men from their position, and drove them backwards into the
> plain. The centre division under Cosby and Wingfield, and
> the rear-guard led by Cuin and Billing, supported in flank by
> the cavalry under Brooke, Montague and Fleming, now
> pushed forward, speedily cleared the difficult country and
> formed in the open ground in front of the Irish lines.
>
> 'It was not quite safe', says an Irish chronicler (in admi-
> ration of Bagnal's disposition of his forces) 'to attack the nest
> of griffins and den of lions in which were placed the soldiers

---

[20]O'Cleary, *Life of Hugh Roe O'Donnell*, 169.

of London.' Bagnal at the head of his first division, and aided by a body of cavalry, charged the Irish light-armed troops up to the very entrenchments, in front of which O'Neill's foresight had prepared some pits, covered over with wattles and grass, and rolled headlong, both men and horses, into these trenches and perished. Still the marshal's chosen troops, with loud cheers and shouts of 'St. George for merry England!' resolutely attacked the entrenchment that stretched across the pass, battered them with cannon, and in one place succeeded, though with heavy loss, in forcing back their defenders. Then first the main body of O'Neill's troops was brought into action, and with bagpipes sounding a charge, they fell upon the English, shouting their fierce battle cries, Lamh-dearg! [the redhand] and O'Donnell aboo! O'Neill himself, at the head of a body of horse, pricked forward to seek out Bagnal amidst the throng of battle, but they never met: the marshal, who had done his devoir that day like a good soldier, was shot through the brain by some unknown marksman. The division he had led was forced back by the furious onslaught of the Irish, and put to utter rout; and, what added to their confusion, a cart of gunpowder exploded amidst the English ranks and blew many of their men to atoms. And now the cavalry of Tyrconnell and Tyrowen dashed into the plain and bore down the remnant of Brooke's and Flemming's horse; the columns of Wingfield and Cosby reeled before their rushing charge—while in front, to the war-cry of Bataillah-aboo! the swords and axes of the heavy armed gallowglasses were raging amongst the Saxon ranks. By this time the cannon were all taken; the cries of 'St. George' had failed, or turned into death shrieks; and once more, England's royal standard sunk.[21]

---

[21]John Mitchel, *The Life and Times of Hugh O'Neill* (New York: P.M. Haverty, 1868), 141-143. See also Cyril Falls' account in *Elizabeth's Irish Wars*, pages 213-219, and G.A. Hayes-McCoy's *Irish Battles* pages 106-131.

Bagnal had made a deadly mistake in tactics. He had placed his regiments too far asunder, approximately 150 paces apart. This distance grew greater during the difficult morning march. The vanguard of the army was annihilated before the second regiment could come to its assistance. The entire army had been literally cut to pieces.[22] Twelve thousand gold pieces, thirty four standards, all the artillery, ammunition and supplies of the vanquished army fell into the hands of the victorious Catholic clansmen. Nearly 3,000 dead, including Bagnal and twenty captains, were left by the English on the field of battle.[23] The remnants of the army fled to the Cathedral of Armagh and were immediately surrounded by the Irish.[24] O'Neill, after receiving a letter from the Dublin Council ("that marks the scummy low-water mark of their oozing courage")[25] which begged him not to kill "in cold blood" the survivors[26], allowed the frightened, dispirited men to return safely to the Pale. All of their arms however were left behind. Armagh was captured, the English garrison in the Blackwater fort surrendered and the reputation of England among the clansmen was nearly destroyed.

---

[22]O'Cleary, *Life of Hugh Roe O'Donnell*, 173-5.

[23]Sullivan, *The Story of Ireland*, 269. According to D'Alton, the Irish lost 200 men with 600 wounded. (D'Alton, *History of Ireland*, 144.)

[24]Clare, *History of Ireland*, 455.

[25]O'Faolain, *The Great O'Neil*, 259.

[26]Bagwell, *Ireland Under the Tudors*, 3:300. D'Alton states that Elizabeth was so annoyed by the subservient tone of the letter that she complained that she, "had never read a letter, which in form and substance was so base." (D'Alton, *History of Ireland*, 3:144.) See also the *Calendar of the Carew Papers*, 4:284. Cyril Falls gives the letter on page 221 of *Elizabeth's Irish Wars*.

Sir Walter Scott, in his colorful poem "Rokeby", refers to the battle of Yellow Ford:

> Who has not heard, while Erin yet
> Strove `gainst the Saxons iron bit,
> Who has not heard how brave O'Neill
> In English blood imbrued his steel;
> Against St. George's cross blazed high
> The banner of his tanistry.[27]

As one might easily imagine, a victory of this magnitude was a poetic theme greatly played upon by the Irish bards. The bards of Erin were constantly striving to enkindle the fire of militant patriotism. For this reason they were severely persecuted by the English government. The following poem written by de Vere fully captures the exuberant spirits of the Irish following their great victory at Yellow Ford:

The War-Song of Tyrconnell's Bard at the Battle of Blackwater

> Glory to God, and to the Powers that fight
>   For Freedom and the Right!
> We have them then, the invaders! there they stand
>   Once more on Oriel's land!
> They have pass'd the gorge stream cloven,
>   And the mountain's purple bound;
> Now the toils are round them woven,
>   Now the nets are spread around!
> Give them time: their steeds are blown;
>   Let them stand and round them stare,
>   Breathing blasts of Irish air:
> Our eagles know their own!

---

[27]Finnerty, *Ireland*, 1:148.

Thou rising sun, fair fall
Thy greeting on Armagh's time-honoured wall
And on the willows hoar
That fringe thy silver waters, Avonmore!
See! on that hill of drifted sand
The far-famed marshal holds command,
Bagnal, their bravest: —to the right,
That recreant, neither chief nor knight,
"The Queen's O'Reilly", he that sold
His country, clan, and church for gold!
"Saint George for England!":—recreant crew,
What are the saints ye spurn to you?
They charge; they pass yon grassy swell
They reach our pit-falls hidden well:
On!—warriors native to the sod!
Be on them, in the power of God!

Seest thou yon stream, whose tawny waters glide
    Through weeds and yellow marsh lingeringly and slowly?
    Blest is that spot and holy!
There, ages past, Saint Bercan stood and cried,
"This spot shall quell one day th' invader's pride!"
    He saw in mystic trance
    The blood-stain flush yon rill:
    On!—hosts of God, advance!
    Your country's fate fulfil!

Hark! the thunder of their meeting!
Hand meets hand, and rough the greeting!
Hark! the crash of shield and brand:
They mix, they mingle, band with band,
Like two horn-commingling stags,
Wrestling on the mountain crags,
Intertwined, intertangled,
Mangled forehead meeting mangled!
See! the wavering darkness through
I see the banner of Red Hugh;

Close beside is thine, O'Neill!
Now they stoop and now they reel,
Rise once more and onward sail,
Like two falcons on one gale!
O ye clansmen past me rushing,
Like mountain torrents seaward gushing,
Tell the chiefs that from this height
Their chief of bards beholds the flight;
That on their he pours his spirit;
Marks their deeds and chaunts their merit;
While the Priesthood evermore,
Like him that rule God's host of yore,
With arms outstretched that God implore!

Glory be to God on high!
That shout rang up into the sky!
The plain lies bare; the smoke drifts by;
Again that cry; they fly! they fly!
O'er them standards thirty-four
Waved at morn: they wave no more.

Glory be to Him alone who holds the nations in His hand,
And to them the heavenly guardians of our Church and
        native land!
Sing, ye priests, your deep Te Deum; bards, make answer
        loud and long,
In your rapture flinging heavenward censers of triumphant
        song.
Isle for centuries blind in bondage, lift once more
        thine ancient boast,
From the cliffs of Innishowen southward on to Carbery's
        coast!
We have seen the right made perfect, seen the Hand
        that rules the spheres,
Glance like lightning through the clouds, and backward
        roll the wrongful years.
Glory fadeth, but this triumph is no barren mundane glory;

Rays of healing it shall scatter on the eyes that read
    our story:
Upon nations bound and torpid as they waken it shall shine,
As on Peter in his chains the angel shone, with light divine.
From th'unheeding, from th'unholy it may hide, like
    truth, its ray;
But when Truth and Justice conquer, on their crowns
    its beam shall play:
O'er the ken of troubled tyrants it shall trail a
    meteor's glare;
For the blameless it shall glitter as the star of
    morning fair;
Whensoever Erin triumphs, then its dawn it shall renew;
Then O'Neill shall be remember'd, and Tirconnell's
    chief Red Hugh![28]

This defeat was the worst disaster Elizabeth suffered in her reign.[29] When the aging Queen heard of it she was horrified and deeply distraught. The security of her own kingdom was threatened not only by the frightening affairs in Ireland, but by Spain which constantly threatened with another Armada.[30] On the same day that the Battle of Yellowford took place, William Cecil, Lord Burghley, the principal architect of Elizabeth's policy, died in London.[31] There were reports from Ireland that O'Neill would not only win the Irish war but carry the crusade into England where he

---

[28]Sullivan, *Story of Ireland*, 270-1.

[29]Lyntton Strachey, *Elizabeth and Essex* (New York: Harcourt, Brace, & Co., 1928), 111.

[30]Garnier, *Popular History of Ireland*, 59.

[31]William Cecil died at seven in the morning surrounded by his family. On July 20th he had written his last letter to his son Robert who was to succeed him stating, "Serve God by serving the Queen for all other service is bondage to the Devil." (Read, *Lord Burghley*, 545.)

would become a leader of the people and re-establish the Catholic Faith.[32]

The contemporary English historian Camden gave the following description of the Irish victory:

> Thus Tirone triumphed according to his heart's desire over his adversary, and obtained a remarkable victory over the English; and doubtless since the time they first set foot in Ireland they never received a greater overthrow . . .[33] it was a glorious victory for the rebels.[34]

In the same manner, another contemporary English historian, Fynes Moryson, relates:

> I term the victory great, since the English from their first arrival in that kingdom (Ireland) never had received so great an overthrow as this. Many of the soldiers slain were of the old companies which had served in Brittany under General Norreys. . . . Tyrone was among the Irish celebrated as the deliverer of his country from thraldom, and the combined traitors were puffed up with intollerable pride.[35]

For months nothing was talked of in England save Tyrone and the defeat of the Blackwater. Moryson himself re-

---

[32]O'Faolain, *The Great O'Neil*, 234. Despite the brutal suppression of the rising of the Northern Earls in England, it is believed that many in England would have supported a restoration of the ancient faith. The fear of the Irish now carrying the war to England with Spanish help was a very real concern at the time in the wake of the magnitude of this victory. See John McGurk's discussion of English war aims and motivation in *The Elizabethan Conquest of Ireland*, pages 13-20.

[33]Murphy, introduction to *Life of Hugh Roe O'Donnell*, 96. William Camden, 1551-1623, was born in London and fiercely anti-Catholic.

[34]Clare, *History of Ireland*, 455.

[35]Moryson, *Itinerary*, 2:217. Fynes Moryson, 1566-1630, served as secretary to Lord Mountjoy in Ireland from 1600-1603.

veals to us that "the generall voyce was of Tyrone amongst the English after the defeat of the Blackwater, as of Hannibal amongst the Romans after the defeat at Cannae."[36]

Envoys were sent secretly between Tyrone and James VI of Scotland. An English spy reported to his government that the Stuart had given him a personal gift when he posed as a messenger from Tyrone. He swore that there was certainly some sort of clandestine agreement between the two. This marks the beginning of the Irish-Jacobite allegiance which alarmed and threatened Elizabeth.[37]

When news of the Irish victory reached Spain, *Te Deums* were sung in the streets throughout the country. For the Spanish, it seemed that, at last, the heretical Jezebel had suffered a serious reverse! The artillery at San Angelo thundered a tributary salute to the joyous news. At the Escorial, Philip II was near death. The courageous king had lived through the summer of 1598 in excruciating pain. The king's condition had grown steadily worse and soon he was covered with maggot infested sores all over his body. Movement of any kind was now out of the question and he lay in the accumulating filth of his own excrements. The odor from the sores and excrements in the room was indescribable. It speaks well for Spanish self-control that so many gentleman, prelates, monks, servants and friends were able to visit the dying king without betraying their nausea and disgust. Doctor Affaro became violently ill

---

[36]*Ibid.*, 274. The reference to Tyrone as Hannibal fits in well with English propaganda at the time, which ironically viewed the English forces as noble "Romans" fighting to bring civilization to the pagan, wild, uncivilized Irish, thereby justifying the conquest.

[37]O'Faolain, *The Great O'Neil*, 263.

from the odor and became bedridden. Through all this suffering, Philip stood fast in his faith awaiting death through this prolonged agony. Never complaining, but thanking God for his suffering, he had the monks read scripture concerning the passion of Our Lord. He received Extreme Unction and as a saint awaited his death. The king had arranged his bed in the oratory so that his weary eyes might rest upon San Lorenzo's high altar and tabernacle in his last moments. On the evening of September 12, 1598 the doctors agreed the end would come soon. Suddenly a messenger entered the room of the dying king with a dispatch from Ireland announcing the glorious victory of the Irish Catholics. This report was tremendously consoling to this man who had been such a staunch defender of the Catholic cause in Ireland and throughout the world.[38] At last his prayers and efforts had been rewarded and the tide had turned. The Catholic monarch dictated a warm letter of congratulations and encouragement to the Confederates. In the letter the king promised immediate aid, the destruction of the heretics and the ruin of Elizabeth. The king then sank back into a holy, tortured stupor. William Thomas Walsh vividly portrays the final hours of Philip II:

> It was all happening there, in the silence of the Escorial, in the soul of the dying King. It was already midnight. The voices continued some high, some low, reading holy words. Whenever they stopped, the King would whisper, 'Padres, decidme mas.'

---

[38]Strachey, *Elizabeth and Essex*, 115. Cyril Falls also makes a brief mention of the consolation which this victory gave to Philip on his deathbed. (Falls, *Elizabeth's Irish Wars*, 222.)

About two o'clock Toledo opened the little box, and took out one of the blessed candles from Our Lady's altar. But the King said, 'Aun no es tiempo.' An hour later Toledo again offered the candle, and Philip said, 'Dad aca, que ya es tiempo.'

With Toledo's help he held the candle in one hand, and the small, wooden crucifix of his Mother and Father in the other. He smiled joyfully. Men about his bed thought of the words of the psalm he had uttered so often during his illness: 'As the heart panteth after the fountains of water, so my soul panteth after thee, O God. My soul hath thirsted after the strong living God; when shall I come and appear before the face of God?' He seemed to become unconscious. They thought him dead; but when someone went to take away the candle and cover his face, he opened his eyes with a sudden parozysm, and fixed them with intense longing and devotion, upon the crucifix, around which his fingers still closed. Thus he remained for some time. He remained fully intelligent after that for more than an hour.

It was five o'clock. In the chapel below there was a stirring of footsteps, a flicker of candles, and the murmuring of voices as priests and acolytes began, on the vigil of the Exaltation of the Holy Cross to say the Mass of Dawn, which they had always offered for the spiritual welfare of the King. Philip gave three little gasps, like a child's. His eyes, still on the crucifix, became stony. At that moment the sun arose over the eastern hill and flooded the white walls of San Lorenzo with the cheerful light of morning.[39]

Although the Irish had lost a valiant friend, the victory at Yellow Ford brought a renewed enthusiasm for the Irish War on the Continent. In Brussels, Paris, Rome and Madrid the names of O'Neill and O'Donnell were spoken of "by all

---

[39]William T. Walsh, *Philip II* (New York & London: Sheed & Ward, 1937), 725-6.

 137

zealous Catholics with enthusiastic admiration."[40] In Rome, Clement VIII prepared to send a bull to Tyrone to excommunicate all heretics, and rumors flew that the Holy Father was preparing a crown for O'Neill's coronation. Books on the Continent such as *La Spada d'Orions* (Rome 1680) which sings the praises of *Ugo, Conte di Tirone Generale Ibernese* began to appear during this date.[41] The war in Ireland was now watched as an integral part of the whole European conflict.

The effect of the battle upon Ireland was profound. Virtually the entire Catholic nation, including several key Anglo-Irish lords, rose to the standard of Church and country, and openly joined the Confederacy. This wave of feeling surged out as a torrent of discontent and swept the English colonists from the land. The new English colonists, unlike the old Anglo-Irish, were Protestants who had illegally seized the lands of several Catholic families at the end of the Desmond War. They now fled helter skelter from their estates, happy to escape with their lives.[42] With the exception of Dublin and a few walled towns defended by garrisons and fugitive colonists, all Ireland was in the hands of the Confederates. Throughout the country men were claiming their old titles and the colonists abandoning them. The Earl of Desmond's nephew, James Fitzthomas Fitzgerald, claimed the Earl's title and now fought for it. O'Neill sent his commandos under Tyrell and Lacy to aid him. They joined Ownies O'Moore and aided the other guerrilla type

---

[40]McGee, *History of Ireland*, 2:430.
[41]O'Faolain, *The Great O'Neil*, 263.
[42]Sullivan, *Story of Ireland*, 273.

groups who were ravaging the colonists in the south. Thiegue O'Brian, who was the brother of the Earl of Thomond, took up arms, as did the Kavanaghs in the province of Leinster led by Donal Kavanaugh Spainneach (the Spaniard).[43] Sir Thomas Norris, President of Munster, only knew of four principle men who remained obedient to the colony and Queen. The country was "impassable for any faithful subject, especially all who wear hose and breeches."[44] By September, O'Neill's commandos had penetrated into Munster. The city of Cork was flooded with refugees "rifled and spoiled, man, woman, and child, yea of the very clothes from their back."[45] The Earl of Ormond, now aged 68, remained at his castle in Kilkenny, powerless and unable to do anything to change the course of events.

Hugh O'Donnell had now established his headquarters twelve miles south of Sligo at Ballymoate. O'Donnell purchased Ballymoate Castle from the local chieftain for L400 and 300 cows. From this vantage point, Red Hugh controlled all of Connaught.[46] By the end of the year 1598, nearly all the inhabitants in southern Connaught had joined the Catholic Confederacy motivated by either personal conviction or practicality. O'Donnell even entered Munster and attacked O'Brien of Inchiquin, the Earl of Thomond,

---

[43]The nickname was due to the fact that he had lived in Spain for four years. (O'Sullivan Bear, *Ireland Under Elizabeth*, 112.)

[44]O'Faolain, *The Great O'Neil*, 261.

[45]*Ibid.* The poet Edmund Spenser lost his estates at this time and had to flee from Kilcolman Castle. The lands that had been seized and given to him were now retaken by the native Irish whom he had despised and hoped to exterminate. He returned to England and died in London that very year. (D'Alton, *History of Ireland*, 147-149.)

[46]McGee, *History of Ireland*, 2:430.

(who accepted the English authority) and aided the Catholic Confederates in that province who sought his help.

Elizabeth wrote an angry letter to the Privy Council stating:

> Though we have sent over great supplies to our excessive charge, yet we receive naught else but news of fresh losses and calamities. Although you have great number of 9,000 men, we do not only see the northern traitor untouched at home and range where he pleases, but the provincial rebels in every province by such as he can spare enabled to give law to our provincial governors.[47]

The exasperated Queen also turned her wrath upon Ormond, the Lieutenant General who did not partake in the battle:

> We must plainly tell you that we did much dislike (seeing this last action was undertaken) that you did not above all things attend it, thereby to have directed and countenanced the same; for it was strange to us, when almost the whole forces of our kingdom were drawn to head and a main blow like to be stricken for our honour against the capital rebel, that you whose person would have better daunted the traitors, and which would have carried with it another manner of reputation and strength of the nobility, of the kingdom, should employ yourself in an action of less importance and leave that to so mean a conduction.[48]

Ormond defended himself claiming that the disaster was caused "to want of good direction and dividing of the army into six bodies, marching so far asunder as one of them could not second or help the other till those in the vanguard

---

[47]Murphy, introduction to *Life of Hugh Roe O'Donnell*, 97.
[48]*Ibid.*, 96.

were overthrown."[49]   And if this answer was not found by the Queen to be satisfactory, he added: "Sure the devil bewitched them."[50]

The major reason why the Anglo-Irish lords now openly took part in the war can be seen in the letter of James Fitzthomas to the King of Spain:

> The government of the English is such as Pharoah himself never used the like, for they content not themselves with all temporal prosperity, but by cruelty desire our blood and perpetual destruction, to blot out the whole remembrance of our posterity, as also our old Catholic religion, and to swear that the Queen of England is Supreme Head of the Church; I refer the consideration hereof to your Majesty's high judgment; for that Nero in his time was far inferior to that Queen in cruelty. Wherefore, myself with my followers and retainers, and being also requested by the bishops, prelates, and religious men of my country, have drawn the sword and proclaimed war against them for the recovery first of Christ's Catholic religion and next for the maintenance of my own right.[51]

By the beginning of 1599 "no English force was able to keep the field throughout all Ireland."[52]

---

[49] *Ibid.*, 97.
[50] *Ibid.*
[51] *Ibid.*, 98.
[52] Sullivan, *Story of Ireland*, 273.

SIX

ESSEX
in ireLand

Were now the general of our gracious empress
As in good time he may—from Ireland coming
Bringing rebellion broached on his sword
How many would the peaceful city quit
To welcome him!
Wm. Shakespeare, Henry V, Act V

I n the year 1599 a list containing 22 articles demanded by
the Irish Confederates were presented to the English
government:

1. That the Catholic, apostolic, and Roman religion be
openly preached and taught throughout all Ireland, as well
in cities as borough towns, by bishops, seminary priests,
Jesuits, and all other religious men.

2. That the Church of Ireland be wholly governed by the
Pope.

3. That all cathedrals and parish churches, abbeys, and
all other religious houses, with all tithes and church lands,
now in the hands of the English, be presently restored to the
Catholic churchmen.

4. That all Irish priests and religious men, now prisoners
in England or Ireland, be presently set at liberty, with all
temporal Irishmen, that are troubled for their conscience,
and to go where they will, without further trouble.

5. That all Irish priests and religious men may freely
pass and repass, by sea and land, to and from foreign countries.

 143

6. That no Englishman may be a churchman in Ireland.

7. That there be erected an university upon the crown rents of Ireland, wherein all sciences shall be taught according to the manner of the Catholic Roman church.

8. That the governor of Ireland be at least an earl, and of the privy council of England, bearing the name of viceroy.

9. That the lord chancellor, lord treasurer, lord admiral, the council of state, the justices of the laws, queen's attorney, queen's serjeant, and all other officers appertaining to the council and law of Ireland, be Irishmen.

10. That all principal governments of Ireland, as Connaught, Munster, etc., be governed by Irish noblemen.

11. That the master of ordnance, and half the soldiers with their officers resident in Ireland, be Irishmen.

12. That no Irishman's heirs shall lose their lands for the faults of their ancestors.

13. That no Irishman's heir under age shall fall in the queen's or her successors' hands, as a ward, but that the living be put to the heir's profit, and the advancement of his younger brethren, and marriages of his sisters, if he have any.

14. That no children nor any other friends be taken as pledges for the good abearing of their parents, and, if there be any such pledges now in the hands of the English, they must presently be released.

15. That all statutes made against the preferment of Irishmen as well in their own country as abroad, be presently recalled.

16. That the queen nor her successors may in no sort press an Irishman to serve them against his will.

17. That O'Neill, O'Donnell, the Earl of Desmond, with all their partakers may peacably enjoy all lands and privileges that did appertain to their predecessors 200 years past.

18. That all Irishmen, of what quality they be, may freely travel in foreign countries, for their better experience, without making any of the queen's officers acquainted withal.

19. That all Irishmen may freely travel and traffic all merchandises in England as Englishmen, paying the same rights and tributes as the English do.

20. That all Irishmen may freely traffic with all merchandises, that shall be thought necessary by the council of state of Ireland for the profit of their republic, with foreigners or in foreign countries, and that no Irishman shall be troubled for the passage of priests or other religious men.

21. That all Irishmen that will may learn, and use all occupations and art whatsoever.

22. That all Irishmen may freely build ships of what burden they will, furnishing the same with artillery and all munition at their pleasure.

(1599, November)[1]

Robert Cecil, in the Calendar of State Papers, sarcastically scrawled the word "Eutopia" along the margin of these demands. The demands show clearly the growing strength of the traditional national identity, staunchly Roman Catholic and Gaelic.[2] Elizabeth was exceptionally angry with Tyrone whom she thought the arch-traitor since he had enjoyed the fruits of an English education. She had at least a dozen names for him—"The Great Divill", "The Running Beast", "The Great Bear", "The Northern Lucifer" and perhaps the most flattering of all, "Beelzebub."[3]

For the Queen, the conditions in Ireland were now both shocking and intolerable. Elizabeth proposed to send Charles Blount, Lord Mountjoy to save the kingdom for the

---

[1]Curtis, *Irish Historical Documents*, 119-20.

[2]This defense of the rights of the Church, the nation and all Irishmen would also have included a defense of the rights of the Catholic Anglo-Irish.

[3]O'Faolain, *The Great O'Neil*, 245.

Crown. Robert Devereux, the second Earl of Essex, the hero of Cadiz,[4] passionately argued against the appointment. The impulsive royal favorite did not feel that Mountjoy possessed the experience necessary to conduct such a war. He persuasively argued that a proficient general was needed. A man must be sent who held the confidence of the Crown and could rise above the petty dissension of the colonists. Needless to say the Queen asked the Earl if he would accept the office. All the members of the Privy council unanimously urged Essex to acquiesce. His friends thought his success in Spain proved his military ability and assured him a victory in Ireland. His enemies on the other hand hoped that his inordinate vanity would lead to disaster and his subsequent downfall.

Essex gave his assent and he was given the title of Lord Lieutenant. His patent gave him more power in Ireland than any other previous Deputy. He was empowered to make and enforce military laws, pardon all crimes (including treason against the Queen's person), appoint to all offices, and distribute dignities as he willed. He was also given, by the Queen, virtually complete freedom to conduct the war as he saw fit.

Essex was gifted by nature with a handsome countenance and he was undoubtedly a man of courage and generosity. He conducted his entire life however with recklessness and frivolity. The members of the court knew that

---

[4]Robert Devereux was born in 1567, the son of Walter Devereux, the first Earl of Essex, who had sought to colonize Ulster. He was made the second Earl of Essex upon his father's death from dysentery in 1576. He achieved a fine reputation during the English assault against Spain, seizing and sacking Cadiz in 1596.

it was nothing other than his personal magnetism which he exercised over Elizabeth that could have saved him from the consequences of his constant caprices and clashes with her. To conduct a war in Ireland, a general needed to possess prudence, patience, ability to organize, and be a good judge of character. Essex was sadly lacking in all these qualities. "I tell you," said a court official, "I know but one friend and one enemy my lord hath: and that one friend is the Queen, and that one enemy himself."[5]

Nevertheless the Earl's personal courage and reputation raised high hopes that England would be defended and that the kingdom of Ireland would be recovered for the crown. All the wealth and power of England was now turned to prosecute the Irish war. Elizabeth opened her purse and prepared to send the most powerful and best equipped force ever to be sent to Ireland. Over 2,000 men were withdrawn from the Netherlands to join the Earl's army bound for the Irish War.

On March 27, Essex, cheered by the citizens of London, departed from Seething Land with a colorfully arrayed troop of horse. Throughout the country prayers were offered in Protestant churches "for his success against the imitators of Korah and Absolom, in whose cases God had manifested to the world his hatred of all rebellion against His divine ordinance, and forshadowing His probable care for an annointed queen."[6] The Anglican divines beseeched heaven praying, "Do not punish our misdeeds by strength-

---

[5]Bagwell, *Ireland Under the Tudors*, 3:318.
[6]*Ibid.*, 3:318-19.

ening the hands of such as despise the truth."[7] As the Earl journeyed through Cornhill and Cheapside, throngs of people turned out to greet their hero crying, "God bless your lordship!" and "God preserve your honour!"[8] Public expectations for the success of the Earl's mission were so high that Shakespeare even suggested a comparison between him and Henry V, the hero of Agincourt.[9] Essex himself boastfully wrote, "I have beaten Knollery and Mountjoy in the Council and will beat Tyrone in the field."[10] A fierce thunderstorm which struck just prior to the Earl's departure however, was taken by many in England as an ill omen.

Essex arrived on April 15, at the head of an army of nearly 20,000 foot and 2,000 horse.[11] This, at the time, was the largest army to have ever been put into action by England and the most complete in equipment, arms and training. As Lord Lieutenant he received the sword of state and Thomas Jones, the Protestant Bishop of Meath and future Bishop of Dublin preached a sermon on the occasion. The Earl united these forces with the relics of Bagnal's and Norris' forces. The staggering cost of the Irish War is witnessed by the fact that over ¾ of the ordinary annual income of England (£340,000 out of £450,000) was put at the disposal of the Queen's favorite who spent it all in seven months.[12]

---

[7] *Ibid.*, 3:317.

[8] *Ibid.*, 3:319.

[9] *Ibid.*, 3:320.

[10] A. J. Neale, *Queen Elizabeth I*, (Garden City, New York: Doubleday, Inc., 1934), 367.

[11] Clare, *History of Ireland*, 455.

[12] McGee, *History of Ireland*, 2:431. Sir Henry Wallop died the day Essex arrived. A new "Treasurer at Wars," Sir George Carew, was

No army sent from England had ever been so well supplied and maintained. The Earl, immediately after being sworn into office at Dublin, issued a proclamation offering a pardon and restoration of lands to all those who would lay down their arms and make peace with the Queen. The Irish revealed now the strength of the Catholic confederate unity as few took the bait and the proclamation was a resounding failure. The Northern clans, in the aftermath of Yellow Ford, had worked unceasingly to strengthen their ties with the Southern clans, who had taken oaths and openly entered into the Confederacy. The Irish Catholics had grown in self-confidence and were not dismayed by the arrival of the large army and its famous commander. O'Neill and O'Donnell had received a letter from Philip III in which he promised to continue his father's policy of aiding the Catholics:

Philip by the grace of God, &c., greeting.—

Your letter reached me at the time I was in very great grief for the death of my dear father. Knowing his good will towards you, I received it with much satisfaction, both because of your constancy in defending the Catholic faith and of the victories which you have gained over its enemies. I congratulate you on both, and I exhort you to persevere courageously in your good work. You need have no doubt about my good will towards you, and you shall see proofs of it when opportunity offers, as you can learn from Hugh

---

sent over with Essex to ensure sufficient funding for the army. Sir William Warren, writing on May 28, 1601, stated of Essex, "His greatness was such he was called the Earl of Excess... or if the wealth of England and Spain had been put into his hands he would have consumed it, winning towns and towers in the air, promising much and performing nothing." (For a more detailed account see chapter four of Sean O'Faolain's *The Great O'Neil*.)

MacDavid, a modest and sensible man, who brought your letter to me.[13]

In June of 1599, one of O'Donnell's messengers returned from Spain in a frigate "in which there were arms for 2,000 men, very long spears and lock guns with necessary and proper implements." O'Donnell split the aid evenly, sending half to O'Neill.[14]

With all the freedom and power Elizabeth had given to her new Viceroy, she did make one stipulation: he was "to pass by all other rebels whatever and to head all his force against the chief traitor Tyrone, and the Ulster rebels, his confederates."[15] Essex, after meeting with the Council in Dublin, was persuaded to first move against the confederate forces in Leinster who had taken a solemn oath of allegiance to O'Neill and O'Donnell at Holy Cross Abbey. Ignoring the wishes of the Queen, Essex set out from Dublin on May 10 with a force of 7,000 men and headed south. The Earl's efforts in Leinster and Munster were succinctly summarized by the Four Masters who whimsically relate that, "The Gaels of Ireland used to say that it would have been better for him if he had not gone on that expedition."[16] Essex's efforts in the south were closely watched by O'Neill and O'Donnell as a good test of the strength of the

---

[13]Murphy, *Introduction to Life of Hugh Roe O'Donnell*, 133.

[14]O'Cleary, *Life of Hugh Roe O'Donnell*, 201. G.A. Hayes-McCoy states that the aid included 10,000 arquebuses, 1,000 pikes, 7 1/2 tons of powder, 5 tons of lead and a supply of match. He places the time of arrival as December 1599 (Hayes-McCoy, *Irish Battles*, 110.)

[15]Murphy, introduction to *Life of Hugh Roe O'Donnell*, 99.

[16]*Ibid.*, 100.

Confederacy and the new spirit which animated the country.

Essex was joined in his expedition by the Earls of Clanrickarde and Thomond, Sir Conyers Clifford and O'Conor of Sligo. The Earl wasted away his strength in many small encounters with the hostile clans in Leinster and the Anglo-Irish of Munster. While Essex was marching to attack Cahir Castle, he was forced to pass through a wooded gorge in Leix. Here, the rear guard of his cavalry was savagely attacked by the O'Mores, led by Owen MacRory O'More, who killed over 500 of his men. So many of the white-plumed English helmets were left behind that the passage way is still called *Bearna-na cleite*—the "Pass of the Plumes." Essex did not seek to avenge this disaster but pressed on towards his objective. Cahir Castle, situated along the Suir, was a strong fortress with many natural defenses. Essex besieged the castle for ten days until it finally fell when the Butler defenders fled during the night. This was the only major success achieved by the Earl, and even this was of a short duration. The castle, whose walls still contain cannon balls fired by Essex, was eventually retaken by James Butler who killed the English garrison which the Earl had left behind. Essex did, however, succeed in bringing supplies to Askeaton, Kilmallock and Adare. In these towns he was greeted with orations and ceremony.[17] Near

---

[17]Concerning these orations, Sir John Harrington relates condescendingly, "I know not which was the more to be discommended: words, composition, or oratory, all of which having their peculiar excellences in barbarism, harshness and rustical both pronouncing and action"; see also John Harrington's *Nugae Antiguae* Vol. II (New York: AMS Press Inc., 1966), 42; Cyril Falls, *Elizabeth's Irish Wars*, 237. Har-

Croom in Limerick he was met by the Geraldines and their allies, who had joined the Catholic Confederacy, and was badly beaten. Sir Henry Norris, the brother of John and Thomas, was shot during this engagement which raged from 9 am to 5 p.m. and died after having his leg amputated on the spot. Elizabeth wrote a letter of condolence to Lord and Lady Norris who had lost their third son in the Irish War.

Essex pathetically wrote the Queen:

> These rebels are more in number than your Majesty's army and have (though I do unwilling confess it) better bodies and perfecter use of their arms than those men whom your Majesty sends over.[18]

The Lord Lieutenant turned around and from Waterford (where he had been welcomed with a "proper Latin oration") led his weakened, dispirited army back to Dublin. For an entire week he was mocked by the victorious, resurgent Geraldines, who "continued to follow, pursue, and press upon them, to shoot at, wound and slaughter them" for six days.[19] The army reached Dublin near the end of June. Essex was profoundly chagrined by this misadventure. Essex wrote discouragingly to Elizabeth that in his judgment all the Irish desire "to shake off the yoke of obedience to Your Majesty and to root out all remembrance of the English nation in this kingdom."[20] Elizabeth sent over

---

rington had translated into English Ariosto's *Orlando Furioso* in 1591.

[18]Murphy, introduction to *Life of Hugh Roe O'Donnell*, 100.

[19]Bagwell, *Ireland Under the Tudors*, 3:331.

[20]R.B. Wernham, *Return of the Armadas: The Last Years of the Elizabethan Wars Against Spain 1595-1603* (Oxford: Oxford University Press, 1994), 304.

many angry dispatches to her commander. As bad news continued to arrive over the angry Irish sea, Elizabeth was thus described, "She walks much in her privy chamber, and stamps her feet at ill news, and thrusts her rusty sword at times into the arras in great rage."[21] The Queen was incensed that the capital traitors had remained unharmed. By July the patience of the aged monarch was running out:

> Your two months' journey hath never brought in a capital rebel against whom it hath been worthy to have adventured a thousand men. . . . There is little public benefit made to us of any things happened in this action. . . . Whereunto we will add one thing that doth more displease us than any charge or expense that happens, which is, that it must be the Queen of England's misfortune (who hath held down the greatest enemy she had) to make a base bush-kern be accounted so famous a rebel as to be a person against whom so many thousands of foot and horse, besides the force of all the nobility of the kingdom must be thought too little to be employed.[22]

The Queen's pride was stung, for every Irish success reached the continent magnified tenfold (thanks to the Jesuits and their fellow priests). She angrily wrote to Essex of Tyrone's joy

> To see such a portion of our fair army, and led by the person of our general, harassed out in encountering those base rogues, who were no way strengthened by foreign armies but only by such of his offal as he was content to spare and let slip from himself, whiles he hath lived at his pleasure, hath spoiled all where our army should come, and preserved

---

[21]Falls, *Elizabeth's Irish Wars*, 241.
[22]O'Faolain, *The Great O'Neil*, 274-5.

 153

for himself what he thought necessary. . . . Little do you
know how he has blazed in foreign parts the defeats of
regiments, the death of captains and loss of men of quality in
every corner.[23]

As Essex continued to hesitate in Dublin, the news of his
failures spread throughout the four provinces of Erin.

Sir Donough O'Conor of Sligo, who had aided Essex in
his southern expedition, had just recently returned from the
English Court. At the court he had been treated with the
highest honors in order that he might aid the Queen by
halting O'Donnell's growing power in southern
Connnaught. He had served with Essex in Munster and his
presence and loyalty was seen as crucial for the war in the
west. Upon returning to his territory he was attacked by
O'Donnell who forced him to take refuge in Coolooney Castle only five miles outside Sligo. For forty days O'Conor
defended the castle until it appeared that he would have to
surrender due to a lack of provisions. When Essex heard of
this he ordered Sir Conyers Clifford, a courageous and experienced soldier, to gather all his forces and march to his
relief. The Earl hoped that this would weaken the Confederates by divorcing O'Donnell from O'Neill. The Lord
Lieutenant would then himself march north against Tyrone.
Clifford dispatched from Galway Theobold Burke, sur-
named *Na long*, with twenty ships and boats carrying stores
and materials for the planned re-fortification of Sligo which
was held for O'Donnell by MacSweeny Fanad with 400
men. Red Hugh sent additional reinforcements under
MacWilliam to the town. Burke and his fleet sailed into

---

[23]*Ibid.*, 275.

Sligo Bay but did not land, preferring to wait for the arrival of Clifford. The Governor himself accompanied by Lord Dunkellin, son of the Earl of Clanrickarde, set out from Athlone with an army of nearly 2,500, with 36 colors of infantry and three of cavalry.[24] He had under him Sir Alexander Radcliffe, Sir Griffin Markhan, Sir Arthur Savage and other experienced officers. The army reached the lovely, Cistercian Boyle Abbey, which had been built by the McDermots in 1220, and prepared for the upcoming battle. From Boyle the road led into the Curlew Mountains which divided Sligo on the southeast from Roscommon. Along this highway, O'Donnell had placed sentries and ordered the trees felled so as to hinder the advance of the army. In the strong pass of Ballaghboy, O'Donnell and his troops awaited the approach of the enemy. He had left the remainder of his forces under his cousin and brother-in-law, Neale Garve to continue the siege of Coloney Castle. Red Hugh, upon hearing of the army's arrival in Boyle and the English Governor's boasting, addressed his men:

> There was an old saying from long ago, that it was not by the number of soldiers, the battle is decided, but by the power of God, and that he is victorious whosoever trusts in the Trinity and believes that the one God is against the crowd that is on the side of cheating and with the few who are on the side of right. . . . The English, whose number is large, are on the side of robbery, in order to rob you of your native land and your means of living, and it is far easier for you to make a brave, stout, strong fight for your native land and your lives whilst you are your own masters and your weapons are in your hands, than when you are put in prison

---

[24]O'Sullivan Bear, *Ireland Under Elizabeth*, 127.

and in chains. . . . My blessing on you, true men; bear in your minds the firm resolution you had when such insults and violence were offered to you, that today is the day of battle which have needed to make a vigorous fight in defense of your liberty by the strength of your arms and the courage of your hearts, as it is not a necessity that the English should be your conquerors. Have no dread or fear of the great number of the soldiers from London or of the strangeness of their weapons and arms, but put your hope in the God of glory. I am certain if you take into your minds what I say to you, that the English will be defeated and the victory will be with you.[25]

It was the eve of the Assumption of the Blessed Virgin Mary (which the Irish call "Mary's Day in Harvest") and the first anniversary of the great victory of the Yellow Ford. Hugh O'Donnell was continually attending Mass which was offered by "a prudent and pious cleric."[26] It was his usual practice whenever he went on a journey or was threatened with any kind of danger to observe a fast, confess his sins to his confessor and receive Holy Communion. On the eve of the Assumption at his request, the Irish army fasted and spent the night in prayer. The following morning Mass was offered and he urged his officers and men to receive with him the Body of Christ, "with great reverence for the Lord Jesus Christ and his holy Mother on her feast that occurred then."[27] After hearing Mass, the Irish went to their tents and prepared a meal. News soon reached the camp that Clifford was advancing from Boyle in an effort to seize the pass by surprise. O'Donnell immediately ordered

---

[25]O'Cleary, *Life of Hugh Roe O'Donnell*, 209-11.
[26]*Ibid.*, 213.
[27]*Ibid.*

the soldiers to take their meal quickly to strengthen them for the fight. He then rallied his forces and addressed them:

> By the help of the Most Blessed Virgin Mary, Mother of God, we will this day utterly destroy the heretical enemy whom we have always hereto worsted. We fasted yesterday in honour of the Virgin, and today we celebrate her feast. Therefore in her name let us fight stoutly and bravely the enemies of the Virgin and we shall gain the victory.[28]

The Irish soldiers were "greatly inflamed to war by this speech."[29] O'Donnell divided his army into two divisions. He sent ahead 600 musketeers under Eugene MacSweeny Tuath, and Hugh and Tuathal O'Gallagher, with orders to attack and delay the enemy until he himself brought up the main body. At 4 p.m. the rain had stopped and the vanguards of the two armies met head on. A fierce encounter with the firing of leaden bullets at long range commenced. Many men in both armies were severely wounded. The Irish gunners began to give way and they were rebuked by their leaders "at their fighting with such faint-heartedness for the Virgin."[30] The soldiers were roused by this zeal and vigorously renewed the struggle. The thundering of the guns could be heard for miles. The Irish advanced and drove the wings of the English army into the center of the pikemen's division. The central division itself was overwhelmed with a discharge of muskets and javelins. Sir Alexander Radcliffe, the leader of the vanguard, was shot and killed. A state of confusion ensued and the leading di-

---

[28]O'Sullivan Bear, *Ireland Under Elizabeth*, 127.
[29]*Ibid.*, 128.
[30]*Ibid.*

vision turned round three times in a circle in an effort to re-organize itself. At this very moment Brian O'Rourke, hearing the fighting from a distance, arrived with 140 men to aid the Catholics. O'Donnell was quickly following behind him with the main body of the Catholic army. The arrival of O'Rourke's men terrified the already badly disorganized royalist army. The English vanguard dropped their weapons and began to flee. Governor Clifford courageously attempted to rally his men but was shot and killed. The battle then became a general rout as the entire English army fled back to the shelter of Boyle Abbey hotly pursued by the Catholics. The felled trees and pits hindered the retreat of the English who discarded their arms and even their clothing. O'Rourke, despite a bullet wound in the hand and thigh, rallied the Catholics and drove back the English cavalry. The Irish, crying *O'Donnell abu*, continued to chase and slaughter the enemy as far as Boyle. Nearly 1,400 of the royalist army were killed, most of them being English or Anglo-Irish of Meath. The Catholics lost 140 men during the battle.[31] Virtually all of the arms, colors, military drums, supplies and clothing of the vanquished army were captured by the Irish. The English fleet under Burke sailed back to Galway, and Colooney Castle was surrendered to O'Donnell. O'Conor astutely submitted to Red Hugh and entered into the Confederacy swearing, "henceforth to aid against the Protestants."[32] Clifford's body was respectfully taken by the Irish and buried in the Holy Trinity monastery of Lough Key.

---

[31]*Ibid.*, 129.
[32]*Ibid.*

The Irish, with joy and great exultation, returned to their camp and "made a thank-offering" to the Lord for their great victory. The army unanimously acclaimed that it was not by force of arms that they had won such a victory, "but by the prayers of O'Donnell to God that he obtained it after receiving the pure mystery of the Body and Blood of Christ in the beginning of that day, and after fasting in honour of the Blessed Mary the day before."[33]

When news reached Essex of Clifford's death and the defeat of his veteran army he was greatly depressed.[34] His fine army, due to sickness, desertion and the hostile encounters with the Irish, had been whittled away to nothing. The Earl asked Elizabeth for 2,000 more fresh troops. He can hardly be blamed for this hesitation as he now had to face the united forces of O'Neill and O'Donnell in the fastness of Ulster. While waiting for the reinforcements from England, Essex sent a detachment of 600 men under Sir Henry Harrington to Wicklow. This force however was severely beaten and driven out of the territory by the O'Byrnes led by Phelim, the son of Feagh (who had been killed by Russell in 1597). Adam Loftus, the son of the Archbishop and Lord Chancellor who commanded the rear, was severely wounded and died in Wicklow. The frustrated Viceroy was infuriated by this new loss. The officers who retreated were tried by court-martial and the survivors executed as an example. By early September the reinforcements he sought arrived along with a galling letter from the

---

[33]O'Cleary, *Life of Hugh Roe O'Donnell*, 219-21.
[34]Strachey, *Elizabeth and Essex*, 135.

Queen. Essex now hurried to make a demonstration against the "arch traitor" O'Neill.

What Essex needed to have planned was a long, strategic two or three year campaign against the Confederates. The Earl, however, had received the military training of a buccaneer. As O'Faolain observed, he was a hit-and-run raider effective at Cadiz but ill prepared for a prolonged campaign in Ireland which required patience and diligence. Accordingly, he set off from Dublin on August 28 with 3,700 foot and 300 horse to attack O'Neill.[35] O'Neill's men skirmished with the Lord Lieutenant as he marched north. When Essex finally reached Ardee in Louth he could see O'Neill's camp strongly entrenched on the high bank over the river Lagan. The next day O'Neill sent Henry O'Hagan to seek a parley with the Earl. Essex refused the overture and dismissed the messenger. On the following day the English army set out for Drumcondra. The army had marched scarcely a mile when O'Hagan approached again, and "speaking so loud as all might hear that were present," he announced that Tyrone "desired her Majesty's mercy, and that the Lord Lieutenant would hear him; which if his lordship agreed to, he would gallop about and meet him at the ford of Bellaclinthe, which was on the right hand by the way which his lordship took to Drumcondra."[36]

Essex agreed and at an appointed time the two commanders rode down unattended to the opposite banks of the river. The advanced guards eyed each other and watched from the uplands with great curiosity. O'Neill ex-

---

[35]Bagwell, *Ireland Under the Tudors*, 3:340.
[36]*Ibid.*, 3:341.

celled at the subtleties of diplomacy and courteously spurred his horse into the stream up to its belly. Tyrone greeted Essex with great respect and, "took his hat and inclined his body and did his duty to his Lordship with very humble ceremony continuing the same observance the whole time of the parley."[37] O'Neill, with all the art for which he was renowned, drew upon his knowledge of the Earl's character. During the meeting he skillfully mentioned the names of those enemies of his own whom he also knew to be at odds with the Lord Lieutenant. He presented his provocations in the most favorable light possible and professed himself ready to submit to the Queen if certain conditions were met. Essex evidently talked to Tyrone of his own private ambition. The secret discussion continued for over half an hour. This was perhaps the most foolish thing Essex ever did. By conversing with the "arch traitor" for such a lengthy time without witnesses he left himself defenseless against his enemies at Court. The day before he had sworn to fight to the end and now his own officers and soldiers watched as he talked familiarly with Tyrone.

A formal meeting with six witnesses on each side followed this initial parley. O'Neill was accompanied by his brother, Cormac MacBaron, Hugh Magennis of Iueagh, Hugh Maguire, Ever MacCooley of Monaghan, Henry Ovington and Richard Owen. Essex was joined by Sir Warham St. Leger, the Earl of Southampton, Sir William Constable, Sir William Warren, Sir Henry Danvers and Sir George Bourchier. The Irish, before discussing the question of a truce, demanded that three conditions be agreed upon:

---

[37]Murphy, introduction to *Life of Hugh Roe O'Donnell*, 106.

1. That the free practice of the Catholic religion should be allowed throughout the whole of Ireland.
2. That the ecclesiastical property which had been seized by the Crown, or given to individuals, should be restored to the Church.
3. That the lands taken from the Irish for the last forty years should be restored to their lawful owners.[38]

Essex evidently considered these reasonable and virtually conceded all as far as he could with royal approval.[39] The Earl then withdrew his army and he marched on to Drumcondra. Essex left William Warren to work out a truce with O'Neill. When O'Neill reiterated his demand for freedom of conscience, Warren told him that "her Majesty would no more yield to that demand than she would do to give her crown from her head."[40] The two met again on September 29 and discussed a continuation of the cessation. O'Neill stated that he would not agree until he received O'Donnell's consent. Essex had now retired to Drogheda "to take physic,"[41] and O'Neill withdrew his troops into the vastness of Tyrone having won without even fighting, as Bagwell later acknowledged, a victory of greater magnitude than Yellow Ford. The Earl of Essex was disgraced and had lost his reputation.

In the meantime, a copy of the journal of the Lord Lieutenant's proceedings was sent to Elizabeth. The Queen immediately saw how completely her favorite had been dominated by O'Neill. Elizabeth wrote him a furious letter

---

[38]O'Faolain, *The Great O'Neil*, 280.
[39]Bagwell, *Ireland Under the Tudors*, 3:341.
[40]*Ibid.*, 3:347.
[41]*Ibid.*, 3:342.

filled with scornful tauntings from Nonsuch, September 17th:

> By the letter and journal received from you we see a quick end made of a slow proceeding. We never doubted but that Tyrone would instantly offer a parley when he saw any force approach, either himself or any of his principal partisans, always seeking these Cessations with like words and upon such contingents, as we gather these will prove by your advertisement of his purpose to go consult with O'Donnell. It appears to us by your journal that you and the traitor spoke together half an hour and without anybody's hearing; wherein, though we that trust you with our kingdom are far from mistrusting you with a traitor, yet both for comeliness, example, and your own discharge, we marvel you would carry it no better. . . . You have dealt so sparingly with us in the substance by advising us only at first of the half-hour's conference alone, but not what passed on either side, by letting us also know you sent Commissioners without showing what they had in charge, as we cannot tell but by divination what to think may be the issue of this proceeding. Only this we are sure (for we see it in effect) that you have prospered so ill for us by your warfare, as we cannot but be very jealous lest you should be as well overtaken by the treaty. . . . To trust this traitor upon oath is to trust the devil upon his religion. To trust him upon pledges is mere illusion, and therefore whatever order you shall take with him of laying aside of arms, recognition of superiority to us, disclaiming from O'Neillship, which were tolerable before he was in his overgrown pride by own success against our power, yet unless he yield to have garrisons planted in his own country to master him, to deliver O'Neill's sons, and to come over to us personally here, we shall doubt you do but piece up a hollow peace, and so the end prove worse than the beginning.[42]

---

[42]Murphy, introduction to *Life of Hugh Roe O'Donnell*, 106-7.

 163

When Essex received this letter he was deeply distressed and his mercurial character was torn between wounded vanity, dismay and anger. He completely lost his head and set sail for England although he had been strictly charged by the Queen not to do so without her express permission. He appointed Adam Loftus, the Protestant Lord Archbishop of Dublin, and Sir George Carew, Treasurer of War, to govern the kingdom in his absence leaving the army in the hands of the aging yet dutiful Earl of Ormond. The rest of Essex's story is well known. Upon his arrival at Nonsuch, he entered into the Queen's bedchamber unannounced and covered from head to foot with mud from his travels. Elizabeth was among her ladies in her dressing gown, without her makeup and bright red wig. The Queen although astonished, graciously welcomed him. The Earl was dismissed; later the Queen's common sense and the advice of Cecil and the Council led to a strong rebuke, imprisonment, disgrace, despondency, rebellion and death in the Tower of London in February, 1601. O'Neill refused any further extension of truce until he heard from Red Hugh.[43] On November 16, 1599, Hugh O'Neill sent a letter to rally the Catholics in the towns of Ireland:

> Using hitherto more than ordinary favor towards all my countrymen who generally by profession are Catholics, and that naturally I am inclined to affect [esteem] you, I have for these and other considerations abstained my forces from tempting to do you hinderance, and because I did expect

---

[43]Sir John Harrington visited Hugh O'Neill at this time. A fine summary of this visit and his reaction to O'Neill's family is found in Cyril Falls, *Elizabeth's Irish Wars*, pages 248-9.

that you would enter into consideration of the lamentable state of our poor country, most tyrannically oppressed, and of your own gentle consciences, in maintaining, relieving and helping the enemies of God and our country, in wars infallibly tending to the promotion of heresy. But now seeing you are so obstinate in that which hereunto you continued of necessity, I must use severity against you (whom otherwise I most entirely love), in reclaiming you by compulsion. My tolerance and happy victories, by God's particular favor doubtless obtained, could work no alteration in your consciences, notwithstanding the great calamity and misery whereunto you are most likely to fall by persevering in that damnable state in which hereunto you have lived. Having commiseration on you, I thought it good to forewarn you, requesting every of you to come and join with me against the enemies of God and our poor country. If the same you do not, I will use means not only to spoil you of all your goods, but according to the utmost of my power, shall work what I may to dispossess you of all your lands, because you are means whereby wars are maintained against the exaltation of the Catholic faith. Contrariwise, whosoever it shall be that shall join with me, upon my conscience, and as to the contrary I shall answer before God, I will employ myself to the utmost of my power in their defence, and for the extirpation of heresy, the planting of the Catholic religion, the delivery of our country of infinite murders, wicked and detestable policies, by which this kingdom was hitherto governed; nourished in obscurity and ignorance, maintained in barbarity and incivility; and consequently of infinite evils which were too lamentable to be rehearsed. And seeing these are motives most laudable before any men of consideration, and before the Almighty most meritorious, which is chiefly to be respected, I thought myself in conscience bound, seeing God hath given me some power, to use all means for the reduction of this our poor afflicted country into the Catholic faith, which can never be brought to any good pass without either your destruction or helping hand: hereby protesting that I neither seek your lands nor goods; neither do I purpose to plant any in your places, if you will adjoin with me; but will extend what liberties and privileges that heretofore you have had, if it shall stand in my power, giving you to understand, upon my salvation, that chiefly and principally I fight for the Catholic faith to be planted throughout all our poor country, as well in cities as elsewhere, as manifestly might appear by that I rejected all other conditions proffered to me, this not being granted. I have already, by word of mouth, protested, and do now hereby protest, that if I had to be king of Ireland without having the Catholic religion, which before I mentioned, I would not the same accept. Take you example by that most Catholic country of France, whose subjects, for defect of Catholic faith, did go against their most natural king, and maintained wars till he was constrained to profess the Catholic religion, duly submitting himself to the apostolic see of Rome, to the which, doubtless, we may bring our country, you putting your helping hand with me to the same. As for myself, I protest before God and upon my salvation, I have been proffered oftentimes such conditions as no man seeking his own private commodity could refuse; but I, seeking the public utility of my native country, will prosecute these wars until that generally religion be planted throughout all Ireland. So I rest, praying the Almighty to move your flinty hearts to prefer the commodity and profit of our country before your own private ends."[44]

For nearly a year, all of Ireland was ruled by the native Irish as an independent Catholic kingdom. O'Donnell ruled supreme in Tyrconnaill and the West of Ireland as

---

[44]C.P. Meehan, MRIA, *The Fate and Fortune of Hugh O'Neill, Earl of Tyrone and Rory O'Donnell, Earl of Tyrconnell* (New York: P.J. Kennedy, 1897), 31-4. This letter reveals fully and clearly O'Neill and the Catholic confederates' intention to defend their ancient Faith and fatherland, including the Catholic Anglo-Irish.

O'Neill in Tyrone and the South. In Rome, Pope Clement VIII had proclaimed a Jubilee, a Holy Year of grace and special indulgences. Over eighty thousand pilgrims gathered at St. Peter's in Rome on December 31, 1599 for the opening of the *Porta Sancta*. Over a million pilgrims were to travel to the Holy City that year. Everywhere Catholic fortunes seemed to revive. The Holy Father prepared to send support to the Catholics fighting in Ireland along with indulgences granted earlier for the crusades and remission of sins for all who would fight in defense of the Faith against the English heretics. Franciscan Matthew d'Oviedo, a Spaniard, had been consecrated Archbishop of Dublin and sent by the Pope to encourage the Irish Catholics. Philip III also was to send 22,000 pieces of gold to help finance the war. In early 1600, Red Hugh's father, Hugh Dubh, had the joy of witnessing from his monastic seclusion his son's triumph. In March of 1600, O'Neill, as was the custom of the ancient Gaelic High Kings of Tara, made a general circuit of the kingdom. He garrisoned his borders and marched south with 3,000 men. Although the English nominally still had over 14,000 men in Ireland, all remained behind walls and dared not challenge him. Everywhere he went he strengthened the National Confederacy and restored the Church. O'Neill himself now increasingly came to be seen at home and abroad as the Prince or King of Ireland. In West Meath, Lord Devlin and Sir Theobald Dillon joined the Catholic Confederacy. Dillon, who initially had opposed Tyrone, saw his property spoiled. O'Neill marched at the head of his men through the center of Ireland as "a kind of royal progress which he thought fit to call a pilgrimage to Holy Cross."[45]   At Holy Cross Abbey in Tipperary on the west bank of the Suir,[46] O'Neill and his men venerated the relic of the true Cross and gave many gifts and alms to the monks.   O'Neill held princely state and organized the southern Irish lords.   He traveled to St. Patrick's Rock at Cashel, and there met James, "the Sugane Earl", of Desmond and the Geraldines. [47]   He then traveled to the city of Limerick.   A document was distributed which announced him as an accredited Defender of the Faith. O'Neill proclaimed a Holy War and urged everyone to join in the cause.   He wrote a letter to Barry Mor of Cork who had remained on the Queen's side, urging him to join the Irish:

> Your impiety to God, cruelty to soul and body, tyranny and ingratitude both to your followers and your country are inexcusable and intolerable. . . . You know the sword of extirpation hangeth over your head as well as ours if things fall out otherwise than well; you are the cause why all the nobility of the south, . . . you being linked to each one of them either in affinity or consanguinity, are not linked together to shake off the cruel yoke of heresy and tyranny with which our souls and bodies are oppressed. All these aforesaid depending on your resolution, and relying to your judgment in

---

[45]Sullivan, *Story of Ireland*, 276.

[46]The great Cistercian House was endowed by Donal Mor O'Brien in 1195 and housed the famous relic of the True Cross which was enshrined in the magnificent 15th century Ormond silver reliquary. The monastery had survived Protestant efforts at suppression and remained a center of Roman Catholic pilgrimage and devotion. It has now been restored and once again houses the sacred relic.

[47]James Fitzthomas Fitzgerald was nephew of the last Earl of Desmond and as a Catholic of noble descent, was set up by O'Neill as the new Earl. He was accepted by the Desmonds but called the "Sugane" (straw rope) Earl by the English.

this common cause of our religion and country, you might forsooth, with their help, and the rest that are combined in this holy action, not only defend yourself from the incursion and invasion of the English, but also by God's assistance, who miraculously and above all expectation gave good success to the cause, principally undertaken for his glory, exaltation of religion, next for the restoration of the ruins and preservation of the country, expel them, and deliver them and us from the most miserable and cruel exaction and subjection, enjoy your religion, safety of wife and children, lands, and goods, which are all in hazard through your folly and want of due consideration.[48]

Barry remained unmoved, however, so O'Neill traversed, pillaged and burnt all his land, "so that no one hoped it could be inhabited for a long time afterwards."[49] In March, the Catholic army moved even further south and encamped at Inniscarra upon the river Lee, approximately five miles west of Cork. Here Hugh O'Neill remained for three weeks strengthening and consolidating the Confederation in Munster. Many of the chiefs of the southern clans, such as O'Mahony, O'Donohue and O'Donovan, visited him and entered into friendship. O'Neill was also greeted by two of the most influential men in the south, Florence McCarthy, lord of Carberry, and the noble hearted

---

[48]Murphy, introduction to *Life of Hugh Roe O'Donnell*, 110. O'Neill also exhorted Corman McDermott "to expel the enemies of the Church". To Barry he also wrote, criticizing him for "serving against us and the Church", and shortly after wrote to him that in failing to join the Catholic cause he had "separated himself from the unity of Christ, his mystical body, the Catholic Church." He also exhorted John FitzEdmonds and his sons to "fight for your conscience and the right." (McGurk, *Elizabethan Conquest of Ireland*, 21.)

[49]Four Masters, *Annals*, 6:2147.

Donald O'Sullivan, lord of Bearhaven. Both of these leaders entered into the Confederacy and Florence was inaugurated, with O'Neill's permission, as McCarthy More. By the summer of 1600 the Catholic Confederacy had achieved what most would have thought impossible. The grip of Protestant England had been shattered. Catholic, Gaelic Ireland emerged apparently triumphant at the opening of a new century. Unfortunately, it is a commonplace irony of history that a political alliance can often withstand any strain it might encounter, with the exception of the victory it was formed to achieve.

seven

LORÒ MOUNTJOY
AND THE CONTINUATION
OF THE WAR 1600-1601

We hold it a very good piece of policy to make
them cut one another's throat, without which this
kingdom will never be quiet.
                    Lord Mountjoy, July 19, 1601.[1]

While O'Neill and his force remained encamped near
Cork, a "disastrous action" occurred. Hugh
Maguire, one of the chief Confederates and the finest cavalry officer in Ireland, set out from O'Neill's camp to raid
the enemy's territory. The chief of Fermanagh was accompanied by Edmund MacCaffrey, O'Durnin (his standard
bearer) and a priest. He encountered a body of English
cavalry led by Sir Warham St. Leger, Marshal of Munster,
who was the finest of England's horsemen. There had been
a rivalry between the two men as to which had the greatest
skill in horsemanship. Although the English were more
numerous, Maguire grabbed his lance and charged them.
St. Leger fired his pistol and shot Maguire. He then bent
low to avoid Maguire's javelin but the chieftain's thrust
pierced the Englishmen's helmet and struck his forehead.
Although severely wounded, Maguire drew his sword and

---

[1]O'Faolain, *The Great O'Neil*, 223.

with his companions heroically fought their way clear of the enemy. St. Leger was carried back to Cork where he died of his wound two weeks later. Before reaching O'Neill's camp, however, Maguire, unable to continue riding, fell from his horse. He received absolution from the priest who was at his side and died. The Four Masters relate that the "death of Maguire caused a giddiness of spirits and depression of mind in O'Neill and the Irish chiefs in general; and this was no wonder, for he was the bulwark of valor and prowess."[2] Hugh Maguire, the Lord of Fermanagh, had put his heart and soul into the war and had been a truly courageous, capable and noble leader within the Catholic confederacy.

Elizabeth, upon hearing of Maguire's death, was quite pleased and had the Privy Council write to the Commissioners of Munster:

> Her Majesty commands us to give you her thanks, it being a great contentment to her to see this change from receiving news of losses and disasters on her Majesty's side, that one of the first traitors hath received that end which, we doubt not shall befall the rest of these monstrous rebels.[3]

Just after the death of Maguire, news reached O'Neill that the new Lord Deputy had arrived in Dublin. Having received the submission of the Irish and Anglo-Irish chiefs of Munster, O'Neill prepared to march north leaving Richard Tyrrell and 1,800 of his men in the southern province. The new Lord Deputy attempted to block O'Neill's passage into the north. O'Neill, however, with a series of brilliant

---

[2]Four Masters, *Annals*, 6:2165.
[3]Murphy, introduction to *Life of Hugh Roe O'Donnell*, 111.

marches which thrilled the country, returned to his own country without loss. Elizabeth and her new Viceroy did not escape "the great dishonour of this traitor passing home to his den unfought with."[4]

The new Lord Deputy, Sir Charles Blount, Lord Mountjoy, and the new President of Munster, Sir George Carew, had landed together at Howth on February 26th. A large army of nearly 20,000 soon followed as England once again directed all her might, both land and sea, against the "rebels." Mountjoy had been initially the rival, the bitter enemy and later, devoted friend of the tragic Earl of Essex. He far exceeded the Earl in judgment, resolve and foresight. At thirty-seven, he was a veteran diplomat, soldier (who had served in the Netherlands), scholar and a Protestant theologian. The new Deputy and Carew were both cunning and unscrupulous. They hoped to succeed in areas where the sword had failed with craft, treachery, bribes and false promises. His situation was a most difficult one and would have appeared daunting for a man of lesser spirit. In Connaught, only the towns of Athlone and Galway remained "loyal". O'Conor of Sligo and Theobald Burke Na Long were still confederated with Red Hugh. The Earl of Clanrickarde was weakening due to the victories of the Catholics but his son, Lord Dunkellin, remained devoted to the royalist cause as was the Earl of Thomond. Crossing the mighty Shannon into the province of Munster, he found that almost all supported the Irish Confederates save Lord Barry. The aged Earl of Ormond still held Kilkenny and Tipperary but the O'Mores, O'Connors and Birminghams

---

[4]Bagwell, *Ireland Under the Tudors*, 3:355.

supported the Catholic cause as did the O'Byrnes and O'Tooles in Wicklow and Wexford. It was reported that even a number of the towns were resentful of England and had been won over and were now giving aid to the Irish Catholic cause. The English forces in Ireland were also badly disorganized and dispirited. Mountjoy, like Essex, was ordered to direct the war against O'Neill and O'Donnell and promote Protestantism although an appearance of tolerance was to be made temporarily lest the "rebellion" be further strengthened. Mountjoy had an army of 14,000 foot and 2,000 horses. He made Lord Dunkellin supreme commander of the forces in Connaught and sent Sir George Carew to the Province of Munster at the head of an army of 3,000.

When O'Neill had returned safely north he received a message from O'Donnell in June: two Spanish ships filled with war materials under the command of Ferdinand de Barranova had anchored at Killybegs in Donegal. Matthew de Oviedo (the Spanish Franciscan) and Martin de la Cerdo came as joint envoys of the Pope and the King of Spain. The Pope granted indulgences and the remission of sins to all those who would take up arms against the English in defense of the Faith. The Sovereign Pontiff also gave a crown of phoenix feathers to O'Neill and sent a letter congratulating him on his victories and encouraging him "to persevere in his glorious struggle, so that the Catholic Kingdom of Ireland might not be subject to the yoke of heresy."[5] Philip

---

[5]Murphy, introduction to *Life of Hugh Roe O'Donnell*, 116. Morn's *Archbishops of Dublin* contains the full text of the papal letter on page 206. Pope Clement was as supportive as possible given the delicate position of the English Catholics in England and the old English Catholics in Ire-

III, in addition to the munitions, gave the Catholics 22,000 pieces of gold. The Irish asked the envoys why the King had so long delayed in sending the promised aid. Oviedo replied that Philip *was* determined to help them with both arms and men but that English emissaries had misrepresented their situation in foreign courts, claiming that the Irish had made peace with the Queen. In order to find out the true state of affairs in Ireland, the King had sent them as his envoys. Oviedo had been made the Archbishop of Dublin by Clement VIII and remained in Ireland for some time gathering information. He was eventually sent back to Spain to solicit further aid.

All the wealth of England was now being poured into Ireland to support a costly military plan which sought to hem in and isolate the Northern Confederates with a ring of garrisoned forts. Elizabeth sent instructions that no peace was to be made with the "Golden Calf" which was her new name for Tyrone. Mountjoy implemented this policy immediately with the forces recently sent from England.

The government had long hoped for some time to plant a northern garrison on the shores of Lough Foyle from which they could attack O'Donnell's and O'Neill's rear. This would force them to divide their forces and fight a war on two fronts. Mountjoy energetically undertook to implement this plan and, in a beautiful stratagem, marched

---

land, many of whom distrusted O'Neill and the native Irish despite the common ties of religion. The city of Waterford, for example, sought to be loyal to the Queen in temporal matters and loyal to the Pope in spiritual matters. A fine treatment of this difficulty can be found in Fr. John Silke, "Hugh O'Neill, the Catholic Question and the Papacy". (*Irish Ecclesiastical Record*, 5th series, 104 [1965], 65-79.)

through the difficult Moiry Pass which led into Ulster to Armagh and feigned an attack on Tyrone. While O'Donnell and O'Neill were drawn to their southern borders to face Mountjoy, an English fleet carrying Sir Henry Docwra with 4,000 foot and 200 horse sailed from Chester in England into Lough Foyle and landed at Culmore without opposition, on the 16th of May. Culmore was fortified and garrisoned with 600 men under Captain Atford. Docwra and the main body marched to Derry and there, at the ancient monastery *Doire Choluim Cille* (the Oakwood of St. Columcille), built a strong fort with the supplies and arms from the fleet. Mountjoy, for his part, diligently set about his task and strengthened the English garrisons at Newry, Carlingford and Dundalk, and then returned to Dublin. O'Donnell and O'Neill whirled around after the Lord Deputy had departed and marched on the new fort at Derry with 5,000 men. The Catholics attacked suddenly but the sentinels were alert and the garrison gave a successful defense and could not be drawn out of the fort. The Irish lacked proper siege implements and the English had strategically positioned several large guns which rendered the fort impregnable. The Irish army withdrew the following day, but O'Donnell left a party of his men under the command of O'Doherty of Innishowen and Neale Garve O'Donnell to continue the siege and hopefully to starve out the garrison. Red Hugh then showed his contempt for the English at Derry by setting off with his army in June, taking the offensive, and driving deep into Connaught, plundering Thomond's and Clanrickarde's lands and strengthening the confederates there. The English in Derry, out of "fear and dread,"[6] remained hemmed in within the defenses of the fort throughout this southern campaign. The English, due to their cramped quarters, began to suffer from dysentery. As the fort had not been re-supplied with food, the garrison was faced with starvation. Due to these hardships, the English plans for landing an additional garrison at Ballyshannon were called off. On June 28th, a portion of the besieged, under Sir John Chamberlaine, made a sally from the defense works but were driven back and the English commander was killed. O'Donnell returned from Connaught in July and promptly returned north to Derry. On the 29th he led a raid on the English cavalry horses which were grazing outside the fort. The Irish seized nearly 200 horses and drove them south. The Catholics had gone nearly four miles when Docwra, with 20 horse and a body of infantry were seen angrily pursuing O'Donnell's men. Red Hugh drew up his men and awaited the English advance. Both sides charged and a furious battle took place, "so that the horsemen of both were mixed with one another."[7] A cousin of Red Hugh, Hugh Dubh O'Donnell, and Docwra met face to face in the battle; O'Donnell hurled his javelin and struck Docwra in the forehead, wounding him severely. The English commander fell from his horse but was saved by his fellow officers who lifted their fallen commander and carried him despondently back to the fort. This was magnified as a great victory for the Irish and even Elizabeth was deeply distressed by the news concerning the defeat and wounding of Docwra. The siege of these forts continued.

---

[6]O'Faolain, *The Great O'Neil*, 292.
[7]O'Cleary, *Life of Hugh Roe O'Donnell*, 249.

O'Donnell surrounded them tightly with 2,000 men and the lack of food and sickness began to take its toll. O'Neill and Red Hugh both offered safe passage for any soldier who would return to England. Mountjoy had to continuously send reinforcements by sea to maintain a strong English presence.

All during this time the Irish continued to write to Spain seeking aid. On June 24th, Oviedo wrote the King:

> Sire, —I wrote by Don Martin de la Cerda giving your Majesty an account of the state of things in this island when we came with your Majesty's letters. As I have been here for two months, seeing everything that has been done, I can give a more exact account of what is taking place in this province. At present we are hemmed in between two armies, one of which came by sea, the other by land, not to speak of the many garrisons which the English have near us and from which they make incursions every day. Yet such is the bravery of these two Earls and of their followers that if they fought with equal arms they would have no fear; but as they have neither muskets nor artillery, they cannot drive them from the forts which they are erecting each day within the province, and as the war has lasted so long they are so exhausted and impoverished that they have not the means of supporting the soldiers or of paying them, and so every day we are afraid they will leave us. The English are making great efforts to bring about a peace, offering excellent terms; and for this purpose the Viceroy sent messengers twice to O'Neill, saying among other things that your Majesty is making peace with the Queen, and that his condition will be hopeless. At other times he says that no greater misfortune could happen to the country than to bring Spaniards into it, because they are haughty and vicious, and they would destroy and ruin the country. To all this they reply most honourably that they will hold out so long as they have one sol-

dier, or there remains a cow to eat. At present they have got together a very good army, so that O'Neill made the Viceroy retreat when he was coming by land, and O'Donnell keeps those who came by sea shut up in their fortresses. The consequence is, that if a help of six thousand men and some large guns were now sent them they could take any city in Ireland. I wish it were possible for me by word of mouth to show the importance of this undertaking and the great service that would be rendered thereby to God and to his Church, and the great advantage it would be to the service of your Majesty and the peace of your states to attack the enemy here. This is the best possible opportunity, and if it is allowed to slip by, I do not know when we shall find another. But as I cannot urge it otherwise than by these few lines, I pray God, in whose hands the hearts of kings are, that He may move the heart of your Majesty to help us at once. Every day I promise the Catholics this help, and in this way I keep them on hands. May the Lord preserve your Majesty for many and very happy years to be the protector and help of all the afflicted.

From Dungannon in Ireland, June 24th, 1600.

Your Majesty's humble chaplain,

Fray Mattheo, Archbishop elect of Dublin.[8]

Hugh O'Neill also continued to send letters to Philip:

Sire, —We have written by Don Martin de la Cerda to your Majesty in acknowledgment of what your Majesty has done for us and in gratitude for what we have received, both arms and money bestowed on us by your generous hand. We have given to the Archbishop of Dublin and to Don Martin a very long account of our condition, that the one in writing and the other by word of mouth may give information to your Majesty and you may rest assured that if we were able with our own forces and those of our friends to resist the

---

[8]Murphy, introduction to *Life of Hugh Roe O'Donnell*, 117.

power of this enemy it would be enough for us to know that we were doing a great service to God and to his Church, and also to your Majesty's interests, in order to make us risk our lives and shed our blood without troubling and wearying your Majesty, who we know has so many and important things to attend to. But, Sire, a war so long and continuous against so powerful an enemy, and against some of our own countrymen, who do us still more harm, as your Majesty will understand, must have so exhausted and impoverished us that it is by a miracle we hold out, and that owing to our reputation. At present, matters stand in so favourable a way in this kingdom that with some help and some large guns to make breaches in walls, this war would end successfully, for we have an army in all the provinces of Ireland, and when the succour reaches us and its arrival becomes known, our strength would be doubled; whereas if the aid fails to come or is delayed, our forces must grow less and melt away, not having means to subsist.

We humbly beseech your Majesty to order this aid to be hastened, since experience has shown us what evils arise from a delay in such matters. The Archbishop of Dublin encourages and strengthens us and revives our hopes, and by his presence has given us much courage and confidence, and in this way his coming has been of great use and benefit. It only remains that the authority of his Holiness, which has been asked for on behalf of your Majesty, should be sent to him, for there is urgent need of it to correct and reform matters concerning religion, and without it this cannot be done. May our Lord watch over and preserve your Majesty, giving you the increase and prosperity which your vassals and humble servants desire.

From our Camp in Ireland, June 28th, 1600.

It is so difficult to send our letters to Spain, that though I sent this off more than a month ago, it has been returned to me. Now it will go by way of Scotland. I can assure your Majesty that the enemy's strength grows daily, and that our people are losing courage, seeing the succour delayed. But I trust in God and in your Majesty that it will not fail us.

From the Catholic Camp, August 3rd, 1600.

Your humble vassal and servant kisses the feet and hands of your Majesty.

Hugh O'Neill[9]

O'Neill hoped to send his son, Henry, to Spain in order that he might be trained for his lofty position and witness the full splendor of the Catholic Faith. He made his wish known to Philip III and received this benign reply:

Noble and Well-beloved,—I have already written a joint letter to you and your relative O'Donnell, in which I replied to the letter of both of you. By this, which I now write to you personally, I wish to let you know my good will towards you, and I mean to prove it not only by word but by deed; and whereas, from intelligence which reached me from Ireland some days past, I understood you wished to send your son here to be reared and instructed in the Catholic faith, and those who brought the letter understood so from you, I wish to let you know hereby that if such is your determination, it will be a pleasure to me to carry it out. If you send him here, he shall be very dear to me, and I will treat him as a youth of fair hopes, and as the son of such a father should be treated. Don Martin de la Cerda will bring him over, and supply his wants on the journey, as we have ordered.

Given at Madrid, the 24th of December, 1599.[10]

The boy, upon his arrival in Spain, was sent to study at the famous University of Salamanca. He was given a pension of 200 ducats a month by the King. Henry lived at the

---

[9]*Ibid.*, 118.
[10]*Ibid.*, 121.

Franciscan convent in Salamanca and evidently was considering joining the Order. The King, however, by the advice of Cardinal Guevara, moved the boy's residence until his father was consulted concerning the matter.

By the end of 1600, the war was raging in every part of the kingdom. The English, having strengthened their position in the north, set out to subdue the rebellious south. The Catholic cause in Leinster had been maintained by Owen O'More, the chief of Leix and leader of the Wicklow Highlanders. The chieftain valiantly defended his territory from the English and his country prospered through his inspired defense. In April, an interview had taken place at Corroneduff between the Earl of Ormond, Sir George Carew, the President of Munster, Lord Thomond and Owen O'More.[11] The illustrious Jesuit preacher, Father James Archer of Kilkenny, who fervently defended the Catholic cause, was with the O'Mores and Ormond was desirous to speak with him having heard of his reputation. O'More called to Fr. Archer who approached the group leaning on a staff. Ormond challenged the priest for supporting rebellion against the sovereign Queen. The priest defended both himself and the legitimacy of the war according to Catholic principles.[12] When the exchange became heated the Jesuit raised his staff. The clansmen, fearing for the priest's safety, charged the group dragging Ormond from his horse as Thomond and the Lord President Carew fled back to Kilkenny. This "kidnapping" caused a veritable sensation in

---

[11]Sometimes called Owen MacRory (O'More).

[12]Ormond challenged the Jesuit's support of "rebellion" to which the Jesuit responded that the Queen was excommunicated and the Pope was the Sovereign of Ireland.

Ireland and greatly distressed the Queen. The Irish were jubilant. Mountjoy himself was not that distressed at the capture of the Earl. He even believed he had cause to suspect his loyalty. He had been friends with O'Neill and had done little to help the new Lord Deputy. His religious sympathies were also unclear, as he seemed to favor the Irish religious cause, although he would not "rebel" against Elizabeth. Upon hearing of his capture, Mountjoy cautiously responded "for as I have reason to conceive of his proceedings I know not whether this be good or evil news... that although the Earl of Ormonde be the last man that I think would have clean quit the estate of England, yet I have great reason to be confident that, despairing in the force of England to protect him, he had already opened his heart to some other foundation to make good his estate in this kingdom."[13] Ormond, a kinsman of the Queen, was held prisoner from April until June. Fr. Archer had numerous conferences with the Earl and had the joy of receiving the Earl into the Roman Catholic Church. The Earl remained true to his confession until his death. He was set free in June with assurances that there would be no reprisals. Mountjoy, however, sought to avenge him as he had promised Elizabeth[14]. Mountjoy left Dublin in August of 1600 and with a large force invaded Leinster. Mountjoy was shocked to see how well tilled the farmlands were and began to destroy the crops with harrows. O'More protested vigorously this attack on the land and its people, but a short

---

[13]Frederick Jones, *Mountjoy 1563-1606: The Last Elizabethan Deputy* (Dublin: 1958).

[14]McGee, *History of Ireland*, 2:53.

time later was tragically killed in a minor skirmish by a musket shot at Maryborough on August 17th. The Lord Deputy began again to systematically destroy all the crops in the province burning houses and driving away cattle. With O'More's death and the famine brought on by the English, many of the Irish chiefs in Leinster lost heart and made their submission to the Queen out of necessity, although Owen's brother, Raymond, sought to continue the struggle. With Leinster for the most part successfully pacified, Mountjoy sent an army with sickles, scythes and harrows into Munster. The Munster horror of famine, so vividly described by Spenser, loomed on the horizon once again. Many of the leading men of the province, although in their hearts remaining faithful to the Confederacy, outwardly made peace with the Lord Deputy. Carew had his soldiers mercilessly destroy all the crops wherever they went in order to induce a famine. From Kinsale to Glandore harbor to Dunmanus bay, not a single grain of corn was left unburned. The English drowned 500 cows to save themselves the trouble of driving them, and "the churls and poor people were treated as enemies and killed."[15] Along with the cold winter came the food shortage and, once again, men, women and children perished by the thousands in Munster.[16] Mountjoy and Carew continually tried to split

---

[15]Bagwell, *Ireland Under the Tudors*, 3:361. D'Alton relates that Carew boasted, "that all the corn and houses near Limerick were burned; and that in Kerry his troops had killed 1,200 men in arms not counting the women, children and husbandmen who had also been slain.." (D'Alton, *History of Ireland*, 3:170.) See also, George Carew, *Pacata Hibernia* 2 Vols. (London: Downey & Co., Ltd., 1896), 158; *Carew Papers*, 4:428-9, 487.

[16]Joyce, *History of Ireland*, 256.

the Confederacy in the south with intrigues and forgeries so that the Catholic leaders did not know whom to trust. For example, letters were forged purporting to have been secretly written to Mountjoy by the Earl of Desmond in which he offered to betray one of his fellow confederates named O'Connor. The forgeries were "disclosed" to O'Connor who was offered £1,000 if he seized the Earl and handed him over to the government. O'Connor captured Desmond and imprisoned him at Castle Ishin. This type of action, inspired by Carew's treachery, further weakened the Confederacy in the south. The brilliant Captain Tyrell, however, continued his guerrilla war in the southern province but was now put on the defensive.

Hugh O'Donnell, in an effort to restore the lagging spirits of the Confederates, left Tirconnaill and again drove far south into Connaught. That he could still do this was indicative of the weakness of Docwra and the English at Derry. He attacked and burned the lands of the Earls Thomond and Clanrickarde who had sided with the English. Thomond's new town of Ennis was also destroyed. O'Donnell's attack in the south renewed the spirit of the Irish in the southern provinces. It probably prevented Carew from seizing the Earl of Desmond who had been imprisoned by O'Connor. Catholic commander Piers Lacy had gathered 4,000 men and quickly surrounded Castle Ishin. Carew, because of O'Donnell's incursion, lacked all his forces. When he finally moved to raise the siege and capture Desmond it was too late. A priest with Lacy had convinced the garrison to release the "Sugane" Earl of Desmond who was restored to the Confederate forces.

Carew complained bitterly that even towns were "so bewitched by Popish priests" they were aiding the rebels.[17] O'Connor, who had been tricked by Carew, once more befriended the Confederates but was never again fully trusted.

Although Docwra was too weak to take the offensive in the north during O'Donnell's absence, he did have other weapons which he effectively used to break up the Confederacy. The English presence on the Irish rear was in itself a moral victory which began to cause the weak men among the Confederates to waver. Art O'Neill, the son of Hugh O'Neill's old rival Turlough, was promised all of Tyrone by Docwra if he joined the Queen's cause. He accepted the offer and with a small body of men came over to the English camp. When Hugh O'Neill heard of his treason he derided him as "Queen Elizabeth's earl that cannot command 100 kerne."[18] The Queen acutely felt the sarcasm as she had seriously contemplated transferring the Earl's titles to his kinsman. There were other serious defections however. The English, during O'Donnell's absence, secretly entreated his cousin Neale Garve to join them promising him the chieftaincy of Tirconnaill and many other rewards. Neale Garve felt he had as good a claim to the chieftaincy as Red Hugh. He was powerful, revengeful and very ambitious. O'Cleary related that he had joined with Red Hugh "not

---

[17]D'Alton, *History of Ireland*, 3:167. Carew thought his principle duty lied in "the supressing and reforming of the loose, barbarous and most wicked life of that savage nation." (Canny, *Elizabethan Conquest*, 127.)

[18]Bagwell, *Ireland Under the Tudors*, 3:373. Art O'Neill, son of Turlough, died a short time after this betrayal.

through love but through fear."[19] Docwra continued to lure him playing upon his envy of Hugh Roe. He eventually went over to the English. Tragically, some of the clansmen who did not look beyond personal attachment followed his example. Docwra thus reported his defection:

> On the third of October came in Neale Garvie O'Donnell with 40 horse and 60 foot, a man I was directed by the State to win to the Queen's service. [20]

The English captain further wrote to Mountjoy that the coming in of O'Donnell was a sign of "how God doth work for her Majesty," and that it was the Divine Power who "hath turned the hearts of two principle men to join with Her Majesty."[21] Both men were knighted and promised the titles to their clan's holdings.

Neale Garve's entire career reflected the diseased weakness of the Irish clan system which both Hugh O'Donnell and O'Neill had tried so desperately to reform. His defection was the only serious case among the northern clans. He was a powerful combatant and now fought for the English with great zeal. The great body of Irish remained true to the cause of their Faith and country. Hugh Roe's sister, Nuala, who was married to Garve, immediately separated from him on account of his treachery.

---

[19]Murphy, introduction to *Life of Hugh Roe O'Donnell*, 125. Neale was the son of Con and nephew of Calvagh who had ruled Tirconnaill as chief. He agreed to serve the English cause but demanded that he be allowed to practice the Catholic Faith. Docwra told him his practice would not be interfered with and he would not be obliged to attend Protestant services.

[20]*Ibid.*, 124.

[21]O'Faolain, *The Great O'Neil*, 293.

 187

Neale Garve was a strong and powerful warrior and proved to be a great asset to the English in Derry. The garrison now received a supply of fresh meat and the Irish guard was greatly weakened by the defection. On October 8th, Docwra sent Neale Garve with 1,000 foot and 30 horse to seize the O'Donnell ancestral seat at Lifford. The town was guarded by a fort which was garrisoned by 30 of O'Donnell's men. Most of the garrison were outside the fortress and taken by complete surprise. They succeeded in burning the houses inside the fort in order that they might not be used by Garve and the English. The town was captured however, and most of the garrison killed. Garve sent supplies to the beleaguered English armies in the forts.

Hugh O'Donnell was in Connaught when one of his men brought him word of the perfidious actions of his kinsmen. Hugh was greatly surprised by this news and marched home as quickly as he could, "none of his soldiers being able to keep with him except a few of his horsemen."[22] O'Donnell arrived on October 12th with 700 foot and 100 horse and encamped three miles west of Castlefin. The next day he led his army before the town. Garve, if nothing else, was a man of great courage and skill in warfare. He boldly led the English garrison in a charge and the two armies skirmished with neither side gaining the upper hand. On the following day Hugh again attempted to recapture the town and Garve with the English sallied forth once again. A fierce cavalry fight ensued and Manus O'Donnell, Red Hugh's younger brother, charged into a group of five Irish royalists. Being surrounded, Manus was

---

[22]Murphy, introduction to *Life of Hugh Roe O'Donnell*, 126.

struck in the right side by a spear thrust from Garve, and under the shoulder by another royalist named Cornelius O'Gallagher. Roderick (Rory) O'Donnell, seeing the desperate situation of his brother, raced to his aid. He hurled his spear at Garve's breast, who, tightening the reins, raised his horse's head which received the blow. The horse under Garve fell dead but he was lifted up by his men. Hugh O'Donnell now led the infantry in a furious charge and drove the royalists back to the fort. Manus O'Donnell died of his wounds fifteen days later after receiving the Last Rites of the Church.[23] Hugh O'Donnell succeeded in capturing Cornelius O'Gallagher and had him hanged. Red Hugh again shut up Garve and the English in the fort and prevented them from preying upon his territory. This difficult period of the war revealed the true greatness of Red Hugh as a field commander fighting a war on many fronts and maintaining discipline within his forces. Rory (Roderick) O'Donnell, who was Hugh's younger brother, returned north and harassed the English in Derry.[24]

On November 10th, two Spanish ships with munitions, arms and money sailed into the harbor at Killybegs.

---

[23]The moving account of Manus' death on October 22, 1600, who died forgiving his enemies including Neale, who inflicted the mortal wound, is found in O'Cleary's *Life of Hugh Roe O'Donnell*, 261.

[24]On one occasion ships carrying English troops and provisions from Derry to Lifford were attacked close to Lifford where the Lough narrowed with "missiles" by Catholic forces along the bank under the command of Rory. The English garrison at Lifford sallied forth but were repulsed by the Catholic army. Rory was slightly wounded in the thigh by a bullet in this engagement but succeeded in capturing the boats and provisions. A large number of the royalists were slain according to O'Sullivan Bear. (O'Sullivan Bear, *Ireland Under Elizabeth*, 137.)

O'Donnell met them and divided the supplies between himself and O'Neill. This additional aid, however, did not imperil Docwra's position although it caused him a certain uneasiness.

Mountjoy, in the meantime, being far more patient than Essex, continued his steady, methodical policy of building and garrisoning forts. Within a year and a half O'Neill found himself being surrounded by a ring of English forts—Bunalong, Newry, Fort Norris, Carrickfergus[25], Carlingford, Elagh, Burt, Coleraine, Strabane, Masserene, Edenduffcarrick, Moyrie, Lecale, Armagh, the Blackwater, Newtown, Castlederg, Castlereagh, Culmore, Derry and Lifford. Many of these forts however suffered from continual sickness and desertion and proved very costly to maintain.[26] Often the supplies sent by the government were rot-

---

[25]Sir Arthur Chichester, who was in charge of the garrison in Carrickfergus, had an intense hatred for the Irish. In May of 1601 he wrote to Mountjoy concerning his efforts to the west of Lough Neagh, which captures the spirit of the war at this time: "I have launched the great boat and have twice visited Tyrone with her, and oftener with lesser [boats]. We have killed, burnt, and spoiled all along the Lough within four miles of Dungannon, from whence we returned hither yesterday; in which journeys we have killed above one hundred people of all sorts, besides such as were burnt, how many I know not. We spare none of what quality or sex soever, and it hath bred much terror in the people, who heard not a drum nor saw not a fire there of long time. The last service was upon Patrick O'Quin, whose house and town was burnt, wife, son, children and people slain, himself (as is now reported unto me) dead of a hurt received in flying from his house, and other gentlemen which received blows in following us in our return to the boat; and Tyrone himself lay within a mile of this place, but kept himself safe sending 100 shot to know the matter, which he seemed to marvel at." (Falls, *Elizabeth's Irish Wars*, 277.)

[26]McGee states that the English had to maintain at least 8,000 men garrisoned in Ulster alone. (McGee, *History of Ireland*, 2:58.)

ten and diseased. Docwra once received food so horribly rotten that he successfully traced it all the way back to an order for corn which had been given and collected for Bagnal who had died back in 1598! Incidents such as these along with the timidity of magistrates, the base corruption of army officials and the dissentions of greedy colonists all hampered and frustrated the English campaign of 1600-1601.

In Munster, Carew continued the English policy of spreading famine and destruction throughout the land. In August he gave an account of the province:

> All our garrisons in Kerry, Askeaton, Kilmallock, Youghal, I thank God do prosper and are now at their harvest which must be well followed, or else this summer service is lost. Wherein I will be careful to lose no time for the destruction of it will procure the next year's famine; by which means only the wars of Ireland must be determined. . . . no day passeth without report of burning, killing and taking prey. . . . infinite numbers of their cattle are taken, and besides husbandmen, women and children, of weaponed men there hath been slain in this province.[27]

The "Sugane" Earl of Desmond had been greatly weakened by this policy and many more of the Irish Confederates, for their own safety, feigned loyalty to the Queen. Robert Cecil, in an effort to further diminish the power of Desmond, sent over to Ireland another member of this illustrious family, James Fitzgerald, who had been imprisoned in the Tower since 1584. This young man was the son of the late Earl Gerald. He was entrusted to Carew who hoped to

---

[27]Bagwell, *Ireland Under the Tudors*, 3:126.

establish him among the people as the Queen's Earl of Desmond opposed to the "Sugane" Earl. The new Earl was greeted at Youghal and Kilmallock with intense joy by the people, who symbolically threw wheat and salt on the heir of the ancient house of Desmond. This joy lasted only one day. The following day was Sunday and the new Earl, having been brought up in the new religion while he was in London, walked off to the Protestant service. The people were shocked and fell on their knees imploring him not to abandon the Faith of his fathers. The Earl was ignorant both of their language and creed and attended the Protestant worship. Upon his return the people showed that even the ties of kindred were subordinate to their Faith. The Earl was reviled, abused and abandoned by the people. Because of this rejection the Earl was found to be useless by his employers and was sent back to London.[28]

The war turned once again to the northern theater. The Earl of Clanrickarde, who had so often been attacked by O'Donnnell, died in May, 1601 and was succeeded by his son Richard, Lord Dunkellin. Mountjoy, desirous of giving the new Earl an opportunity to prove his courage and loyalty, ordered him to gather his forces and the English from several garrisons in Munster and lead this army to Sligo against O'Donnell. The Lord Deputy hoped to use Clanrickarde to create a diversion which would draw O'Donnell from his own territory. If this succeeded, Docwra could

---

[28]Cecil wrote to Carew that he should simply have him put to death in some way. During the fighting in Munster, Fitzthomas, the "Sugane" Earl of Desmond, was finally seized and sent to London where the unfortunate man was imprisoned and eventually died in the Tower.

then further strengthen his strongholds and extend his power by seizing other places. When O'Donnell heard of the Earl's approach at the head of a large army, he left a force under his younger brother Rory O'Donnell to keep Garve and the English contained in Lifford and marched south with his army. Hugh Roe did not stop until he crossed the Curlew mountains and the Boyle River into Moylurg where he pitched his camp directly opposite his enemies.

> They remained thus for some time face to face, spying and watching each other. Many were the conflicts, slaughterings, and affrays which took place between them while they remained thus in readiness for each other, until at length the English army became weary and returned in sorrow to their homes.[29]

Neale Garve and Docwra were not inactive during this time. The two men having conferred, decided to seize the beautiful Franciscan monastery which had been built by the O'Donnell's in 1474. Docwra stated his reasons for attempting to capture the monastery, observing that

> the abbey of Donegal was kept only by a few friars, the situation of it close to the sea and very convenient for many services especially for a step to take Ballyshannon with, which was a work the manifold attempts and chargeable preparations the Queen had been at to accomplish.[30]

---

[29]Four Masters, *Annals*, 6:2251. O'Donnell was also at this time seeking to assist the selection of a new chieftain for the O'Doherty's of Innishowen as their chief had died earlier that year.

[30]Murphy, introduction to *Life of Hugh Roe O'Donnell*, 127.

Garve was sent an additional 500 English soldiers with which he set out to capture the monastery on the 2nd of August. O'Donnell's small force attacked the first body of English troops which had been sent ahead to reconnoitre the road and beat them back. When the main body led by Neale Garve arrived, Hugh O'Donnell's men could do little against the superior force and withdrew, allowing them to march to Donegal and take possession of the monastery. Here is a description of the state of the monastery by a Franciscan friar named Fr. Mooney who lived there during this time:

> In 1600 our community at Donegal consisted of forty brethren, by whom the divine office was sung day and night with great solemnity. I had charge of the sacristy, and I had in it forty priest's vestments with all their belongings; many of these were of cloth of gold and cloth of silver, some of them interwoven and wrought with gold ornaments; all the rest were of silk. We had, moreover, sixteen large silver chalices of which two only were not gilt. And we had two ciboriums for the Blessed Sacrament. The church furniture was very respectable. The windows were all glazed. But when the war grew more fierce and the heretics were getting a firmer footing, they made their way to the town of Donegal while the Lord O'Donnell was busily engaged elsewhere, and on the feast of St. Laurence the Martyr they placed a garrison of soldiers in the monastery. Some of the brothers who had been warned of their coming fled into the woods some miles off, having first put on board a ship the church furniture in order to save it. I was the last to leave the monastery and I came away in that ship.[31]

---

[31] *Ibid.*, 128.

 194

The Earl of Clanrickarde and his army had just returned south when O'Donnell's men brought him word that Garve had seized the monastery. Hugh Roe prepared to return north and hid his sorrow from his men "for it was his constant practice whenever he heard anything which caused sorrow or saddness, not to exhibit any signs of his thoughts at all, but his countenance was merry and agreeable when he appeared in public before all who were in his presence."[32]

O'Donnell soon arrived to avenge the sacrilege. He surrounded the English who had since turned the monastery into a solid defensive position. He placed strong and vigorous watches which did not allow the English to venture forth. The garrison was supplied by the English fleet which due to the deep water could sail in close to the monastery. The struggles between the two armies were described by O'Cleary as follows: "wrathful, vindictive, fierce attacks were cutting, sharp, destructive, venomous, . . . large bodies of soldiers, recruits and warriors were slaughtered and slain."[33]

The struggle continued in this way until the end of September. Then, on the night of September 29th, for some unknown reason, a fire in the monastery ignited the stores of English powder. There was a tremendous explosion as men, stone and wood "were mixed up in their flight and motion upwards for a long time and fell on the ground charred corpses, and some of them fell on the heads of the

---

[32]O'Cleary, *Life of Hugh Roe O'Donnell*, 287.
[33]*Ibid.*, 289.

people beneath when coming to the ground, so that many were consumed by fire then."[34]

Red Hugh, taking advantage of his enemy's confusion, made a ferocious assault on the English, as the flames illuminated the surrounding darkness and were reflected in the deep waters of Donegal Bay.[35] A violent hand-to-hand encounter began. The English ship in the harbor, while attempting to assist the English in the monastery with covering fire, was dashed against a rock. Hundreds were killed on both sides and the English forces who survived were driven out and sought refuge in the earthen defense works which they had dug in another nearby Franciscan Monastery at Magherabeg.[36]

During the campaign of 1601 O'Neill and O'Donnell fought with the heroism of Thermopylae rather than that of Marathon or Plataea. The two Hughes carried on a successful defensive war back to back as it were with O'Donnell defending the north and O'Neill the south. The two friends, who were "flames of mutual love and affection"[37], contin-

---

[34]*Ibid.*, 291. O'Cleary attributes the explosion to "the Lord displaying his power" against those who had desecrated the cells of the sons of life.

[35]The beautiful Franciscan monastery which was a center of art, learning and piety was never fully restored. When the Franciscans returned to the site, huts were set up on the shore and the ruined chapel was still used for the Holy Sacrifice. A moving account of the sacrilege and destruction is given by the former prior and Franciscan provincial, Fr. Mooney, to Fr. Purcell in C.P. Meehan, MRIA., *The Rise and Fall of the Irish Franciscan Monasteries and Memoirs of the Irish Hierarchy in the Seventeenth Century* (Dublin: James Duffy, 1869), 1-16.

[36]O'Sullivan Bear states that nearly 1,000 royalists perished in this fierce encounter including Neale Garve's brother Con. (O'Sullivan-Bear, *Ireland Under Elizabeth*, 139.)

[37]O'Cleary, *Life of Hugh Roe O'Donnell*, 155.

ued to hold the overwhelming numbers of the Queen's army at bay. Their mutual friendship and loyalty is one of the true glories of Irish History. In June, Mountjoy resorted to treachery and offered a record L2,000 for the head of O'Neill. So great was the loyalty inspired by the brilliant commander that none took the offer. An attempt was made to assassinate him, but the Englishman, named Walker (who even drew a sword on O'Neill in his own tent), was disarmed and eventually allowed to return to his company!

Fierce battles continued to occur similar to the bitter encounter which took place between O'Neill and Mountjoy in the Battle of Moiry Pass.[38] In the southern provinces the English had accomplished little of lasting importance except in Munster where the famine was taking its toll. Irish guerrilla forces in Leinster were again raiding the Pale. Mountjoy, ignoring the protestations of the colonists, continued to pour all his resources into the war in Ulster. During late September and early October of 1600, the Lord Deputy had succeeded, despite O'Neill's repeated attacks,

---

[38]An excellent description of "Tyrone's trenches", used effectively in this encounter in which O'Neill bested a frustrated Mountjoy, is found in Hayes-McCoy's *Irish Battles*, 132-43. Cyril Falls also acknowledges begrudgingly the excellence of O'Neill's resistance. (Falls, *Elizabeth's Irish Wars*, 265.) See also, Frederick M. Jones, *Mountjoy 1563-1606: The Last Elizabethan Deputy*, 82. The Four Masters relate that O'Neill's men were "like swarms of bees issuing from the hollows of bee-hives who compelled him to return by the same road, after the killing of countless numbers of the gentlemen and recruits. He did not go beyond Moiry Pass for some time after this." (Four Masters, *Annals*, 6:2225.) The confident Irish cavalry openly taunted the English horsemen, calling them "churls", baiting them to fight. Mountjoy and the English were forced to withdraw in early October from this difficult pass.

in building Fort Norris in memory of Sir John Norris eight miles north of Newry.

Often, in many historical writings, one of the most misleading errors is the oversimplification of complex historical situations which occurs from the historian's foreknowledge of the outcome of events. The narration may become more intelligible but is less plenary as it loses much of the apprehension, anxiety and unpredictability of the time. Neither side was certain of success. Mountjoy continued to move cautiously and slowly as the Catholics were still a powerful enemy. In August, the Lord Deputy wrote to Cecil reminding him that

> Whatsoever others have undertaken I beseech you, sir, to remember that in all my dispatches I have declared that the uttermost you could look from us in this summer should be to plant such garrisons as must take effect next winter, and that we should proceed slowly, and come short of our purpose, if we were not continually supplied with means, and in time of victuals and all kinds of munitions.[39]

The staggering cost of maintaining the war was draining England of both her wealth and influence as well as the flower of her manhood. Conscription for service in Ireland was avoided by Englishmen like the plague. Elizabeth was so dissatisfied with the progress of her Lord Deputy that she suspected him of being partial to Tyrone. Mountjoy, in response, resorted again to offering a handsome reward for O'Neill's capture or assassination.

Day by day the war continued with a feverish intensity. The armies fought tenaciously face to face with their nerves

---

[39]O'Faolain, *The Great O'Neil*, 305.

tense and strained. The battles during this period, although fierce, were never more satisfying than a partial success. O'Donnell re-took fort Newtown and Mountjoy wrote to Cecil that Tyrone had "poured 3,000 shot into our camp"[40] and was barely prevented from seizing their position. How frustrating and truly frightening the attack referred to in this one passage of a long and distant dispatch must have been. The war continued to drag exhaustingly on with no end in sight. A number of the clans in the Catholic confederacy were forced to make peace with the Queen due to the exhaustion of their resources, although they did not aid the English in the war.

The Irish in 1601 still held the trump card of Spanish aid. For the past two years the Irish had daily expected the arrival of a Spanish army. The English were fully aware of these rumors which filled the country and that the Catholics would rejoice at their arrival. Carew wrote to the Privy Council informing them that

> by intelligences that can be learned the Irish do persuade themselves that this summer the King of Spain will send them succours; which if he do, no part of that kingdom—no, not the cities—will be free from rebellion, as well in regard of the affection they have to that nation and their religion as the inveterate malice they have to our religion and us.[41]

An army from Spain had been promised for a number of years by both Philip II and Philip III to aid the Catholic cause, but when would it arrive?

---

[40]*Ibid.*, 306.
[41]Murphy, introduction to *Life of Hugh Roe O'Donnell*, 131-2.

eight

the spanish
and the battle of kinsale

The disaster which shattered the Spanish Armada would have broken the resolve of any nation less courageous than Spain. The kings of Spain were singularly dedicated to the advancement of the Catholic cause throughout the world. Philip III, although not as able a ruler as his father, viewed his father's good will towards Ireland as a sacred trust which had been bequeathed to him. There can be no doubt however that the continual delays and the bureaucracy of the Spanish administration weakened the Catholic effort in Ireland.[1] After many delays, a fleet of 33 ships[2] sailed from Lisbon in late August of 1601 for Ireland under the command of Don Diego Brochero.[3] The ships carried an army of 4,000 men under Don Juan de Aquila. A violent squall arose and the fleet was divided with Don Pedro de Zubiaur and seven ships being

---

[1]Although aid was frequently sent, the longed for army took nearly ten years to arrive and was not the size requested by the Confederates. (John J. Silke, *Kinsale, The Spanish Intervention in Ireland at the End of the Elizabethan Wars* [New York: Fordham University Press, 1970].)

[2]Atkinson, *History of Spain and Portugal,* 172.

[3]Davies, *Golden Century of Spain.*

driven to Corunna. On September 20, word was sent to the Governor of Cork that a Spanish fleet had been seen on the horizon sailing for Cork. The Governor was panic-stricken and immediately dispatched a horseman with letters to inform Mountjoy and his council in Kilkenny castle.[4] When the strange fleet had neared the mouth of the harbor, the wind suddenly changed directions and they tacked round and headed for Kinsale some twenty miles to the south along the coast. The Spanish army landed on September 23 and Aquila marched towards the town near the mouth of the Bandon River with 2,500 men. The English garrison under Captain William Saxeys fled in horror to Cork. The townsmen graciously received the foreigners and the Sovereign of Kinsale, with white wand in hand, quartered the troops in various houses. The Spanish also seized and garrisoned the two strong castles which controlled the entrance to the harbor: 125 men were placed in Rincorran on the east side and 50 in Castle ny parke on the west. The Spanish commander issued a proclamation that no one in the town would be molested in any way and that if any desired to leave the town they were free to do so.[5]

With the arrival of the Spaniards, the entire complexion of the war changed. The Irish Catholics throughout Ireland were thrilled and elated by the news. Mountjoy abandoned Ulster and flew down to Cork as fast as he could. He knew full well what this landing meant. The Anglo-Irish Privy

---

[4]Carew, Ormond and Sir Richard Wingfield were present with Mountjoy.

[5]Carew complained that they were "billited through the town more readily than if they were the Queen's forces." (D'Alton *History of Ireland*, 3:174.) Carew, *Pacata Hibernia*, 1:277-8.

Council immediately ordered a concentration of all the English forces in the south and prepared for a winter campaign. The Lord Deputy acted with a vigor and determination which indicated his conviction that if Ireland was to be saved for the Queen the Spanish must be quickly crushed. Reinforcements were sent from England and the Lord Deputy marched out of Cork and encamped on the north side of Kinsale with over 15,000 men.[6] The English burned all the corn within five miles of Kinsale and laid siege to the town. A proclamation was issued warning the inhabitants "not to take part with the Pope and the King of Spain, who were unjustly maintaining the rebels against their annointed sovereign."[7] Matthew de Oviedo, who for years had supported the Irish Catholics, accompanied Don Juan from Spain and issued a counter proclamation in Latin which defended the Papal power of deposition as it had been exercised by Pius V, Gregory XIII and Clement VIII. The Irish were absolved from all allegiance to Elizabeth who was declared a mere usurping heretic.[8]

---

[6]McGee, *History of Ireland*, 2:447. Nearly 5,000 men were sent immediately from England and the siege began in earnest by mid October.

[7]Bagwell, *Ireland Under the Tudors*, 3:400.

[8]The following is the text of the Archbishop's proclamation: "Don Juan de Aquila, general of the war, and the Catholic King of Spain's chief commander in God's war, which is made in Ireland for defence of the faith. To all the Irish Catholics living in Kinsale, the city of Cork, and in all other villages, cities, and castles, wisheth health in Him who is the true happiness. There is come unto our ears a proclamation, or certain libel, made in the city of Cork, in the name of the Deputy; which because it containeth many untruths and such things as offend the ears of honest men, lest they may lead and seduce the minds of simple men into error and turn them from the truth, I am compelled to show their falsehood, to lay open the truth, and in few words to signify the pretence and intention of our most excellent King

Philip in this war, which is, with the apostolic authority, to be administered by us; and (to speak the truth) I could very easily retort upon them those reproaches which they object to us, and make them lose the pleasure which they have taken in ill-speaking by hearing of the like; notwithstanding, we will not, like weak and unarmed women, go to reproachings, but, setting these things aside, answer to those that are objected with sound truth and Christian modesty.

First of all, ye feign that we would lead away the pretended subjects of the Queen of England from their obedience, to bring them under our yoke, which is a very untruth; for we endeavour not to persuade anybody that he should deny due obedience (according to the word of God) to his prince. But ye know well that, for many years past, Elizabeth was deprived of her kingdom and all her subjects absolved from their fidelity by the Pope, unto whom He that reigneth in the heavens, the King of Kings, hath committed all power, that he should root up, destroy, plant, and build in such sort that he may punish temporal kings, if it shall be good for the spiritual building, even to their deposing, which things hath been done in the kingdoms of England and Ireland by many popes, viz. by Pius Quintus, Gregory the Thirteenth, and now by Clement the Eighth, as it is well known; whose bulls are extant amongst us. I speak to Catholics, not to forward heretics, who have fallen from the faith of the Roman Church; seeing they are blind leaders of the blind and such as know not the grounds of the truth, it is no marvel that they do also disagree from us in this thing. But our brethren, the Catholics, walking in the pureness of the faith, and yielding to the Catholic Church, which is the very pillar of the truth, will easily understand all those things. Therefore it remaineth that the Irish, which adhere to us do work with us nothing that is against God's laws or their due obedience, nay, that which they do is according to God's word and the obedience which they owe the Pope.

Secondly, ye affirm that we Spaniards go about to win the Irish with allurements and feigned flatteries, which is a thing far from our nature, and that we do it but for a while; that after we have drawn the minds of simple men to us we might afterwards, exercising our cruelty towards them, show our bloody nature. O the immortal God! Who doth not wonder at your bitter and inexpressible cruelty and your boldness showed in these words? For who is it that doth not know the great cruelty which you English have exercised and cease not to exercise, toward the miserable Irish? You, I say, go about to take from their souls the Catholic faith which their fathers held, in

The Spanish commander was annoyed that he had not been greeted by friends upon his arrival. Both Aquila and Oviedo sent letters to O'Neill and O'Donnell in the far north urging them to hasten south with their armies. Although the Spanish had landed in the worst possible location,[9] O'Neill and O'Donnell prepared to leave guards in their own territory and march south to the assistance of the Spanish. The Irish lords had repeatedly asked for an army of six to seven thousand, with heavy ordinance to achieve

---

which consists eternal life; truly you are far more cruel than bears and lions, which take away the temporal life, for you would deprive them of the eternal and spiritual life. Who is it that hath demolished all the temporalities of this most flourishing kingdom but the English? Look upon this and be ashamed. Whereas, on the other hand, we commiserating the condition of the Catholics here, have left our most sweet and happy country, Spain, that is replenished with all good things, and, being stirred with their cries, which pierce the heavens, having reached the ears of the Pope and our King Philip, they have, being moved with pity at last resolved to send to you soldiers, silver, gold and arms with a most liberal hand, not to the end they might, according as they feign, exercise cruelty toward you, O Irish Catholics, but that you may be happily reduced (being snatched out of the jaws of the devil and free from their tyranny) to your own pristine ingenuousness, and that you may freely profess the Catholic faith. Therefore, my most beloved, seeing that which you have so many years before desired and begged for with prayers and tears; and that now, even now, the Pope, Christ's vicar on earth, doth command you to take arms for the defence of our faith, I admonish, exhort and beseech you all - all, I say, unto whom these letters shall come - that as soon as you possibly can you come to us with your friends and weapons. Whosoever shall do this shall find us prepared, and we will communicate to them those things which we possess. And whosoever shall (despising our wholesome counsel) do otherwise, and remain in the obedience of the English, we will persecute him as a heretic and a hateful enemy of the Church even unto death." (Carew, *Pacata Hibernia*, 1:295-98.)

[9]See Curtis' assessment in *A History of Ireland*, pages 216-17.

victory over the English. Earlier, while the war raged in Munster, a landing had been envisioned in that province. An Ulster landing would have been a more difficult journey for the Spanish and Munster had ports that could easily be supplied. When the Spanish finally sailed with Aquila's army, there had been no final confirmation with the Irish as to the site. Mountjoy, in September of 1601, had moved down from Ulster to Trim in county Meath in anticipation of a landing in the south. The Spanish forces strategically hoped to aid the Catholics in Ireland, thereby hurting England and also forcing the recall of English troops out of the Netherlands.

Archbishop Matthew de Oviedo, who had been in Ulster in 1600, had returned to Spain. He sailed with the Spanish and with dated information had urged the Munster landing as the firm desire of the Irish princes. Prior to the expedition, a Spanish messenger sent to O'Donnell was told by Red Hugh, speaking for O'Neill as well, that any landing should now take place in the west at Limerick or Galway. If these key locations could not be reached by the Spanish seamen, then a strategic spot should be selected between the mouth of the Shannon and Lough Foyle. The war in Munster had been for the most part suppressed by the end of the summer of 1601. Oviedo was not aware of this changed situation. The Spanish messenger sent from O'Donnell arrived at Corunna on October 1st. The Spanish fleet, however, had already set sail. O'Neill had sent a communication asking the Spanish if they could tack and sail around the west coast to Ulster but Aquila was unwilling.

The Irish, who had fought brilliantly defending their homes and land in Ulster, now had to journey 300 miles to the far south during the winter. It would have been difficult to leave their territory, especially for O'Neill with the likes of Chichester and Docwra. Red Hugh also had to turn his back on his lordship and leave off his confrontation with Docwra and Neale Garve in the heart of his country. Rory O'Donnell temporarily was left behind to try to hold Garve in check. Most government spies thought that O'Donnell, like O'Neill, would not leave Ulster. They were wrong. Hugh O'Donnell, with his usual ardor, was the first to set off with 2,500 men,

> For it was through him that the Spaniards and their King had begun the war. He was full of joy at their coming and he thought it of little importance that the English should dwell in the castles which they had seized in his territory, for he was sure they would escape from them at once if the Irish and the Spaniards were victorious in the contest with the Lord Deputy at Kinsale.[10]

Red Hugh knew Kinsale would be decisive. He set his country in order as best he could and gathered his forces at Ballymoate in County Sligo. The MacSweeneys, Brian O'Rourke, O'Dogherty, MacDermot and many of the clansmen from northern Connaught rallied to him as did his two younger brothers, Rory and Cathbarr. Together they celebrated the feast of All Saints. On November 2nd, filled with hope, he began his courageous march to the far south. When Red Hugh led his army across the Erne he had crossed the Rubicon. They had turned their backs on

---

[10]Murphy, introduction to *Life of Hugh Roe O'Donnell*, 138.

their native province and territory, which was endangered, and for the sake of the Faith and the Irish nation began the long journey to the south.[11] Mountjoy, with aid from the English fleet under the capable command of Admiral Levison, drove off the Spanish ships and began to bombard Rincorran and Castle ny parke. Both forts were eventually won from the Spanish and their Irish auxiliaries. Rincorran fell first and Castle ny parke followed, but only after bitter fighting. Having won these positions the Lord Deputy was able to move his artillery closer to the town and assault it from both land and sea. The English guns blazed unceasingly night and day. He hoped to force the Spanish to surrender before the Irish could bring their united forces south. O'Donnell had already crossed the Shannon into Tipperary and encamped near Holy Cross Abbey. On the feast of St. Andrew he attended Mass at the famous Abbey, prayed for divine assistance and visited the community of monks where "he presented them with oblations and offerings and alms, and they were grateful."[12] Captain Tyrrell joined his forces to O'Donnell's army here. Due to the recent rains and snows, the Irish were hindered in their advance. Mountjoy, fearing the arrival of the Irish, sent Carew with 4,000 men to intercept O'Donnell. The two armies met and encamped opposite each other. Red Hugh wished to save his strength and avoid a battle if possible. To his west were the Slieve Felim mountains which were

---

[11]As Hayes-McCoy comments, there had been "no precedent for this in Irish history. . . . we must not omit to commend them for what they did. Their march across Ireland was heroic." (Hayes-McCoy, *Irish Battles*, 155.)

[12]O'Cleary, *Life of Hugh Roe O'Donnell*, 303.

impassable for an army with baggage on account of the heavy rains. On the night of November 22, there came a sudden and severe frost which hardened up the bog and morass making a journey possible. O'Donnell, having lit large fires to present to the English the appearance of a camp, instantly took advantage of the weather with which the Lord of the Elements had blessed them. With a brilliant stratagem, Red Hugh set out on that icy night and crossed the mountains. He relentlessly drove his men till they reached Croom near Limerick the next night after a march of forty miles. The English were caught flat-footed and Carew was stunned. He called O'Donnell's trek "the greatest march with incumbrance of carriage that hath been heard of."[13] Pursuit being impossible, Carew returned with his forces to Kinsale. Mountjoy was becoming increasingly impatient. On November 28th he sent a trumpet to summon the town to surrender. The Lord Deputy's messenger was rebuffed at the gate and informed that Aquila held the town: "First for Christ and second for the King of Spain *contra tanti inimici.*"[14] The Spaniards defended the walls and hurled verbal abuse at the English calling them *"meschini"*. The English, hearing of O'Donnell's advances, renewed their bombardment, concentrating on the eastern wall of the town where they eventually made a breech. The Span-

---

[13]Joyce, *History of Ireland*, 259. Carew, *Pacata Hibernia*, 2:12.

[14]O'Faolain, *The Great O'Neil.*, 325. Mountjoy complained that the population in Ireland, even the "old English", had "Spanish and Papist hearts" and that "in the cities of Munster the citizens were so degenerated from their first English progenitors as that the very speaking of English was forbidden by them to their wives and children." (Curtis, *History of Ireland*, 217.)

ish busily repaired the wall during the night. They worked so well that the following morning, when the English attempted to storm the breach with 2,000 men, they had to report that despite the pounding the wall had taken, the attack had to be abandoned. The Spanish, on several occasions, sallied forth from the town and successfully encountered the English. Mountjoy continued to move his artillery closer to the town. He had twenty cannon at his disposal and the Spanish only four. The Earl of Thomond commanded the west side of the town while Mountjoy and Carew were on the east. On December 2nd, the Spanish, in the blackness of the night, made one of their most successful attacks. They sallied out with 2,000 men and feinting a move to the west, whirled about with all their strength on the English batteries to the east. An English eyewitness reported that the Spaniards attacked "with exceeding fury"[15] and began to disable the English guns. The English camp, hearing the commotion, rushed to defend the trenches and a fierce battle ensued. Once again however the Spanish swung around and rushed the English defense works in the west and slaughtered the garrison. It was the bloodiest but most successful sortie of the siege. Thus far, the Spanish had fought magnificently. The Earl of Clanrickarde arrived with reinforcements just in the nick of time and rallied the English forces to stop this Spanish assault. The following day the English withdrew further south for greater safety.

O'Donnell, after his extraordinary march, turned west to Castlehaven. Here, thirty miles to the west, the remainder of the Spanish fleet under Pedro de Zubiaur, which had

---

[15]O'Faolain, *The Great O'Neil*, 326.

been separated from Aquila, landed an additional thousand men. The English fleet under Admiral Levison, which had sought to prevent the Spanish landing, succeeded in damaging some of the landing craft, but the Irish under the courageous chieftain O'Sullivan Bear and the Spanish assaulted the English fleet and inflicted significant damage. Levison was forced to withdraw and sailed back to Kinsale with a battered fleet and the loss of over 500 men.[16] O'Donnell, with foresight, strategically sent some of these veterans to hold the Irish forts at Castlehaven, Baltimore and Dunboy which defended three of the best havens in Munster. The remainder of the Spaniards under Don Alphonso Ocampo now joined O'Donnell's army. The tide of the war had turned again in favor of the Irish. When O'Donnell and the Spaniards arrived at Belgoley, the English forces began to be alarmed. O'Neill, who had been moving more slowly than O'Donnell, was now drawing close as well.[17] On November 9th, he had left Dungannon with Conor Maguire (the brother of Hugh), O'Reilly, the MacMahons and others. He had broken through Mountjoy's ring of forts and raided the Pale. He had hoped to draw the Lord Deputy away from the siege of the Spanish to aid the Palesmen lords and their lands. Mountjoy knew, however, that everything depended on the defeat of the Spanish and stubbornly refused to raise the siege or split his forces. He continuously

---

[16]See O'Sullivan Bear, whose father was present, for an account of this battle. (O'Sullivan Bear, *Ireland Under Elizabeth*, 143.) Cyril Falls and Jones also speak of this encounter.

[17]It had been reported that O'Neill would "better trust himself with twenty kearne naked in a wood than with five hundred Spaniards in a town." (Hayes-McCoy, *Irish Battles*, 155.)

pleaded for additional reinforcements and received them. With 4,000 men, O'Neill overran the province of Leinster, burning the crops of the colonists and seizing large numbers of cattle to sustain his army. The dazed colonists witnessed this nightmare which passed before their eyes and were left to their fate by Mountjoy. O'Donnell and O'Neill were joyfully greeted as heroes and liberators by the Catholics as they journeyed south. The Confederacy was once again strengthened and the Catholics were filled with high hopes.

On December 8th Mountjoy received reports that O'Neill's cavalry were only two miles away. By December 13th all supplies for the English camp had been cut off. Mountjoy sent dispatches to England entreating Cecil to create a diversion in the North to draw off O'Neill. The Lord Deputy hoped to receive supplies by sea but this could not be done. It has become one of the clichés of history, observed O'Faolain, that the weather always aided England against her invaders. At the siege of Kinsale, however, the wind blew to the east for weeks. With the Irish controlling the roads, the English were faced with starvation. O'Sullivan Bear, O'Driscoll and O'Connor of Kerry joined the Catholic army. The Irish Catholics combined their forces and began to besiege the besiegers. It was like a game of chess and a war of nerves. The English were in a precarious position and disease as well as hunger were ravaging their camp. All of Munster began to doubt that the English would be victorious. A current of nationalism strengthened the Catholics who daily grew more hopeful and confident. A number of Mountjoy's own men as well as his Anglo-Irish auxiliaries began to desert freely. Carew, in a foreboding dispatch describing the condition of the English camp, relates,

> There has never been a more miserable siege than this in which many die, many more are too sick to serve, and others run away from faintness of heart. . . . I do not think we have by Poll, able men in the camp to serve the Queen above 1,500.[18]

The English who sought to forage for their animals were attacked by the Confederates and soon were forced to remain within their camp. The Irish commanders hoped to starve the English into submission as they had done so many times during the course of the war. O'Neill besieged the English from the north as O'Donnell had done from the west. Aquila, however, grew impatient and not being familiar with this type of warfare sent urgent messages to the Irish pressing them and calling for them to attack the English without another day's delay. The Spaniards themselves were now running so low on food that they began eating rushes soaked in water. The Irish leaders held a council of war on the night of December 23 at Coolcarron. O'Donnell called for an attack pointing out that the Irish themselves could not maintain their position indefinitely "except under conditions of such hardship as would disspirit even the toughest of men."[19] Such was the price of maintaining a winter campaign in Ireland. O'Donnell told

---

[18]O'Faolain, *The Great O'Neil*, 328-9. Although disease and illness would have been high, especially during a winter campaign, this must have been an exaggeration.

[19]O'Faolain, *The Great O'Neil*, 332.

the chieftains that he was "oppressed at heart and ashamed to hear the complaint and distress of the Spaniards without relieving them."[20] The Spanish had fought well and a joint attack would achieve their goal. It appeared that Hugh O'Neill, true to his nature, vigorously opposed this plan of action and wished to continue the siege. The stakes were high. No war however, could ever be won by caution alone.[21] For the first time in the war the two friends were angrily at issue. Some writers allege that they even fought over who was to lead the initial assault.[22] A vote of the council was taken and the Irish, with their Spanish auxiliaries, sided with O'Donnell and the besieged Spaniards. O'Neill acquiesced and loyally prepared to do his duty.

The details of this historic battle are difficult to unravel. The Catholics forces decided that the Irish were to make a surprise attack upon the English, striking both Mountjoy's and the Earl of Thomond's camps, whereupon the Spanish would sally forth and second the blow. All battle accounts agree with this general plan. The two armies would then unite and decimate their common foe freeing Ireland forever from the yoke of tyranny, celebrating the birth of the Savior the following day.

---

[20]Bagwell, *Ireland Under the Tudors*, 3:407.

[21]Many modern historians with hindsight have blamed Red Hugh for this decision. The arguments in favor of a joint attack at this time were convincing. O'Neill was much more like Fabius Cunctator (the Delayer) of the Punic Wars. Red Hugh had been called by the English "the firebrand of all the rebels."

[22]Hayes-McCoy denies the authenticity of these stories. O'Cleary's sad account states that the dispute weakened the fighting spirit of the Irish.

The Irish left their camp to defend their faith and nation the following night on Christmas Eve in three divisions. Each division initially marched side by side and then moved to their positions. Captain Tyrrell commanded the van made up of men from Meath, Leinster, Munster and a small force of Spaniards led by Alonzo de Campo. The main body led by O'Neill was made up of men from Tyrone. O'Donnell commanded the rear with men from Tirconnaill and Connaught. Evidently Tyrrell was to unite with the sallying Spanish and attack Thomond's camp to the west while O'Neill and O'Donnell together were to attack Mountjoy. The night was dark without a moon and the heavens apocalyptically roared with peals of thunder, as brilliant flashes of lightening illuminated the sky. The weather could not have been worse. Due to the storm and darkness the Irish divisions were separated and the guides lost their way. They continued throughout the night to advance silently towards the English camp. The route taken that night by the Irish was approximately six miles. As the gray, wet morning approached the Catholics prepared for their surprise attack. At dawn, O'Neill, O'Sullivan and Ocampo ascended a small hill to view the English camp. They were shocked to see the English fully armed and prepared to fight, with the cavalry organized in troops under Sir Richard Wingfield assembled in front of their quarters. The brilliant plan for a surprise attack had backfired! Somehow the English had learned of the Catholic strategy. There are several traditions concerning how this knowledge had been obtained but it is not known with absolute certainty.[23] The Battle of Kinsale now began in the cold dawn of Christmas Eve day.

O'Neill withdrew his forces across a ford and began to reassemble his men. This delay and hesitation, though understandable, led to the Irish loss of initiative. O'Neill formed his men to fight in the Spanish style using the *tercios* formation. This formation was large and unwieldy and required the army to stand firm even if surrounded and fired upon and also to fill in the gaps continuously but not to yield the ground. The formation was made up of 3,000 men, mostly heavy infantry armed in part with pikes, muskets and calivers.[24] Although O'Neill had trained his men for this encounter, nothing could have been more awkward or foreign to the clansmen from Ulster. Throughout the war, the Irish forces had been highly mobile, flying columns, who had perfected the hit and run style of assault. This more traditional, fast moving type of tactic, which had been perfected by O'Neill and O'Donnell, was not used in this engagement. Wingfield, in the light of day, saw the confusion of the Irish forces and sensed O'Neill's surprise. He advanced against the Irish with 3,000 men. The sound of gunfire and battle reverberated in the cold morning. For some reason the Spanish in Kinsale had not yet sallied forth to attack the English camp as expected. Red Hugh also had

---

[23]O'Faolain, *The Great O'Neil*, 355. The English expected the attack daily and naturally would have been in a state of continual preparation. The story of Brian MacHugh Oge McMahon, an officer of O'Neill's, and the betrayal of the Irish plan for a bottle of aquavitae seems unworthy of belief. The story is related by Moryson and Carew.

[24]Hayes-McCoy gives an excellent description of the formation. (Hayes-McCoy, *Irish Battles*, 164.)

not yet arrived with his men. The first assault by the English was driven back by the Irish who held their ground. Wingfield sent out more musketeers who pressed the Irish van back on the center. On the side of the bog the ground was firm enough to support an all out attack by the English horse and foot. The Irish foot received the full brunt of the attack and held their position driving the enemy back. The battle had been in progress now for nearly an hour and still the Spaniards did not stir from the town. Archbishop Oviedo passionately appealed to Aquila to lead out his men but the Spanish commander thought the firing just a ruse by the English to draw him out.

The Lord Deputy, who had been observing the battle from a distance, saw the English retreat and called up all the remaining horse. O'Neill withdrew and crossed a ford in an effort to reform his cavalry. Some of the Irish thought he was retreating and began to waver. It was just at this moment that the English cavalry led by Mountjoy, Clanrickarde, Graeme and Captains Taaffe and Fleming, fell on the Irish center and broke their lines. The Irish foot, caught on the open plain, began to flee. O'Donnell, at that moment, belatedly arrived with his forces on the field of battle. His men were dismayed by the flight of the Irish foot. He tried to steady them but they grew increasingly alarmed. O'Donnell charged with his cavalry and drove back a wing of the English cavalry across the ford. While this was going on a portion of his horsemen either by "accident or treachery"[25] turned back their horses and ran into the ranks of O'Donnell's infantry. The infantry, being thrown into con-

---

[25]O'Sullivan Bear, *Ireland Under Elizabeth*, 147.

fusion, began to flee with the rest of the Irish. Enraged, Red Hugh sought to call them back and rally them. The Castle-haven Spanish under Ocampo stood firm and most were killed with the commander and a remnant were taken prisoner. What was left of the Irish center tenaciously held their position but all but a few score were decimated. The battle then became a general rout. The conflict lasted scarcely three hours during which time Aquila and his Spaniards, who had so vehemently urged the attack, did not even venture out of the town. O'Neill, O'Donnell and O'Sullivan tried to call back their men to the battle but in vain. The English horse pursued the Irish for two miles until they were forced to halt from sheer exhaustion. The fleeing Irish did not halt until they reached Innishannon eight miles to the northwest along the Bandon River. They were shocked, confused and shamed by their sudden collapse. According to English records, the Irish had left 1,200 dead on the field. On the English side fell Sir Richard Graeme and approximately 400 others.[26] All Irish prisoners taken were executed immediately. Neither side really knew what had happened. The Irish clearly had bungled their approach. The use of the unfamiliar *tercio* formation described by Hayes-McCoy in the open field clearly was a serious miscalculation. O'Donnell's late arrival prevented him from giving timely aid to O'Neill and Tyrell's forces. This is perhaps why O'Neill withdrew his men. The problem of Aquila's failure to sally forth is hotly debated. Fr. James Archer, S.J. and the papal legate, Fr. Ludovico Man-

---

[26]Captains Danvers and Godolphin were also wounded in the engagement. (Sullivan, *Story of Ireland*.)

soni, S.J.,[27] who were present in Kinsale during the siege and battle, strongly blamed Aquila. Fr. Archer, several days after the battle, stated emphatically: "If, even when the battle was on, he had done nothing more than display his troops before the enemy, victory would certainly have been ours." Due to Aquila's failure to sortie out the Irish "lost heart and are convinced that they are betrayed." Archbishop Matthew de Oviedo, who was also present, agreed claiming either treachery or incompetence. There can be no doubt that the Spanish commander had made a serious error in judgment. How culpable he was is unknown. The Irish themselves however, had enough to blame on their own poor performance. Carew immediately after the battle wrote that "No man can yield reasons for this miraculous victory."[28]

The battle had been brief yet was very important. It was a devastating blow to the prestige of the Catholic leaders in Ireland and the longed for dream of Spanish aid.

---

[27]Fr. Ludovico Mansoni had been sent by Clement VIII as papal legate *a latare* to Ireland after the pontiff had consulted with Cardinals Bellarmine and Mathei.

[28]O'Faolain, *The Great O'Neil*, 355.

nine

O'DONNELL in spain
THE WANING OF IRISH RESISTANCE

Oh, my Dark, Rosaleen
Do not sigh, do not weep!
The priests are on the ocean green
They march along the Deep.
There's wine .. from the royal Pope
Upon the ocean green;
And Spanish ale shall give you hope.
My Dark Rosaleen
My own Rosaleen
Shall glad your heart, shall give you hope,
Shall give you health, and help and hope,
My Dark Rosaleen!

All day long, in unrest,
To and fro, do I move,
The very soul within my breast
Is wasted for you, love!
The heart .. in my bosom faints
To think of you, my Queen,
My life of life, my saint of saints.
My Dark Rosaleen
My own Rosaleen
To hear your sweet and sad complaints
My life, my love, my saint of saints
My Dark Rosaleen!
   —(Red Hugh addresses Ireland,
      from the Irish, 16th century)[1]

---

[1]Garrity, *Irish Poetry*, 269-70.

hen the Irish forces re-assembled that night at Innis-hannon, their camp was filled with dejection, melancholy and division. O'Donnell, who was so angered by the disaster that he did not sleep for three days, urged the Irish to resume the fight. O'Neill also wished to maintain the war in Munster. The various Irish chiefs however decided to return north and defend their own lands against the English. O'Donnell, with the unanimous approval of the Catholic princes, resolved to go in person to seek further aid from the King of Spain. He delegated his authority to his brother Rory during his absence and "commanded O'Neill and Rory to be friendly to each other as they themselves both had been."[2] The two men both promised him that they would do as he had requested.

O'Cleary vividly describes the reaction of O'Donnell's men when they learned of their prince's decision:

> When this resolution became known to all publicly the great clapping of hands, and violent lamentations and loud wailing cries which arose throughout O'Donnell's camp the night before he went away were pitiful and saddening.[3]

The Catholic army broke up into its component parts and each clan struggled northwards under its own chief.

O'Sullivan gathered together his own Munstermen, as well as the Spaniards sent by Zubiaur, and united with Richard Tyrrell and William Burke in an effort to cut off the English supplies. He sent a letter to Aquila exhorting him not to lose courage and maintain the defense of the town.

---

[2]Four Masters, *Annals*, 6:2327.
[3]O'Cleary, *Life of Hugh Roe O'Donnell*, 321.

Three days after the battle on January 6th (new calendar) Red Hugh, accompanied by his confessor, his secretary and some military personnel, set sail from Castlehaven for Corunna in a Spanish ship. He arrived in Spain on January 14th and was received with the highest distinction by the Marquis of Caracena, who was the Governor of Galicia, and many other nobles. He resided with the Marquis "who evermore gave O'Donnell the right hand, which within his government, he would not have done to the greatest Duke of Spain."[4] The Marquis gave a gift of 1,000 ducats to O'Donnell who began his journey through Galicia on January 27th. Red Hugh was accompanied by Caracena and "many captains and gentlemen of quality."[5]

After spending the night at Santa Lucia, the party reached the famous shrine of Santiago de Compostella on the following day. Hugh O'Donnell was magnificently received by the bishops, citizens and religious who prepared accommodations for him at St. Martins. The Archbishop beseeched him to lodge at his house but Hugh politely declined. On the 20th of February the Archbishop said a Mass with pontifical solemnity at the Church of St. James for O'Donnell's intentions and Hugh received the Blessed Sacrament from his hands. After this the Archbishop royally entertained the Irish prince and provided a sumptuous feast for him in his house. O'Donnell witnessed several bull fights on the stately Alameda but longed with a passionate zeal to plead his country's cause before the King. Philip III, hearing of O'Donnell's arrival, wrote to Caracena concern-

---

[4]Murphy, introduction to *Life of Hugh Roe O'Donnell*, 145.
[5]*Ibid.*

ing his reception and the affairs of Ireland. Carew, in his *Pacata Hibernia,* describes Philip's letter as "one of the most gracious letters that ever the King directed."[6] O'Donnell ardently traversed the mountains of Galicia and Leon and did not halt until he reached Zamora where Philip was holding his court. He hoped to convince the King to send a full army rather than the detachment which had landed at Kinsale. O'Donnell was nobly received at court. When he came into the King's presence he knelt and made three requests:

> His first petition was that an army should be sent with him to Ireland with suitable engines and with the necessary arms. The second petition was that he would not place any of the nobles of Ireland, unless he was of his own nobility, in power or authority over him, or over his successor so long as they lived, if the King obtained power and sovereignty over Ireland. The third request was that he should not lessen or impair the rights of his ancestors as regards himself or whosoever should succeed him in any place where their power and sway existed long before that time in Ireland.[7]

Philip firmly promised all that he had sought and bade him to rise from his knees. The King lavishly entertained the Irish prince and treated him with great respect, "for his appearance, his fame, and his eloquence, the extent of his wrongs and his lordly language impressed him much."[8]

When Red Hugh left the court he returned to Corunna at the King's request and there awaited the preparations of the fleet. Each day he would gaze out to the great western

---

[6]Carew, *Pacata Hibernia*, 2: 115.
[7]O'Cleary, *Life of Hugh Roe O'Donnell*, 323.
[8]*Ibid.*, 325.

sea toward his beloved homeland. He was filled with joy when he thought upon the King's promised aid and sorrow when he contemplated the length of his stay and the plight of his friends who were waiting for him. The gracious reception he had received everywhere filled him with hope that his mission would be successful. On February 28th, O'Donnell wrote to Philip:

> Sire, —All we have learned about Ireland, we have informed the Council of State of. In this letter we merely beseech your Majesty with all humility that you would be pleased to look into this business, for if we know that you take it in hand we shall have more confidence in you than in all the world besides to advance the welfare of our poor country, and you will see the need of making haste. I pledge my word to your Royal Majesty that, once landed there, we shall make the whole country subject to your Majesty in a very short time; this I promise knowing the state of the country just now. May God preserve your Majesty for many years.
>
> From Corunna, February 28th, 1602.
> Hugh O'Donnell.[9]

Back in Ireland, when the Irish army had dispersed, Mountjoy and Carew prepared once again to attack Kinsale. When Aquila heard that the Catholic army had broken up, he asked Mountjoy for terms. A letter was sent from the King of Spain which commanded the General to maintain the town and informed him of the large reinforcements which were being prepared for O'Donnell in Spain. This letter was intercepted by the English however and never

---

[9]Murphy, introduction to *Life of Hugh Roe O'Donnell*, 145.

reached the Spanish Commander.[10] Aquila abandoned the Irish cause and agreed to surrender not only Kinsale but the Irish castles at Castlehaven, Baltimore and Dunboy which were garrisoned by Spanish soldiers.

Mountjoy treated the Spanish honorably and gave them the following terms of surrender:

> 1. That Don Juan should quit the places which he held in the kingdom, as well as the town of Kinsale as also those held by the soldiers under his command in Castlehaven, Baltimore and the Castle of Bearhaven, the Lord Deputy giving him safe transportation to Spain.
> 2. That the soldiers under his command should not bear arms against the Queen of England if supplies came from Spain till the said soldiers were unshipped in some port in Spain.
> 3. He might depart with all things he had—arms, munition, money, ensigns displayed, artillery and all other provisions of war, as well in Kinsale as in other places.[11]

The articles were agreed to on January 12th and the siege was lifted on the 19th. Donal O'Sullivan and the Catholic Confederates of Munster were enraged when they learned of Aquila's capitulation. O'Sullivan's own castle of Dunboy in Bearhaven had been surrendered without his consent. Before the Spanish defenders could surrender the castle however, O'Sullivan with 1,000 men surprised the Spanish garrison and seized the castle. He strengthened the fortress' defenses and placed in it an Irish garrison under the command of Richard MacGeoghegan. O'Sullivan sent

---

[10]Bagwell, *Ireland Under the Tudors*, 3:412.
[11]Murphy, introduction to *Life of Hugh Roe O'Donnell*, 143.

letters to Philip III protesting the actions of Aquila and asking for more troops. When Aquila was informed that the castle had been lost to the Irish he offered to capture it for the English by force of arms. The Lord Deputy, whose only anxiety was to get him quietly out of the country, declined the offer and urged his immediate departure. After the siege of Kinsale had been lifted, Mountjoy and Don Juan dined together and became good friends. The General lived familiarly with Carew in Cork for sometime. Before his departure he presented the Governor with a book on military fortifications which the Englishman gratefully received. Aquila and the Spanish forces set sail from Kinsale on April 26th and returned to Spain. Upon his arrival the King promptly ordered his arrest. The disgraced Spanish general died soon after his imprisonment. When Queen Elizabeth heard of her army's victory and the subsequent departure of the Spanish she was quite pleased. She thought that the Spanish had escaped too easily but sent her congratulations to the Lord Deputy.

While Mountjoy had been occupied with the surrender and departure of the Spanish in Kinsale, O'Neill fought his way north to Tyrone and carried on a successful defensive war against the English garrisons. The Irish, despite Kinsale, were still hopeful. They knew that Red Hugh would work unceasingly to bring a Spanish Army with Irish auxiliaries back to Ireland. This time the army would land in the north, probably sailing into Lough Swilly in Donegal, there to unite with O'Neill's forces and sweep the English out of Ireland. Rory O'Donnell, while passing by Lough Sewdy in Meath, was foolishly attacked by some English townsmen and an Anglo-Irish garrison which desired to prove their loyalty. The townsmen were armed with staves, swords and spears but quickly fled at the first onset of Rory's cavalry. The garrison tried to rally the fugitives but were themselves surrounded by the Catholic cavalry and slaughtered. Rory eventually reached Tirconnaill but suffered for several months from dysentery. Docwra and the English had strengthened their hold on the country during the Catholic army's absence. The royalists now made expeditions by land and sea from Donegal without opposition. They now besieged and battered with cannon O'Donnell's stronghold, the castle at Ballyshannon. Tuathal O'Gallagher defended the castle with 56 Irish and 4 Spaniards. The garrison made a brave and protracted defense of the walls until these were eventually shattered by the cannon. The garrison, now realizing their situation to be hopeless, withdrew during the night. The English finally captured their long-desired strategic objective the following day and slaughtered those Irish in the area who had assisted the garrison. Sir Oliver Lambert, who was the English Governor of Connaught, along with Clanrickarde and Sir Arthur Savage, set out in August with an army to establish a garrison at Sligo. Rory O'Donnell, who had now fully recovered from his illness, established his headquarters at Roscommon. He was supported by O'Conor of Sligo who aided him in protecting the large herds of cattle which had been driven north from Munster. Lambert and the English followed the same path which had been taken by Clifford and his army in 1599. The English once more marched from Boyle Abbey and entered the Curlew Mountains. History again repeated itself as Rory O'Donnell and O'Conor, with an army which included 400 musketeers, routed the English governor and his army on the great bog at the summit of the mountain pass. All other English efforts to reach Sligo by land failed. Eventually seven companies of English soldiers were gathered under the command of Sir Leonard Guest and taken by ship to Sligo. This assault by sea resulted in the town being taken by surprise and quickly fortified by the English. Rory immediately ordered all the crops near the city to be cut down. The English garrison sallied out of the town to prevent this and Rory attacked to defend his reapers. A sharp battle followed in which the English were driven back in the city with a loss of 300 men.[12]

Hugh O'Neill and Rory O'Donnell continued to fight an exhausting defensive war. Their hopes were kept alive with daily rumors that Red Hugh would soon land in the northwest with an army of 10,000 Spaniards. Both men knew full well that Hugh O'Donnell would continue to work himself to the bone in Spain to avenge the loss at Kinsale and succor his comrades in arms.

Red Hugh continued to wait impatiently for the dilatory Spanish to prepare the fleet. From Corunna he would often gaze at the Western Sea with "anguish of heart and sickness of mind when he reflected on the state in which the Irish were, without aid or help, while waiting for him."[13] On April 15th he wrote another and still more pressing letter to the King:

---

[12]O'Sullivan Bear, *Ireland Under Elizabeth*, 146.

[13]O'Cleary, *Life of Hugh Roe O'Donnell*, 325.

Sire, —I, faithful, humble and favoured servant of your Majesty, should commit a great crime if I doubted about the accomplishment of what, for such well-founded reasons, worthy of Christianity and of your Majesty, you have been pleased to offer me, and assure me of, it being in every way so conformable to the Catholic sentiments of your Majesty. But having such experience in the matters I mention, that no other, from acquaintance with them, can judge better of them, and knowing that the whole of the success of what I desire arises from succour being sent immediately, and seeing time pass by so quick, and the cruel knife coming so near each day to the throats of this persecuted people, who put their hopes in the mercy of God and in the clemency of your Majesty, I cannot refrain from renewing my sad entreaties. This resolution I have taken in consequence of what I hear today (the 15th of April) will happen in Ireland, and I say it with all the earnestness and zeal which I owe to God and to your Majesty, that if within a month from this day there do not land on the northern coast of that kingdom 2,000 soldiers, or at least 1,500, with arms, provisions, and money to enable us to raise and bring together 5,000 or 6,000 of the inhabitants and revive the war, so as to expel the enemy from the Earl O'Neill's territory and from mine and to make them abandon that quarter, even though in the whole of June a great fleet with aid should reach there, I doubt very much whether they will reach in time, or whether they will find anything but the blood and ashes of that multitude of faithful men.

Most humbly do I beg of your Majesty to allow me to set off with 2,000 soldiers, a thing that can be done very well this month, and will be most useful until more forces can go; and if any one asserts the contrary, I ask your Majesty to allow me to go in all haste to the Court, that I may, in presence of the Council, give good reasons for my assertion. If this force is not sent I take it as certain that the whole of the north will fall away, and all the rest will soon follow, and all will come under the intolerable yoke of the heretics. The States

of your Majesty will suffer thereby. I say this in God's presence. But I will submit myself in all things to your Majesty's will, putting my hope in God and in your Majesty.
May God preserve your Majesty for many years.
Hugh O'Donnell.
From Corunna, April 15th, 1602.[14]

In spite of the exasperating delays, O'Donnell was hopeful and sought to boost the Irish morale. On May 14th he wrote from Corunna to O'Connor Kerry: "Of one thing you can assure yourself, the King will not fail to gain Ireland, though it cost him the greater part of Spain."[15]

O'Donnell's presence in Spain greatly disturbed the English government. Their spies in Spain reported that O'Donnell was held in high estimation throughout the country.

In Munster, after the Spaniards had departed from Kinsale, Mountjoy sent Carew to capture Dunboy Castle which had been garrisoned by O'Sullivan. Carew, after recovering from an illness, finally marched from Cork with 3,000 men and sent his artillery and supplies by sea.[16] At Bantry he was joined by Sir Charles Wilmont with an additional 1,000 men. In June the entire army was conveyed by sea to Great Beare Island where they encamped near the castle. Tyrell fought to try to prevent the landing but was wounded in

---

[14]Murphy, introduction to *Life of Hugh Roe O'Donnell*, 146.

[15]*Ibid.*, 147. The full text may be found in Carew's *Pacata Hibernia* Vol. 2 pages 246-7.

[16]While Carew was recovering, the Earl of Thomond was sent with 1,250 men to suppress "the rebels and reconoitre Dunboy Castle." Although he achieved partial success, he was unable to reach Dunboy as the only pass available was ably defended by Tyrell. Thomond left a garrison on Whiddy Island in Bantry Bay and returned to Cork.

the encounter and forced to withdraw. Despite the overwhelming numbers, the powerful guns and Carew's promises, Richard MacGeoghegan, who had been placed in command by O'Sullivan, firmly resolved to defend the castle with 143 men and three cannon. The Irish defenders had taken courage with the arrival of a Spanish ship at Kilmakilloge in Kenmare Bay. The vessel carried L12,000, ammunition and letters urging the Irish chiefs to remain firm. Most importantly the ship brought Owen MacEgan, who was the Bishop designate of Ross and Papal Nuncio. He possessed ecclesiastical authority over Munster. The nuncio told the defenders of Dunboy of the great Spanish army which would soon come to their relief.[17] The garrison, due to the natural strength of the castle felt they could hold out for at least two or three months. Against overwhelming odds 143 men planned to fight and hold off the disciplined attack of an army of 4,000. The English batteries were well supplied with ammunition and opened up on the castle on June 6th. The battle raged continuously. By the 17th the castle walls had been so severely shattered that MacGeoghegan sent an offer to surrender to Carew if the Irish were allowed to march out with arms. The English governor responded by hanging the messenger and issuing orders for the final assault. The garrison desperately resisted the storming party with undaunted courage. Many were killed on both sides as the defenders were driven from turret to turret by the sheer force of numbers. The Irish retreated to the eastern

---

[17]MacEgan stayed with the MacCarthys in Carbery. He was eventually killed on the field of battle by an English force under Captain Taafe on January 5, 1603, while ministering to the wounded and dying. His tragic death led to the final submission of the MacCarthys.

wing of the castle which had not yet been assaulted. This wing could only be reached by a narrow passage way in which firearms could not be used. For an hour and a half a savage hand-to-hand struggle was continued as the defenders hurled down stones and bullets which wounded and killed many of the assailants. While this was going on the English cleared away a large pile of rubble and entered the castle from the rear. The defenders were now pressed on both sides. Forty of them sallied out of the castle and headed for the sea in an effort to swim to safety. All but eight were killed before they reached the water. The remainder were killed by the English who patrolled the area in their boats. Throughout the long summer day and into the night the bitter battle continued. The castle was now a heap of ruins and the English eventually won all the upper levels of the castle. MacGeoghegan had been severely wounded and the numbers of the garrison had been greatly reduced. When the defenders had been driven down into the cellars, Carew left a strong guard at the entrance and withdrew with his men so that they might rest that night. On the following morning the Irish prepared to fight to the bitter end with the exception of 23 who put down their weapons and surrendered. Carew began to bombard the cellar with his cannon and the ceiling collapsed on the defenders. At last the remaining men forced the acting commander, Taylor, to surrender. As a party of English entered to seize the captives, MacGeoghegan grabbed a candle from Taylor's hand and with his remaining strength staggered toward the barrels of gunpowder which were in the corner. One of Carew's officers grabbed him however and the others stabbed him with their swords. Fifty-eight of those who surrendered were hanged immediately.[18] Taylor and fourteen others were saved to see if they could be induced to give valuable information or renounce their faith. These courageous men stoutly refused and were executed without mercy. One of the prisoners, a Jesuit named Dominic Collins, was offered "ecclesiastical dignities"[19] if he would apostatize. He remained true to his faith and was taken to his home town (Youghal) where he was cruelly tortured and executed. O'Sullivan Bear recorded October 31st as the date of his martyrdom.[20]

The defense of Dunboy had been a glorious and magnificent struggle against impossible odds. Carew, in his own account of the siege, concludes by saying of the 143 defenders of Dunboy "no one man escaped but were either slaine, executed, or buried in the ruins; and so obstinate and resolved a defense had not been seen within this kingdom."[21]

---

[18]O'Sullivan Bear claims they had been promised clemency and that several women were also hung.

[19]O'Sullivan Bear, *Ireland Under Elizabeth*, 156.

[20]O'Sullivan relates that Fr. Collins (O'Colan) "was dragged at the tails of horses, hanged with a halter, and his breast being cut open with sharp knives." (O'Sullivan Bear, *Ireland Under Elizabeth*, 156.)

[21]Carew, *Pacata Hibernia*, 2:204. Joyce, *History of Ireland*, 265. The heroic defense of the Dunboy castle was not forgotten in Ireland and inspired the following verse:

Long, long in the hearts of the free
Live the warriors who died in the lonely Dunbui -
Down time's silent river their fair names shall go,
A light to over race the long coming day;
Till the billows of time shall be checked in their flow.

(A.M. Nolan, *A History of Ireland* [Chicago: J.S. Hyland & Co. 1928], 156.)

The fall of Dunboy was important for it signaled the collapse of the war in the south. Carew, having received an additional 1,000 fresh reinforcements from England, sought to punish the MacCarthys of Carbry and therefore sent a strong force under Sir Charles Wilmont who devastated Kerry. The MacCarthy's were forced to flee to Limerick. The whole region south of Cork was also wasted. This devastation was designed to prevent O'Sullivan and Tyrrell from continuing the conflict. If the Spanish were to return, Carew made sure there would be nothing for them in all of Kerry. He also had strong garrisons placed in Kinsale, Bantry and Baltimore. Doubting the loyalty of Cormac MacCarthy, he cast him into prison, seized his castles at Blarney and Macroom thereby capturing and imprisoning his wife and children.[22] In Spain, Red Hugh's impatient spirit was sorely tried by ongoing Spanish vacillation. He asked his friends in Ireland to let him know the whole truth but to keep all bad news from the Spanish for fear that they might abandon the project. This was virtually impossible, however, and the arrival in Spain of the Jesuit, Fr. Archer, with a number of Irish fugitives after the fall of Dunboy must have caused the King to falter. Despite the promises made to him, time continued to pass without any sign of immediate aid being sent to Ireland.

It was anguish of heart and sickness of mind to him that the Irish should remain so long without being aided or relieved by him, and deeming it too long that the army which

---

[22]Cormac eventually escaped and entered into communications with Tyrrell but fearing the power of the English did not openly join the Catholic cause fearing the loss of his lands and family.

had been promised to him did not come together to one place he prepared to go before the King to know what it was that caused the delay in raising the army which he had promised.[23]

On June 10th Caracena wrote to the King demanding of him the favor of an audience with O'Donnell in which he could set before him the true state of affairs in Ireland and the tremendous need for aid:

> Sire, —The Earl O'Donnell is in a state of great affliction, thinking of the straits to which the Catholics of Ireland are reduced and particularly the Earl O'Neill; yet he holds his own condition to be worse; since they can but lose their lives, while he will forfeit his honour to the good name he acquired by continuing the war for so many years, being now absent from his country. This he supports by many reasons and proofs. In fine, what he desires now is that your Majesty would immediately give orders for his departure to that kingdom in whatever way your Majesty may be pleased, though he has no doubt whatever but that your Majesty means to help them, and he is equally sure that the delay has been the cause of his enemy. He says what he feels most is that your Majesty does not give him an audience; in twelve days he will go by the post to where your Majesty may be in case you are pleased to allow him, and all the more readily because he thinks the success of his expedition depends on this interview. And it seems to me that the matter is so very urgent and important that it is my duty to write to your Majesty. Your Majesty in all this will command whatever best suits your service; which I will always carry out as I am obliged. May God watch over your Catholic Majesty.[24]

---

[23]Four Master, *Annals*, 6:2295.

[24]Murphy, introduction to *Life of Hugh Roe O'Donnell*, 148.

A week later O'Donnell wrote to the King:

> Sire, —Several times I have written to your Majesty
> what I thought likely to advance the service of your Majesty
> and the safety of the persecuted Catholics of the poor king-
> dom of Ireland. To these letters I have received no answer
> whatever; and I am weary of seeing how I am wasting my
> time here, and I fear that things are going on badly at home.
> It concerns the interests of your Majesty to learn exactly the
> fallen state of the Catholics of Ireland. I beseech your Maj-
> esty to deign to send me permission to proceed to the Court
> for the purpose; and not to trouble you further, I end by ask-
> ing God to prosper and preserve your Majesty in all your
> undertakings, as we your favoured vassals need and desire.
> From Corunna, 20th of June, 1602.
> Hugh O'Donnell.[25]

O'Donnell was finally granted an audience with the
King and immediately set off on August 9th. The King was
holding his Court at Valladolid where the royal family had
usually resided until Philip II built the Escorial. On his
journey the fiery young prince stopped at the royal castle of
Simancas where he suddenly and mysteriously took ill. For
sixteen days, Hugh valiantly struggled against this strange
illness which had seized hold of him. By his bedside to
console him in that foreign land were Father Flaithri
O'Mulchonry and Father Maurice Ultach, a poor friar of the
Order of St. Francis from Donegal Monastery. Despite his
courageous struggle, his time had come.

> At last he died at the end of that time, the tenth day of Sep-
> tember exactly, lamenting his faults and transgressions, after
> rigid penance for his sins and iniquities, having made his

---

[25]*Ibid.*

confession without reserve to his spiritual confessor, and receiving the Body and Blood of Christ, and being duly anointed by the hands of his confessor and his ecclesiastical elders, who were in his company always up to that time.[26]

O'Cleary gives the following description of O'Donnell's funeral and burial in Spain:

> His body was then taken to Valladolid to the King's Court, in a four-wheeled hearse, with great numbers of state officers, of the Council, and of the royal guard all round it, with blazing torches and bright flambeaux of beautiful waxlights blazing all around on each side of it. He was buried after that in the chapter of the monastery of St. Francis with great honour and respect and in the most solemn manner any Gael ever before had been interred. Masses, and many hymns, chants, and sweet canticles were offered for the welfare of his soul, and his requiem was celebrated as was fitting.[27]

---

[26]O'Cleary, *Life of Hugh Roe O'Donnell*, 325. He further mentions O'Mooney who knew Red Hugh and described him as "being of middle height, ruddy of comely face, and beautiful to behold. His voice was like the music of a silver trumpet. His morals were unimpeachable." The Four Masters relate that "the look of amiability on his countenance, captivated everyone who beheld him," and emphasize, "his great powers of command."

[27]O'Cleary, *Life of Hugh Roe O'Donnell*, 235-7. John Mitchel comments, "the stately city of Valladolid holds the bones of as noble a chief and as stout a warrior as ever bore the wand of chieftancy, or led a clan to battle." (Mitchel, *Life and Times of Hugh O'Neill*, 215.) Peter Lombard, the Primate of Armagh, wrote at a later date to Rory O'Donnell concerning his elder brother Red Hugh: "By your honorable brother a worthy enterprise was begun for the maintaining and restoring of the Catholic religion, who, being received to eternal glory, where his prayers are of greater efficacy with the Lord of heaven than his forces were upon the earth . . . " (Meehan, *The Fate and Fortune*, 186-7)

For almost 300 years it had been assumed that his death was from natural causes. It has now been discovered in an English State paper with almost absolute certainty that O'Donnell was poisoned by an English agent named William Blake, who had been sent by Carew with Mountjoy's approval.[28]

Red Hugh was only twenty-eight when he died. He was truly one of the brightest and noblest characters in any history. His captivity and escape as a boy, his brilliance as a commander, his numerous victories, his unfaltering opposition to the English invaders, his loyalty to O'Neill, his sincere piety, devotion to the Catholic Faith, and the entire romance of his story has attracted Irish hearts to him as a symbol for centuries. Seamus MacManus gives the following evaluation of his character:

> His voice was sweet and musical. He loved justice and was faithful to his promises. He showed courage and resource in the presence of difficulties; was quick to seize opportunities; maintained a rigid discipline in his army; was patient in hardships; courteous and affable in manner; absolutely open and sincere. He never married; his private life was without stain. One who knew him said "he was a great despiser of the world." Noble, generous, with tireless activity, daring,

---

[28]Murphy, introduction to *Life of Hugh Roe O'Donnell*, 149. Blake, a merchant from Galway, had approached Carew in Cork in the month of May and had offered to poison Red Hugh. Carew approved and hoped, "God would give him strength and perseverence". (D'Alton, *History of Ireland*, 3:188.) A full copy of Carew's letter to Mountjoy concerning the assassin is found in Murphy, *Historical Introduction*, CXIIX-CL and in the *Carew Papers* Vol. 4, pages 241, and 350-351. According to Carew, Red Hugh was originally suspicious of Blake, who sailed out of Cork, but eventually was admitted into the Prince's company.

with his handsome person, his splendid spirit as one of the last of Ireland's princes his name has been a star in the nation's memory.[29]

On October 15th Carew received full confirmation of O'Donnell's death and wrote to Mountjoy expressing his satisfaction and of the death's political effects in Ireland and abroad.

> O'Donnell is certainly dead. The report is both brought and sent to me from Lisbon by merchants from this town, which I employed into Spain. I know that they dare not deliver untruths to me. The death of this traitor will much advance the Queen's service in Ireland, for the other Irish which live in Spain are not of the estimation which O'Donnell was of.[30]

Few intelligence reports were more acceptable to Elizabeth and the English government than those of O'Donnell's death. Gilbert, the Earl of Shewsbury, writes concerning it to Carew on October 27, 1602:

> The death of O'Donnell is very welcome news to us here, and no less cause to you there. There goeth withal a report here that a kind of snake or serpent was found within him. It may be that he was troubled with worms, as many children and men be; but if he was not tormented with the worm of conscience whilst he lived for his hateful treasons and other villanies against his natural sovereign, which

---

[29]MacManus, *Story of the Irish Race*, 393-4. O'Donovan in *Annals of the Four Masters* Vol. 6, page 2385, writes, "History does not present a more chivalrous and devoted Irishman than Hugh Roe proved himself to be during his short and eventful career."

[30]Murphy, introduction to *Life of Hugh Roe O'Donnell*, 152. See Cyril Falls' *Elizabeth's Irish Wars*, pages 316 and 339, for an English assessment of Red Hugh.

made him no doubt carry a black soul away with him, it were to be wondered at.[31]

The remnant Catholic forces left in Munster divided themselves into three groups. O'Sullivan held on in the Beare peninsula with about 700 fighting men. The McCarthys of Carbry held on fighting a guerrilla type of war with 400 men and Tyrrell traveled to desolate Kerry with a force of 500.

Continuously harassed by the English, Donal O'Sullivan, who had held out for six months against overwhelming forces, realized he could not maintain himself in Munster and resolved to march north leaving his beloved Kerry to join O'Neill since the hope of immediate Spanish aid had dimmed. He resolved to fight his way north as quickly as possible, nobly taking with him 400 men and 600 women and children. Every step of the way he was attacked by both English and Irish hoping to demonstrate their loyalty to the crown. The heroic chief and clansmen fought brilliantly with a desperate courage, traveling 20-30 miles a day. Upon arriving on the banks of the mighty Shannon River where it enters Lough Oerg, he was compelled to kill his horses using their skin to hurriedly construct currachs. At Aughrim they routed an English force under Lord Clanrickarde's brother and Captain Henry Malby who was killed along with several other officers. All this took place during the bitter cold of January with icy winds and heavy snow. Many of these refugees died on the journey or dropped behind and were assisted by friendly

---

[31]Brewer, *Carew Papers*, 4:370.

Irish. Of the 1,000 who left Glengarriff at the beginning of this noble yet sad saga, which lasted two weeks, only 35 men, 16 servants and one woman were welcomed into the safe shelter of O'Rourke's castle at Dromhair in Leitrim in the distant north although other stragglers later made their lonely way to safety.[32] O'Sullivan eventually joined O'Neill in Glenconkeine in March of 1603.

Hugh O'Neill and Rory O'Donnell continued to fight a defensive war but their resources had been entirely exhausted. When news reached them of Hugh O'Donnell's death in Spain their resolve was broken and they knew their cause to be hopeless. Red Hugh had been the heart and soul of the Catholic cause. Mountjoy offered favorable terms to Rory who called his advisors to deliberate with him in council. Rory was in desperate straits being attacked from Ballyshannon and Sligo. He called together his counselors and comrades and after a fierce debate, O'Donnell and O'Connor both reluctantly made peace with the Lord Deputy at Athlone in the bleakness of December. The Lord Deputy treated Rory with great honor. This effectively ended the war in Tirconnaill. O'Neill however continued to hold out in the Ulster wilderness hoping against hope that Spain would still send the promised aid. The once powerful prince was now little more than a guerrilla leader. Cormac Art O'Neill and MacMahon continued faithful to

---

[32]MacManus, remarking on this extraordinary march from Kerry to Leitrim states, "It has all the elements of the great Tragedies; indomitable souled men; defiance of fate; encounters with foes; encounters with elements, with storms, frost and snow; men with dying bodies and unquenchable spirit, battling, marching, praying." (MacManus *Story of the Irish Race*, 394.)

O'Neill and remained with him. So great was O'Neill's reputation that the Lord Deputy still feared him. Mountjoy, joined by Docwra at Lifford and Sir Arthur Chichester from Carrickfergus, marched into the heart of Tyrone with 8,000 men and shattered into a million pieces the ancient throne chair at Tullaghoe upon which the O'Neills had been inaugurated for centuries. The 8,000 men, in the autumn of 1602, covered the fertile fields along Bann and the Roe destroying all the grain with fire where it was possible or using the *praca*, a special type of harrow, which tore up the grain by its roots. The horror of the Munster famine was now unleashed with an all out war on the civilian population in Ulster. All the crops in the territory were trampled by horsemen and cut down with swords by the infantry. For the odious results of Mountjoy's cruel policy of ending the war through starvation of the entire people we have his own horrifying words:

> We have seen no one man in all Tyrone of late but dead carcasses merely hunger starved, of which we found divers as we passed. Between Tullaghoe and Toome (17 miles) there lay unburied 1,000 dead, and since our first drawing this year to Blackwater there were about 3,000 starved in Tyrone.[33]

Mountjoy still was not satisfied and continued his work: "Tomorrow by the grace of God I am going into the field as near as I can to utterly waste the county Tyrone."[34] He then gives several cadaverous details showing, if showing was

---

[33]Joyce, *History of Ireland*, 273-4.
[34]*Ibid.*, 274.

necessary, that women, children and peaceable poor people suffered as did the rebels:

> And no spectacle was more frequent in the ditches of the towns than to see multitudes of these poor people dead with their mouths all coloured green by eating nettles, docks and all things they could rend up above ground.[35]

O'Neill continued to retire with his few men into the impenetrable bogs and forests. He could no longer take active measures against the English but was thoroughly occupied with preserving himself and his men from utter destruction. Nevertheless O'Neill continued to show his military genius in these defensive operations. He refused to submit and even in his fallen state was dreaded by the English government which was still apprehensive of another Spanish armada. Many of his allies were forced to make peace due to the strength and numbers of the English forces, in a desperate attempt to save their people and land. Heavily garrisoned forts were established such as Fort Mountjoy, in order to encircle and hem him in. O'Neill made his way into Fermanagh and was joined by Brian MacArt and his own brother, Cormac. They traveled from the shores of Lough Erne to Glenconkeine, a densely wooded area to the northwest of Lough Neagh. Against now overwhelming odds, he brilliantly continued to hold out in hope of Elizabeth's death or additional Spanish aid. Despite enticing offers from Mountjoy, no one could be

---

[35] *Ibid*. Horror stories abound in Moryson and Carew's accounts including tales of three small children found alone in a small cottage. Their mother had starved to death and these terrified little children were living on the flesh of their dead mother.

found who would betray Hugh O'Neill. News of Tyrone's plight reached the continent and Henry IV of France, recalling O'Neill's greatness and fearing the power of Spain, begged Elizabeth to forgive the man who had shamed her and cost so much in honor and gold, bankrupting the Elizabethan state.

The Queen herself was now dying. On January 31st, a cold rainy day, Elizabeth was moved from Westminister to Richmond. Pressured by Robert Cecil and Mountjoy, she allowed the Lord Deputy to work terms with "the archtraitor" in February of 1603. As historian Theodore Maynard observed, "The deathbed of Elizabeth is one of the most dreadful in history."[36] She who had outlived so many of her foreign rivals, advisors and suitors would not live to see the final end of the war in Ireland. Her days were now literally numbered. The death of her beloved Essex, the intrigues of James in Scotland, the threat of Spain and the victories of the Irish Catholics preyed upon her spirits. O'Neill was seldom out of her mind and she constantly asked her godson, Harrington, who had served in Ireland, concerning him. The French ambassador to the Queen thought that the Irish war was one of the chief causes which totally destroyed her peace of mind. Her temper grew worse and became more abrupt with each passing day. She took little nourishment other than "manchet and a succory pottage."[37] The Queen constantly kept a sword by her and when a nerve storm came upon her "she would snatch it up, stamp

---

[36]Theodore Maynard, *Queen Elizabeth* (Milwaukee: The Bruce Publishing Co., 1954), 276.

[37]Strachey, *Elizabeth and Essex*, 276-7.

savagely to and fro and thrust it in fury into the tapestry."[38]
For days at a time the aged monarch sat silently possessed
of a strange melancholy which was occasionally broken by
savage outbursts and lamentations. In an effort to bring a
successful conclusion to the war which was still costing her
thousands of pounds, the Queen, having ordered Mountjoy
to open negotiations with Tyrone, longed to hear of his surrender. The Queen's final days are vividly described by
Lyntton Strachey:

> There were no very definite symptoms, besides the
> growing physical weakness and the profound depression of
> mind. She would allow no doctors to come near her; she ate
> and drank very little, lying for hours in a low chair. At last it
> was seen that some strange crisis was approaching. She
> struggled to rise, and failing, summoned her attendants to
> pull her to her feet. She stood. Refusing further help she re-
> mained immovable, while those around her watched in
> awe-stricken silence. Too weak to walk, she still had
> strength to stand; if she returned to her chair, she knew that
> she would never rise from it; she continued to stand, then;
> had it not always been her favorite posture? She was fight-
> ing Death and fighting with terrific tenacity. The appaling
> combat lasted for fifteen hours. Then she yielded—though
> she still declared that she would not go to bed. She sank on
> the cushions spread out to receive her; and there she lay for
> four days and nights, speechless, with her finger in her
> mouth. Meanwhile an atmosphere of hysterical nightmare
> had descended on the Court.[39]

---

[38]*Ibid.*, 277. She frequently spoke tormentedly of O'Neill especially
to her cousin Sir John Harrington.

[39]*Ibid.*, 283-4.

Many of the great men of the kingdom implored her to obey the physicians and let herself be taken to bed. Finally Cecil boldly said, "Your Majesty, to content the people you must go to bed." "Little man, little man," she weakly replied, "the word must is not used to princes."[40] Eventually she was moved to her bed and the Protestant Archbishop of Canterbury, Whitgift, (whom Elizabeth had called her "little black husband") was called in to pray fervently for the Queen's soul.[41] On the 24th of March, in the chilly dark hours of the early morning, Elizabeth died.

Mountjoy had been instructed to "sound" the defeated, but unsubdued and still dangerous O'Neill, as to terms of peace. Negotiations were opened and Sir William Godolphin and Sir Garrett More (a close friend of O'Neill) were sent as commissioners to arrange the terms. They reached O'Neill in early March at his retreat near Lough Neagh. O'Neill promised to meet Mountjoy at Melifont Abbey.[42]

---

[40]*Ibid.*, 285. About the same she said to Lady Scrope, her maid of honor, who tried to convince the Queen to go to her bed, "I saw one night my own body, exceedingly lean and fearful, in a light of fire. Do you see sights in the night?" When her commander of the navy, Admiral Lord Howard, attempted a similar remonstrance she replied, "If you were in the habit of seeing such things, such things in your bed as I do in mine, you would not persuade me to go there. I am tired, I am tired, and the case is not altered with me." (Maynard, *Queen Elizabeth*, 278.)

[41]When Whitgift first entered the Queen's presence "in order to bring the consolations of religion" he was driven out. (Maynard, *Queen Elizabeth*, 278.) According to William Thomas Walsh, she referred to Whitgift at this time as "only a hedge-priest", i.e. a sham priest. (Walsh, *Philip II*, 709-10.)

[42]The ancient monastery, at this time in the hands of a layman, Sir Garret Moore, was the first Cistercian monastery in Ireland established by St. Malachy of Armagh with monks sent with him from

These negotiations were hurried on the deputy's part by private information which he had of the Queen's death; and fearing that O'Neill's view might be altered by that circumstance, he immediately desired the commissioners to close the agreement and invite O'Neill under safe conduct to Drogheda to have it ratified without delay.[43]

On the 30th of March, 1603, Hugh O'Neill and Lord Mountjoy met at Melifont Abbey. Hugh undertook the necessary forms and declarations of submission and the articles of peace were ratified by both sides. The very favorable conditions which were conceded to O'Neill show the high estimation held by the English government of their victory over him and their respect of his still formidable influence. He was given total amnesty for the past; he was to be restored in blood, despite his attainder and outlawry; he was to be reinstated in his dignity as the Earl of Tyrone; he and his people were to enjoy full and free exercise of their religion; and new "letters patent" were to be issued re-granting to him, Rory O'Donnell and others, virtually all the land occupied by their respective clans. For his part Hugh was to renounce the title of "The O'Neill" and accept

---

France by St. Bernard through the generosity of O'Carroll, King of Oriel, "in honor of God and for the welfare of his soul *pro remedio animae suae.*" The ruins of this venerable monastery are still quite impressive. For five centuries it had been served by the Cistercians till it was brutally suppressed and plundered by order of Henry VIII and given to the father of Sir Garret. Ironically, Devorgilla, who had been instrumental in bringing the English into Ireland as MacMurrough's paramour, had spent her final days in repentance in the precincts of this monastery which she richly endowed and in which she was interred.

[43]Sullivan, *Story of Ireland*, 325.

the English title of "Earl"; he was to allow English sheriffs and law to enter his territories; and lastly he was to disavow all foreign alliances. O'Neill, although he did not know it for several days, had surrendered his sword to his friend who was now James I of England, not to Elizabeth. Although several other Irish chieftains continued to carry on a desultory war, with the surrender of O'Neill it may be said that the Nine Years War which had exhausted both England and Ireland had come to a fizzling conclusion.

epilogue

That glory is short lived which is taken and given by men
The glory of this world is always accompanied by sorrow
The glory of good men is in their own consciences,
not in the mouths of men
The joy of the just is from God and in God they rejoice
in the truth.—Thomas a Kempis

T he Irish greatly rejoiced when James I ascended the throne of England. The people thought him to be a Catholic at heart. The repugnant Tudor dynasty had ended and they beheld one they believed to be a Gaelic prince wearing the crown of England. *Hibernia* and *Caledonia* had been on friendly terms for centuries. James himself had been friendly to O'Neill and the Confederate chieftains. In May of 1603, Hugh O'Neill, Rory O'Donnell and Lord Mountjoy visited London to make their submission to the new King. They set sail from Fyans Castle in the harbor of Dublin for Holyhead on the ship *Tramontana*.[1] They were hooted at and assaulted by the London rabble. The King, however, graciously received them as friends at Hampton Court. O'Neill was reinstated as the Earl of Tyrone, Rory was made the Earl of Tirconnaill, and both men were given

---

[1] A sudden, dense fog near the Skerries almost led to the destruction of the ship which was nearly dashed to pieces. This would probably have killed all on board.

back all the lands that had belonged to their clans. The English colonists in Ireland were furious when they heard of the kind reception and favors these "rebels" had received from the new sovereign. Sir John Harrington, the cousin of the late Queen, wrote,

> I have lived to see that damnable rebel, Tyrone, brought to England honored and well liked. Oh, what is there that does not prove the inconstancy of worldly matters! How did I labor after that knave's destruction! I adventured perils by sea and land, was near starving, ate horse flesh in Munster, and all to quell that man, who now smileth in peace at those who did hazard their lives to destroy him; and now doth Tyrone dare us, old commanders with his presence and protection.[2]

These were the arch-traitors who cost England so dearly in blood and wealth! Neale Garve, who received only the lands which he held before his treachery, was enraged. He indignantly raved against the Dublin Council which had promised him all of Tirconnaill and led a rash rebellion against the English. He eventually was captured and sent to the Tower of London, where he died after an imprisonment of 18 years. O'Neill and O'Donnell returned and settled peacefully on their land. O'Neill had been promised that his people could freely practice their Catholic Faith. This had been the major goal of the war. All over Ireland Catholics began to claim their old churches and practice their religion openly. The Cathedrals of Limerick, Cork, Cloyne and Cashel as well as the churches of Wexford, Clonmel, Kilkenny and Ross were re-dedicated and restored. The Mass was said openly throughout the land. In Cork all

---

[2]Meehan, *The Fate and Fortunes*, 39.

Protestant Bibles and prayer books were publicly and solemnly burned. The Blessed Sacrament was carried through the streets of the city "with great pomp and incredible joy of the whole town."[3] Mountjoy marched from Dublin to Waterford with a royalist army. He was met by a priest named John White and a Dominican friar who entered his camp carrying a crucifix and a deputation from Waterford. He informed the Viceroy "that the people of Waterford would never willingly yield allegiance to any prince who would attack and persecute the Catholic religion."[4] Mountjoy, on account of the difficulties of the times and his own confusion as to the King's will in the matter, peacefully entered the town and treated the priests fairly.[5]

When Mountjoy returned to England, Sir George Carew was made Lord Deputy. He wrote to Cecil bitterly complaining of the influence of the Roman clergy in Ireland:

> This country of late so swarms with priests, Jesuits, seminarists, friars and Romish bishops, that I assure your lordship that if there be not speedy means used to free this kingdom of this wicked rabble, which labor to draw the subjects' hearts from their due obedience to their prince, much mischief will burst forth in very short time; for there are here so many of this wicked crew that are able to disquiet four of the greatest kingdoms in Christendom. It is high time they

---

[3]O'Sullivan Bear, *Ireland Under Elizabeth*, 179.
[4]*Ibid.*
[5]The Lord Deputy permitted the wearing of clerical garb and the celebration of Mass in private homes. The English soldiers during this incident mocked and ridiculed the two priests for bringing an "idol" (a crucifix) into their camp. Sir Richard Wingfield offered to end the discussion between Fr. White and the Lord Deputy by running the priest through with his sword. Meehan gives a good account of this incident in *Fate and Fortunes* pages 27-30.

were banished from hence, and none to receive, or aid, or relieve them. Let the judges and officers be sworn to the supremacy; let the lawyers go to the church and show conformity, or not plead at the bar; and then the rest by degrees will shortly follow. Here will be much ado at Michaelmas, when this great caste of 4,000 shall be. I would God the king had some use of their services in some other place, for here will they live upon spoil and to do mischief; labor will they never, and rob will they still. The heavenly God bless your lordship always, and give me grace to deserve your favor.

Dublin, September 3, 1603.

Your lordship's always to do you service,

George Carew[6]

The necessity of conciliating the Catholic party in England, of maintaining peace in Ireland and continuing the Spanish negotiations (not to mention his own personal bias against the Puritans) led James to treat the Catholics favorably. Because of this, the Protestant English colonists were rendered impotent for they could do little without the King's support. They thought they had won the war, yet they found their enemies exalted and popery triumphantly rising throughout the kingdom. This dream of Catholic restoration lasted for only two years however. James, in attempting to enforce the Anglican Canons which had been adopted in 1604 against the Puritans, was accused by the same party of favoring the Papists. This accusation alarmed the weak King who knew the strength of Presbyterianism in

---

[6]Meehan, *Fate and Fortunes*, 50-51. Meehan relates that earlier when news of the defeat of the Spanish Armada reached Ireland the Protestant Archbishop Adam Loftus commanded all the Catholic lawyers to assist at prayers of thanksgiving in Protestant churches recently seized from the Catholics! The lawyers refused and left the city.

the country. To convince the skeptical of his Protestantism, James drank "to the eternal damnation of the Papists" at a solemn state dinner.[7]

On the 28th of September, 1605, James issued the following proclamation in Dublin:

> We hereby make known to our subjects in Ireland that no toleration shall ever be granted by us. This we do for the purpose of cutting off all hope that any other religion shall be allowed, save that which is in consonant to the laws and statutes of this realm.[8]

All the magistrates were ordered to strictly enforce all penal laws against Catholics. Robert Cecil set up an elaborate spy system to entrap all possible recusants. The reign of fear and treachery drove several desperate men into the web of Cecil's "Gunpowder Plot" in the following year. This event rendered the King's returning to a position of toleration an impossibility.

This was just what the English colonist in Ireland had been waiting for. The entire country, although completely drained, was again thrown into turmoil. The Protestant colonists vengefully turned their wrath and avarice upon the Catholics. The Victor-Apostolic of Waterford and Lismore wrote a detailed account of the sufferings of the Irish nation for the Faith. In a letter addressed to Cardinal Baronius from Waterford dated the 1st of May, 1606, he says:

---

[7]Clare, *History of Ireland*, 464.
[8]*Ibid*.

There is scarcely a spot where Catholics can find a safe retreat. The impious soldiery, by day and night, pursue the defenseless priests, and mercilessly persecute them. Up to the present they have succeeded in seizing three; one is detained in Dublin prison, another in Cork, and the third in my opinion, is the happiest of all, triumphing in heaven with Christ our Lord; for in the excess of the fury of the soldiery, without any further trial or accusation, having expressed himself to be a priest, he was hanged on the spot.[9]

The Papal Nuncio, in another letter to Rome, further describes the state of the Catholics:

2,000 florins are offered for the discovery of a Jesuit, and 1,000 for the discovery of any other priest, or even of the house where he lives. Whenever the servants of any of the clergy are arrested, they are cruelly scourged with whips, until they disclose all that they know about them. Bodies of soldiers are dispersed throughout the country in pursuit of bandits and priests; and all that they seize on, they have the power, by martial law, of hanging without further trial. They enter private houses, and execute whom they please, vieing with each other in cruelty. It is difficult to define the precise number of those who are thus put to death. All who are greedy and spendthrifts, seek to make a prey of the property of Catholics. No doors, no walls, no enclosures can stop them in their course. Whatever is for profane use they profess to regard as sacred and bear it off; and whatever is sacred they seize on to desecrate. Silver cups are called chalices, - and gems are designated as *Agnus Deis*; and all are therefore carried away. There are already in prison one bishop, one vicar general, some religious, very many priests, and an immense number of the laity of every class and condition. In one city alone five of the alderman were thrown into prison successively, for refusing to take the nefarious

---

[9]*Ibid.*, 465.

oath of allegiance, on their being nominated to the mayor-
alty; in another city, no less than 30 were likewise thrust into
prison at Easter last, for having approached the holy communion in the Catholic Church.[10]

Such was the condition of the Catholics in Ireland three
years after the peace of Melifont. The situation in Ireland
was watched closely by the Holy See. Pope Paul V[11], in a
special letter to the Irish Catholics dated from St. Mark's on
the 22nd of September, 1606, mourns over their sufferings,
commends their wondrous constancy, which he said "could
only be compared to that of the early Christians."[12] The
Pontiff continued to encourage the Irish and sent them the
following letter:

> Your glory is that faith by which your fathers procured
> for their country the distinguished apellation of the Island of
> Saints. Nor have the sufferings which you have endured
> been allowed to remain unpublished; your fidelity and
> Christian fortitude have become the subject of universal ad-
> miration; and the praise of your name has long since been
> loudly celebrated in every portion of the Christian world.[13]

---

[10]*Ibid.*, 465-6.

[11]Camillo Borghese was elected Pope on May 16, 1605 and reigned
until January 28, 1621. He was born in Rome although his family was
Sienese. A devout, reforming Pontiff, he promoted the Tridentine de-
crees; approved St. Philip Neri's Oratory; beatified Ignatius Loyola,
Francis Xavier, Teresa of Avila and Philip Neri. He supported the
Church missionary effort and had a deep love for Rome, finishing the
nave, portico, and facade of St. Peter's and restoring the aqueduct of
Trajan, bringing water to the city and the Janiculum Hill.

[12]Clare, *History of Ireland.*, 467.

[13]*Ibid.* The full Latin text may be found in J. Hagan "Misellanea Vaticano-Hibernica 1580-1631". (*Archvium Hibernicum*, Vol. 3, [   ], 260-64.)

Hugh O'Neill and Rory O'Donnell protested the persecution, reminding the new Lord Deputy, Sir Arthur Chichester, a fierce anti-Catholic who had come to power in February of 1605, that the King had promised them the free practice of their faith. Despite the protests, manifestos issued by Usher, King James's uncle, who had been made the Protestant Bishop of Armagh[14], were promulgated in Dungannon and Donegal bidding the chiefs and their people to apostatize from the Faith of their fathers. The chiefs and their people however courageously remained true to Him who said, "fear not for I have overcome the world," and held fast to the Faith.

The frustrated colonists sought to entrap O'Neill and O'Donnell in some scheme by which they might legally seize their great possessions and the rich land of Ulster. The Irish princes, although still powerful, had been so weakened by the war that their was little hope of armed resistance. O'Neill and O'Donnell were invited by Sir Christopher St. Lawrence, the Lord Howth, to a meeting at the Castle of Maynooth around Christmas in 1606. The two Earls agreed and met, with O'Kane and the Lords Delvin and Howth. The conference was held under the pretext of a Christmas party. What actually occurred at this meeting is not known. An anonymous letter which was directed to Sir William Usher, the Clerk of the Council, was dropped in the Council Chamber of Dublin Castle in March of 1607. This letter is now generally believed to have been written

---

[14]Peter Lombard, the true primate, was in Rome unable to take possession of his rightful see due to the hostility of James and the belief that he could do more for his country in Rome.

by Howth who was thought to have been employed by the crafty Cecil to entrap the Catholic Earls and betray them. The letter stated that O'Neill, O'Donnell and O'Kane had discussed the preparation of another Confederacy to defend the Catholic Faith. It further alleged their intention to seize Dublin Castle and kill the Lord Deputy. The Earls were ordered to appear in London to answer the charge. O'Neill and O'Donnell knew that the colonists and planters were just waiting for the word to fall upon their territories and that the crafty Cecil had already decided upon their destruction. They made a disturbing and painful decision to leave their ancient patrimonies and into exile they had to go for safety could be found only in flight. Their situation was desperate and yet the thought of leaving Ireland filled them with bitter sorrow. There were men on the continent who would welcome them: the Archduke in Brussels, Philip III, and the Pope in Rome. They thought perhaps that with the Irish swordsmen in the continental armies an invasion of Ulster might be attempted. Perhaps one of their sons might even lead the expedition. Hugh O'Neill's son, Henry, who had been sent to Spain, now sent a ship from the Netherlands to save his father and carry him to the continent. Word reached the chieftains that the French ship had arrived and was waiting for them, anchored in Lough Swilly.

O'Neill, as he journeyed northward, stopped at Melifont Abbey, where he had surrendered to Mountjoy four years earlier, and visited his friend Sir Garrett More. Hugh "wept abundantly when he took his leave giving every child and every servant in the house a solemn farewell, which made them all marvel, because in general it was not his manner to use such compliments."[15] He remained two more nights in his beloved castle at Dungannon making his final preparations. He must have been severely tormented in his soul. Earl, prince, chieftain, statesmen, soldier, a victorious general and defender of the Faith he had been; now all seemed over. On the border of old age, surrounded by vicious enemies, what did fate hold in store for him? And what was to be the fate of his beloved country?

He made his final journey to Lough Swilly with his wife Catherine, his three sons and other relations. The French ship awaited them at Rathmullen near the forlorn ruins of the Carmelite priory. A tearful Rory O'Donnell was already there having departed from his clan with his two brothers, his sister Nuala, his hereditary bard Owen Roe MacWard and accompanying attendants. Conor Maguire, the brother of the courageous Hugh who had perished during the war was also there. A total of ninety-nine people boarded the ship at noon which set sail for the open sea at midnight on the 14th of September, 1607, the Feast of the Exaltation of the Holy Cross. This moving event is called in Irish history "The Flight of the Earls." The ominous news of their departure was mournfully related from province to province. The Irish bards dirged it, and the Gaelic clansmen wept. They sensed that something had ended with the departure of that ship. The last bulwark against the Saxon sheriff and Saxon law had blown away with the northeastern wind. The Four Masters relate:

> It is certain that the sea has not borne, and the wind has not wafted in modern times a number of persons in one ship,

---

[15]Sullivan, *Story of Ireland*, 331.

more eminent, illustrious noble in point of geneology, heroic deeds, valour, feats of arm and brave achievements, than they. Would that God would have permitted them to remain in their patrimonial inheritances until the children should have arrived at the age of manhood! Woe to the heart that meditated—woe to the mind that conceived—woe to the council that recomended the project of this expedition, without knowing whether they should to the end of their lives be able to return to their ancient principalities and patrimonies.[16]

The Gaelic princes sailed directly to Normandy.[17] They sailed up the Seine, south of Havre de Grace, on the morning of October 4th, the Feast of St. Francis of Assisi, twenty-one days after leaving Donegal. Upon their arrival in France, the English minister demanded their arrest as "rebels." The chivalric Henry IV responded to the demand with a resolute no. The Irish were warmly welcomed and royally entertained by Henry who greatly admired the military ability displayed by these famous Catholics in the Irish Wars.[18] The chieftains journeyed from France through the Spanish Netherlands, now modern day Belgium, and were received with dignity and marked honors by Archduke Albert and Isabella. In all the courts of Europe (to the acute embarrassment of England), as the princes passed on their

---

[16]Four Master, *Annals*, 6.

[17]On this journey they sailed past Aran Island, off the Donegal coast, past Sligo, glimpsing Croagh Patrick, beyond Galway for Corunna. The wind however, blew them toward Brittany. The sea was stormy and several of the nobles were nearly swept off the deck of the ship.

[18]James issued a "Proclamation Touching the Earls of Tyrone and Tyrconnel" which reveals the baseness of the King. See Meehan, *Fate and Fortunes*, pages 175-6.

way to the Eternal City, they were treated as men deserving
of attention, respect and honor by various princes and po-
tentates. The princes visited Rouen, Amiens, Arras, Douai,
Brussels and Louvain. In Belgium they visited some of the
shrines, such as Malines, desecrated by Norris and his English soldiers during Elizabeth's reign. The Belgians were
delighted that O'Neill's sword had "avenged their desecrated altars" when Norris was wounded and defeated near
Armagh. The princes resolved to spend the winter in Louvain. A number of the exiles remained there, including
Hugh O'Neill's young nephew, Owen Roe. On February
28, 1608, thirty-two of the exiles began the journey to Rome
via Lucerne where they celebrated St. Patrick's Day. They
crossed the Alps, stopping at the hospice of St. Gothard.
They entered Italy and traveled to Faido, Bellinzona, Como,
Milano, Parma and Reggio, arriving in Bologna on April 10,
1608. They continued to Imola and Faenza and spent some
time at the Holy House of Loreto. The journey was resumed through Foligno, Assisi, Narni and Civita-Castellana
until, at the beginning of May, they finally reached the famous Ponte Milvio. It was in the Holy City of Rome, the
common asylum of all Catholics, that these illustrious fugitives were given the truest, warmest and tenderest welcome. The Catholic Primate of Ireland, Peter Lombard[19],

---

[19]Lombard had written an important and eloquent defense of
Hugh O'Neill and the Catholic war in Ireland for the Holy Father in
1600 entitled *De regno Hiberniae sanctorum insula commentarius*. A fine
overview of this important Irishman who was involved in the great
events of his day including the misunderstood Galileo case, the Robert de Nobilo case and the dispute between Molinists and Thomists
can be found in John J. Silke, "The Irish Peter Lombard", *Irish Studies*,
64, No. 254 (1975), 143-55.

with a large retinue of Cardinals, greeted them and brought them through the Flaminian gate (Porto del Popolo) to the palace prepared for them by the Pope in Borgo Vecchio. They visited the tomb of St. Peter and the next day they met the Holy Father at the Quirinal Palace. Pope Paul V conferred upon them every mark of affection and every honorable distinction. The Pontiff, along with all the prelates and princes of Christendom, regarded them as confessors of the faith. Each of them were given by the Pope and Philip III liberal annual pensions befitting their royal birth and princely state. On the Thursday before Trinity Sunday, the Pope solemnly canonized St. Frances of Rome, so beloved of the Roman people, for her charity and mystical favors and gave O'Neill and O'Donnell the seats of honor under the Dome of St. Peter's.[20] Together they visited the many pilgrimage sites of the Holy City with fervent prayers for their loved ones and their beloved native land.

One by one, however, the Irish princes began to die in that foreign climate. On July 28, 1608, Rory O'Donnell died.[21] He was soon followed by his brother Caffar who died on the 17th of September. Both princes were interred with royal honors in Rome in the church of San Pietro in Montorio on the Janiculum Hill. This church, according to

---

[20]For a sense of the devotion the Irish princes had for Rome, the capital of Christendom, see Tadhg O'Cianain's *The Flight of the Earls* pages 169-259. (Tadhg O'Cianain, *The Flight of the Earls*, ed. and trans. Paul Walsh [Dublin: M.H. Gill & Son Ltd., 1916].)

[21]Although suffering from a severe fever, he made a pilgrimage to the seven patriarchal basilicas in the summer heat before his death. On July 27th, he received the Last Sacraments and commended his soul to God, vested in the habit of St. Francis like so many of his forefathers.

tradition, was believed to be where St. Peter met his death. Conor Maguire died at Genoa on the 12th of August, while he was heading for Spain. O'Neill's young son Hugh, whom he had hoped would succeed him, died about a year afterwards on the 23rd of September, 1609. Another son who had been left in Brussels was found strangled in his bed. Thus, after only two years from his departure from Ireland, O'Neill found himself virtually alone. Often he would climb the slopes of the Janiculum Hill, with its glorious view of the city, to pray for his son and fallen compatriots, kneeling by their tombs under the gaze of Raphael's Transfiguration whose brilliant colors dominated the sanctuary. English spies surrounded him during his exile and reported that in the evenings after dinner, if O'Neill was "warm with wine," he would strike the table and exclaim that they would "have a good day yet in Ireland."[22] For eight more years O'Neill continued to live in Rome. In the last few years he began to lose his sight and eventually went blind "like another Belisarius". At last, on the 20th of July, 1616, this great Irish patriot, who in intellect, courage and renown was an international figure, died at the age of 76 after receiving the last rites of the Church and was clothed in the habit of St. Francis. By uniting Ireland's struggle for freedom with the whole movement of the Catholic Reformation he had helped bring his country from its slumbering isolation into the mainstream of European thought. The following entry of his death is made by the Four Masters in the year 1616,

---

[22]Sullivan, *Story of Ireland*, 333.

O'Neill (Hugh), son of Ferdoragh, who was styled Earl of Tyrone at the parliament of 1585, and who was afterwards styled O'Neill, died at an advanced age, after having passed his life in prosperity and happiness, in valiant and illustrious achievements, in honour and nobleness. The place at which he died was Rome, on the 20th of July, after exemplary penance for his sins, and gaining the victory over the world and the devil. Although he died far from Armagh, the burial-place of his ancestors, it was a token that God was pleased with his life that the Lord permitted him no worse burial-place, namely Rome, the head city of the Christians. The person who here died was a powerful, mighty lord, with wisdom, subtlety, and profundity of mind and intellect; a warlike, valorous, predatory, enterprising lord in defending his religion and his patrimony against his enemies; a pious and charitable lord, mild and gentle with his friends, fierce and stern towards his enemies until he had brought them to submission and obedience to his authority; a lord who had not coveted to possess himself of the illegal or excessive property of any other except such as had been hereditary in his ancestors from a remote period; a lord with the authority and praiseworthy characteristics of a prince, who had not suffered theft or robbery, abduction or rape, spite or animosity to prevail during his reign; and had kept all under the law as was meet for a prince.[23]

O'Faolain gives the following evaluation of O'Neill's character and career:

Men are fated to do what their talents demand of them, and there was after all, little of cold reason in anything he had done who had merely fulfilled himself and God's will in him. He could never have lived like old, obese, tipsy Turlough, or blustered like Sean the Proud. Win or lose; we have to fight because if a man does not know how to fight he

---

[23]Four Masters, *Annals*, 6:2373-75.

does not know how to live. It had been Heaven's plan that he had worked it; and if the plan did not succeed then that was another of those mysteries of Heaven and nature whose apparent errors so profoundly puzzle all men.[24]

The Holy Father ordered a public funeral for O'Neill and personally directed the arrangements on a scale of grandeur fit for royal princes and kings. The world prostrates itself in worship before the altars of Success and Vain-Glory; but Catholic Rome, ever the friend of the unfortunate and oppressed, never judges men or nations by the standards of their worldly accomplishments. The English religious revolutionaries who had driven these Princes from their native land in order that they might die ignominiously in exile, now suffered to see all of Christendom assigning to them an exalted place among the martyrs and heroes of Christian patriotism. O'Neill was buried with magnificent solemnity on the Janiculum in the Franciscan church of San Pietro in Montorio next to Rory and Carfar O'Donnell and his son Hugh.

Meehan gives the following description of the funeral:

Clothed in the Franciscan habit, and laid on a bier, the lugubrious trappings of which showed the cognizance of the Red Hand, his corpse was born by twelve stalwart Irishmen along the Longara, the Spanish ambassador and three of the chiefest of the Roman nobility holding the pall. Religious of all orders, with lighted torches, preceded and followed the bier, chanting the psalms with which the Church accompanies her departed faithful to the frontier of eternity; and as the long procession slowly ascended the acclivity of the Janiculum, the tolling of a hundred bells, the throb of the muf-

---

[24]O'Faolain, *The Great O'Neil*, 357.

fled-drum, and the minute-guns of S. Angelo, announced to the imperial city, the shepherds of the Campagna, and the vine-dressers among the Alban hills, that an illustrious personage was then about to be laid in his last resting-place. in obedience to the pontiff's command, the church of Montorio was draped in mourning, and nothing was omitted that could lend deepest solemnity to the funeral pomp. Cardinals, Roman patricians, and ambassadors from various foreign courts, assisted at the Mass of Requiem; and when the last absolution was pronounced, the hands of his fellow-exiles deposited the remains of their great chieftan beside those of his son, the baron of Dungannon, and those of the O'Donels, lords of Tyrconnel.

Together, side by side, they had fought in life; side by side they sleep in death. The following simple epitaph was carved on O'Neill's tomb, *DOM, Hic Quiescunt Ugonis Principis, O'Neill Ossa,* "To the Best and Greatest God, Here lie the bones of Prince Hugh O'Neill.[25]

---

[25]Hugh O'Neill was interred with his son who received the following epitaph: "To Hugh, the Baron of Dunganon, first-born of Hugh O'Neil grand prince and count of Tironia. (Who) according to his own devotion toward God and his parents followed to Rome—the common city of Catholic exiles—His Father and Uncle Roderick, count of Tirconallia, for the sake of the Catholic faith which they had defended for many years against heretics in Ireland—after he abandoned his own states remaining in exile on his own accord, Whose premature death took away the hope—conceived by all in his regard because of his outstanding qualities of mind and body—of restoring some day the Catholic religion in those areas and joined (him) to the aforementioned uncle Roderick ruined by a similar fate. He died worthy of weeping both to his own people and to the entire curia on September 23rd, 1609, in the 24th year of his life."

The following is Paul V's epitaph for Rory O'Donnell: "Prince Roderick O'Donnell, count of Tirconallia in Ireland Who—having gone through the greatest dangers both in war and in peace on behalf of the Catholic religion, a most firm supporter and defender of the

There is probably not in the elegiac poetry of any language anything comparable to the "Lament for the Princes of Tyrone and Tirconnaill" which was written by O'Donnell's bard, Owen Roe MacWard. MacWard, in this moving poem, fully captures the sorrowful fate of Ireland by addressing Lady Nuala O'Donnell and her attendant mourners as they wept at the grave of the princes. This magnificent English translation by Managhan preserves the spirit and tenderness of the original Gaelic.[26]

> 0 woman of the piercing wail!
> Who mournest o'er yon mound of clay
> With sigh and groan,
> Would God thou wert among the Gael!

Apostolic Roman faith for the protection and preservation of which (he was) an exile from the fatherland, after having visited the important monuments of the Saints in Italy, France, Belgium, and having been received in the same places with the special love and honor of the Christian Princes and also with the paternal affection of His Holiness the Pope/ and Catholic Lord/ Paul the fifth—Brought—amid the most fervent prayers of Catholics for his prosperous return—the greatest sorrow to his own people and grief to all the social-categories in this city By the premature death which he suffered on July 31 in the year of salvation 1607, the 32nd of his own life; Which (death) soon his brother Calfurnius—the companion of dangers and exile—having followed by the same path so that he might enjoy with the same bliss, in the midst of the highest hope and expectation of good people based on the nobility of his spirit, which virtue and outstanding character adorned, left a grief-filled loss of himself and sadness to the co-exiles on September 15th of the immediately following year, the 25th of his own life; Both of them by age and the order of fate preceded the first-born brother Prince Hugh, whom feeling piously and catholically for the faith and the fatherland Philip the Third King of the Spains both cherished kindly as living and having died took care to have buried honorably in Valladolid in Spain on September 10th in the year of salvation 1602.

[26]Sullivan, *Story of Ireland*, 335.

Thou wouldst not then from day to day
Weep thus alone.

And who can marvel o'er thy grief,
Or who can blame thy flowing tears,
That knows their source?
O'Donnell, Cunnasava' s chief,
Cut off amid his vernal years,
Lies here a corpse
Beside his brother Cathbar, whom
Tirconnell of the Helmets mourns
In deep despair—
For valour, truth, and comely bloom,
For all that greatens and adorns,
A peerless pair.

When high the shout of battle rose
On fields where Freedom's torch still burned
Through Erin's gloom,
If one—if barely one—of those
Were slain, all Ulster would have mourned
The hero's doom!
If at Athboy, where hosts of brave
Ulidian horsemen sank beneath
The shock of spears,
Young Hugh O'Neill had found a grave,
Long must the North have wept his death
With heart-wrung tears!

What do I say? Ah, woe is me!
Already we bewail in vain
Their fatal fall!
And Erin, once the Great and Free,
Now vainly mourns her breakless chain
And iron thrall!
Then, daughter of O'Donnell, dry
Thine overflowing eyes, and turn

Thy heart aside,
For Adam's race is born to die,
And sternly the sepulchral urn
Mocks human pride!

Look not, nor sigh, for earthly throne,
Nor place thy trust in arm of clay;
But on thy knees
Uplift thy soul to God alone,
For all things go their destined way
As He decrees.

'T were long before, around a grave
In green Tyrconnell, one would find
This loneliness;
Near where Beann-Boirche's banners wave,
Such grief as thine could ne'er have pined
Companionless.

Beside the wave, in Donegal,
In Antrim's glens, or fair Dromore,
Or Killilee,
Or where the sunny waters fall
At Assaroe, near Erna's shore,
This could not be.
On Derry's plains,—in rich Drumcliff,—
Throughout Armagh the Great, renowned
In olden years,
No day could pass, but woman's grief
Would rain upon the burial-ground
Fresh floods of tears!

O no!—from Shannon, Boyne, and Suir,
From high Dunluce's castle walls,
From Lissadill,
Would flock alike both rich and poor.
One wail would rise from Cruachan's halls

To Tara's hill;
And some would come from Barrow side,
And many a maid would leave her home
On Leitrim's plains,
And by melodious Banna's tide,
And by the Mourne and Erne, to come
And swell thy strains!

Two princes of the line of Conn
Sleep in their cells of clay beside
O'Donnell Roe;
Three royal youths, alas! are gone
Who lived for Erin's weal, but died
For Erin's woe!
Ah! could the men of Ireland read
The names these noteless burial stones
Display to view,
Their wounded hearts afresh would bleed,
Their tears gush forth again, their groans
Resound anew!

Embrace the faithful crucifix,
And seek the path of pain and prayer
Thy Saviour trod;
Nor let thy spirit intermix
With earthly hope and worldly care
its groans to God!

And Thou, O mighty Lord: whose ways
Are far above our feeble minds
To understand;
Sustain us in those doleful days,
And render light the chain that binds
Our fallen land!
Look down upon our dreary state,
And through the ages that may still
Roll sadly on,

Watch Thou o'er hapless Erin's fate,
And shield at last from darker ill
The blood of Conn![27]

The Nine Years War was Gaelic Ireland's last stand as a nation under her own laws against England and English law. The War, however, had not been fought in vain. The cause of the Catholic Reformation on the Continent was certainly aided by the severe strains it placed on Protestant England. Charles Wilson, who was so critical of Elizabeth's failure to adequately aid the Protestant cause in the Netherlands, in all fairness observes that "The argument that she was short of money, that the demands of home defense, Ireland especially had to be first priority is cogent."[28]

The Irish War indirectly allowed Spain to maintain Belgium as a Catholic country. Hugh O'Neill and Red Hugh O'Donnell together had laid the ground work for a future nationalism. If they had not done so, Catholic Gaelic Ireland would have died, leaving behind only ruins, records, and artifacts for the archaeologist and philologist. At the conclusion of the Elizabethan Wars, Ireland appeared to be finally conquered. The beginning of the 17th century saw the ruin of the clan and communal system, the overthrow of the great Gaelic Houses and the establishment of centralization by a foreign despotic power. The truly amazing fact, however, is that the conquest was not complete but merely superficial. The Catholic Confederacy had impressed upon the Irish character something infinitely more profound and deep. A Catholic nation had emerged without a state. On

---

[27]*Ibid.*, 335-40.
[28]Wilson, *Revolt of the Netherlands*, 134.

the surface, the English Law ran and her armies freely moved. But the soul of Ireland remained free and unconquered. The overwhelming majority of the people, despite one of the most savage and barbaric persecutions in history, remained true to their Catholic Faith.

> Against the loss of Britain, which had been a Roman province, the Faith, when the smoke of battle cleared off, could discover the astonishing loyalty of Ireland. And over against this exceptional province—Britain—now lost to the Faith, lay an equally exceptional and unique outer part which had never been a Roman province, yet which now remained true to the tradition of Roman men; it balanced the map like a counter-weight. The efforts to destroy the Faith in Ireland have exceeded in violence, persistence, and cruelty any persecution in any part or time of the world. They have failed. As I cannot explain why they have failed, so I shall not attempt to explain how and why the Faith in Ireland was saved when the Faith in Britain went under. I do not believe it capable of an historic explanation. It seems to me a phenomenon essentially miraculous in character, not *generally* attached (as are all historical phenomena) to the general and divine purpose that governs our large political events, but *directly* and specially attached. It is of great significance; how great, men will be able to see, many years hence or tomorrow, when another definite battle is joined between the forces of the Church and her opponents. For the Irish race alone of all Europe has maintained a perfect integrity and has kept serene, without internal reactions and without their consequent disturbances, the soul of Europe which is the Catholic Church.[29]

---

[29]Hillaire Belloc, *Europe and the Faith* (London: Cox & Wyman Ltd., 1920), 182-83. This remained true for the greater part of the twentieth century. The success of the recent secular challenge remains unsure. See the papal address to the Irish bishops in *L'Osservatore Romano*, 26

Ireland's body had been bound by fetters, but her soul and mind were free. The divine dignity of the defeated typified in the passion and death of Christ was followed by the glory of Easter. God, in His providential design, used this war to deepen the Catholic identity of the people through the cross of suffering and thereby spread the Faith throughout the world. During the centuries of suffering, God in his design allowed this bleeding and lacerated nation to be flung all over the world. As this stream of the brokenhearted and destitute traveled to distant lands, everywhere they went they have carried with them their Catholic Faith and ideals.

A nation's true greatness lies ultimately not in wealth and commercial success nor in the vast conquest of territories which so impresses the world's jaundiced judgments. A nation's greatness, like an individual, is to be found in its moral integrity and spiritual glory. Ireland, until quite recently, suffered from a cruel poverty because her people, in remaining true to their ancient faith, lived primarily for eternity, not time; and for spiritual riches, not temporal.

This steady stream of emigrants sought, in desperate exile, for those goods which they sadly could not find in their own homeland. Lacordaire preached eloquently in the nineteenth century of "the martyr race"; and truly, just like the early Roman martyrs and the martyrs of our own day, these poor are the glory of Erin. This suffering is not, however, to be a cause for bitterness or hatred, for such is not worthy of the true Christian. We must, however, remember

(6/30/99), 3-4.

their courage and heroism. Catholic Ireland stoutly refused to die and each succeeding generation asserted its right to nationhood and freedom of worship by force of arms. The suffering of the faithful and the nation led many noble and generous Protestants also to serve and fight for the freedom and independence of Ireland. As William Butler Yeats placed upon the mouth of Patrick Pearse reflecting upon the 1916 uprising, "There's nothing but our own red blood . . . can make a right Rose Tree." After the passion and death came a truly glorious rising.

When G. K. Chesterton observed a papal flag being flown outside an Irish farmhouse for the Eucharistic Congress in Dublin he wrote:

> I continued to stare, I know not why, at that little lonely house with that large and lordly flag. In the first flash of the fantastic, it had seemed as if the house could have been wrapped up in the flag; but as I looked more closely, I saw the house was larger than I thought, being low and rambling, with outhouses; being the small farmhouse of what seemed to be a very solid and prosperous farm; I saw the people moving to and fro among the barns, going about their duties as the sun went down. And I began to remember the other side of the argument and the end of the story. These men, now tilling their own soil, had once been hunted in it as modern laws would hardly suffer us to hunt wild beasts. The Irishry had hardly been treated like a race, but rather like a rash; like a disease that had broken out upon the soil and must be suppressed. They were hardly men, they only existed in the plural like measles. Fine poets and fastidious gentlemen, sent over from England, could only screw up their noses and suggest that some insecticide should remove the very smell of such sub-human humanity. It became not only sub-human, but subterranean; its creed was

driven underground; its culture and language were assumed to have already died out, like the aborigines of Tasmania. And then, as if in a dream, it seemed that the scene altered and all the world was changed; and old powers began to play new parts . . . 'The poor should as far as possible become owners.' . . . The wiser statesmen of the later nineteenth century begin to hear older and more universal theories of the State, more generous than a cheap Radicalism or a tribal Toryism; property as a natural right of men and not a legal privilege of lucky men; economics as the servant of ethics; the servant of the servant of God. I looked again at the great gold-and-silver banner and suddenly forgot all the nonsense about national political conquest; and the idiocy that imagines the Pope as landing on our shores with a pistol in each hand. I knew there was another Empire that has never declined nor fallen; and there rolled through the heavens of pure thought the thunder of the great Encyclicals, and the mind of the new Europe in which the new nations find that the Faith can make them free. The great flag began to flap and crackle in the freshening evening wind; and those who had been toiling on the little farm, those whose fathers had been hunted like vermin, those whose religion should have been burnt out like witchcraft, came back slowly through the twilight; walking like lords on their own land.[30]

The fact that Ireland stands today, a free and overwhelmingly Catholic nation, is perhaps the greatest tribute which can be made to the War and the vision of those brave men who fought and died to make that dream a reality. May we never forget the sacrifices they made in defense of the Faith and Fatherland. *Requiescant in pace.*

FINIS

---

[30] G. K. Chesterton, *Christendom in Dublin* (London: Sheed & Ward, 1933), 24-27.

BIBLIOGRapʰy

Archivium Hibernicum or *Irish Historical Records* Vols. 3 & 4. Dublin: M. H. Gill & Sons, Ltd., 1914.

Atkinson, William C. *History of Spain and Portugal*. Middlesex, England: Penguin Book Inc., 1960.

Bagwell, Richard. *Ireland Under the Tudors* Vol. 3 Reprint, London: The Holland Press, 1963.

Baxter, S. B., ed. *Basic Documents of English History*. Boston: Houghton Mifflin Co., 1968.

Belloc, Hillaire. *Characters of the Reformation*. Garden City, New York: Image Books, 1958.

————. *Europe and the Faith*. London: Cox & Wyman, Ltd. 1920.

Bindoff, S. T. *Tudor England*. Vol. 5 of *The Pelican History of England*. Baltimore, Middlesex, England: Penguin Books Inc., 1950.

Bradshaw, Brendan. "Sword, Word and Strategy in the Reformation in Ireland", *Historical Journal*, 21 (1978): 475-502.

————. *The Irish Constitutional Revolution of the Sixteenth Century*. Cambridge: Cambridge University Press, 1979.

Brewer, J. S., and William Butler, eds. *Calendar of the Carew Papers in the Lambeth Library* Vols. 2 & 4. Nendeln/Liechtenstein: Kraus-Thompson Ltd., 1974.

Campion, Edmund. *A Historie of Ireland*. New York: Scholars', Facsimilies and Reprints, 1940.

Canny, Nicholas P. *The Elizabethan Conquest of Ireland: a pattern es-*

tablished, 1565-76. New York: Barnes & Noble Books, 1976.

———. "Hugh O'Neill, Earl of Tyrone, and the Changing Face of Gaelic Ulster", *Studia Hibernica,* 10 (1970): 7-35.

Carroll, Warren. *The Cleaving of Christendom* Vol. 4 of *The History of Christendom.* Front Royal, VA: Christendom Press, 2000.

Carew, George. *Pacta Hibernia* 2 vols. London: Downey & Co. Ltd., 1896.

Clare, M. F. *History of Ireland.* London: Longmands, Green & Co., 1873.

Cornish, P.J. *The Irish Martyrs.* Dublin: 1989.

Curtis, Edmund. *A History of Ireland.* New York: Barnes & Noble, 1936.

———, ed. *Irish Historical Documents 1172-1922.* New York: Barnes & Noble, 1968.

D'Alton, E.A. *History of Ireland* Vol. 3. London: Gresham Publishing Co.

Daniel-Rops, Henri. *The Catholic Reformation* Vols. 1 & 2. Garden City, New York: Image Books, 1965.

Davies, R. Trevor. *The Golden Century of Spain.* New York: Harper & Row, 1961.

Dawson, Christopher. *The Dividing of Christendom.* Garden City, New York: Image Books, 1967.

Dickenson, A. G. *The English Reformation.* New York: Schocken Books, 1964.

Edwards, R. Dudley. *Church and State in Tudor Ireland.* New York: Russell & Russell, 1972.

———. *Ireland in the Age of the Tudors.* London: Croom Helm, 1977.

Ellis, Steven G. *Ireland in the Age of the Tudors, 1447-1603: English expansion and the end of Gaelic rule.* New York: Longman, 1998.

———. *Tudor Ireland: Crown Community and the Conflict of Cultures, 1470–1603.* New York: Longman Inc., 1985.

Esdaile, A., ed. *The Age of Elizabeth 1547-1603*. London: G. Bell & Sons Ltd., 1931.

Falls, Cyril. *Elizabeth's Irish Wars*. New York: Barnes & Noble, 1970.

Finnerty, John F. *Ireland* Vol. 1. New York: P.F. Collier & Sons, 1904.

Fitzgerald, T. W. H. *Ireland and Her People*. Chicago: Fitzgerald Book Co., 1909.

Ford, Alan. *The Protestant Reformation in Ireland, 1590-1641*. Frankfurt: Verlag Peter Lang, 1987.

Foster, R. F. *Modern Ireland 1600-1972*. New York: Penguin Books, 1989.

Four Masters. *Annals of the Kingdom of Ireland* Vol. 6. Dublin: Hodges, Smith, & Co., 1856.

Froude, James Anthony. *The English in Ireland*. 3 vols. New York: AMS Press, 1969.

Garnier, Charles-Marie. *A Popular History of Ireland*. Baltimore: Helicon Press, 1961.

Garrity, Devin A., ed. *Irish Poetry*. New York: The New American Library, 1965.

Hagan, J. "Misellanea Vaticano-Hibernica 1580-1631". *Archvium Hibernicum*, 3, 260-64.

Hayes-McCoy, G. A. *Irish Battles: A Military History of Ireland*. Belfast: The Appletree Press Ltd., 1990.

Hayes-McCoy, G. A. "Gaelic Society in Ireland in the late Sixteenth Century", *Historical Studies*, 4 (1963): 45-61.

Hinton, Edward M. *Ireland Through Tudor Eyes*. Philadelphia: University of Pennsylvania Press, 1935.

Harrington, Sir John. *Nuguae Antiquae* Vol. 1. New York: AMS Press, Inc. 1966.

Harrison, G. B., ed. *The Letters of Queen Elizabeth*. N.Y.: Funk and Wagnalls, 1968.

Hughes, Philip. *Rome and the Counter Reformation in England*. London: Burns Oates, 1944.

Jones, Frederick M. *Mountjoy 1563-1600: The Last Elizabethan Deputy*. Dublin: 1958.

Joyce, P. W. *History of Ireland*. London: Longmans, Green, & Co., 1923.

Mattingly, Garrett. *The Armada*. Cambridge, Massachussetts: The Riverside Press, 1951.

MacManus, Seamus. *The Story of the Irish Race*. New York: The Devin-Adair Co., 1944.

Maynard, Theodore. *Queen Elizabeth*. Milwaukee: The Bruce Publishing Co., 1954.

McGee, T. D. *History of Ireland* Vols. 2 & 8. New York: D. & J. Sadlier and Co., 1863.

McGurk, John. *The Elizabethan Conquest of Ireland*. Manchester, UK: Manchester University Press, 1997.

Meehan, C. P., MRIA. *The Fate and Fortune of Hugh O'Neill, Earl of Tyrone and Rory O'Donnell, Earl of Tyrconnell*. New York: P.J. Kennedy, 1897.

———. *The Rise and Fall of the Irish Franciscan Monasteries and Memoirs of the Irish Hierarchy in the Seventeenth Century*. Dublin: James Duffy, 1869.

Mitchel, John. *The Life and Times of Hugh O'Neill, Prince of Ulster*. New York: P.M. Haverty, 1868.

Morgan, Hiram. *Tyrone's Rebellion; The Outbreak of the Nine Years War in Tudor Ireland*. Woodbridge, England: Boyall Press, 1993.

Moryson, Fynes, *The Itinerary of Fynes Moryson*, 4 Vols. Glasgow: James MacLehose & Sons.

Murphy, Denis, S.J. *Historical introduction to The Life of Hugh O'Donnell by L. O'Cleary*. Dublin. Fallon & Co., 1895.

Neale, A. J. *Queen Elizabeth I*. Garden City, New York: Doubleday Inc., 1934.

Nolan, A. M. *A History of Ireland*. Chicago: J.S. Hyland & Co., 1928.

O Cianain, Tadhg. *The Flight of the Earls*. Ed. and trans. Paul Walsh. Dublin: M.H. Gill and Son, Ltd., 1916.

O'Cleary, L. *The Life of Hugh Roe O'Donnell* with a historical introduction by Denis Murphy. Dublin: Fallon and Company, 1895.

O'Dwyer, Peter, O. *Towards a History of Irish Spirituality*. Blackrock: The Columba Press, 1995.

O'Faolain, Sean. *The Great O'Neil*. New York: Duel, Sloan & Pearce, 1942.

O'Rahilly, Alfred. *The Massacre at Smerwick*. London: Longmans, Green and Co., Ltd., 1938.

O'Reilly, Myles. *Lives of the Irish Martyrs and Confessors*. New York: James Sheehy, 1878.

O'Sullivan Bear, Don Philip. *Ireland Under Elizabeth*. London: Kennikat Press, 1970.

Quinn, D. B. *The Elizabethans and the Irish*. Ithaca: Cornell University Press, 1966.

Read, Conyers. *Lord Burghley and Queen Elizabeth*. New York: Alfred A. Knopf, 1960.

Shakespeare, William. *The Complete Works of William Shakespeare*. Ed. W. A. Wright. Garden City, New York: Doubleday & Co, 1936.

Silke, John J. *Kinsale, The Spanish Intervention in Ireland at the End of the Elizabethan Wars*. New York: Fordham University Press, 1970.

———. "Hugh O'Neill, the Catholic Question and the Papacy". *Irish Ecclesiastical Record*, 5th series, 104 (1965), 65-79.

———. "The Irish Peter Lombard", *Irish Studies* 64, No. 254 (1975), 143-55.

Spenser, Edmund. *A View of the State of Ireland*. Eds. Andrew Hadfield and Willy Maley. Oxford: Blackwell Publishers Ltd., 1997.

Strachey, Lyntton. *Elizabeth and Essex*. New York: Harcourt, Brace & Co., 1928.

Sullivan, A. M. *The Story of Ireland*. Dublin: M.H. Gill & Sons, 1861.

Thebaud, A. J. *The Irish Race*. New York: P.J. Kennedy, 1883.

Walsh, Michelene Kerney. *Hugh O'Neill and the Flight of the Earls*. Rathmullen: The Flight of the Earls Heritage Center, 1991.

Walsh, Reginald, "Irish Manners and Customs in the 16th Century". *Archivium Hibernicum* or *Irish Historical Records* Vol. 4, (1917): 183.

Walsh, William T. *Philip II*. New York & London: Sheed & Ward, 1937.

Watt, John. *The Church in Medieval Ireland*. Vol. 5 of *The Gill History of Ireland*. Dublin: Gill and Macmillan Ltd., 1972.

Waugh, Evelyn. *Edmund Campion Jesuit and Martyr*. Garden City, New York: Image Books, 1946.

Wernham, R. B. *The Return of the Armadas: The Last Years of the Elizabethen Wars Against Spain 1595-1603*. Oxford: Oxford University Press, 1994.

————, ed. *The New Cambridge Modern History* Vol. 3. Cambridge: The University Press, 1968.

Wilson, Charles. *Queen Elizabeth and the Revolt in the Netherlands*. Berkeley & Los Angeles: University of California Press, 1970.

ındex